STATEMENT CONCERNING PUBLICATIONS OF RUSSELL SAGE FOUNDATION

Russell Sage Foundation was established in 1907 by Mrs. Russell Sage "for the improvement of social and living conditions in the United States of America." While the general responsibility for management of the Foundation is vested in the Board of Trustees, the responsibility for facts, conclusions, and interpretations in its publications rests with the authors and not upon the Foundation, its Trustees, or its staff. Publication under the imprint of the Foundation does not imply agreement by the organization with all opinions or interpretations expressed. It does imply that care has been taken that the work on which a manuscript is based has been thoroughly done.

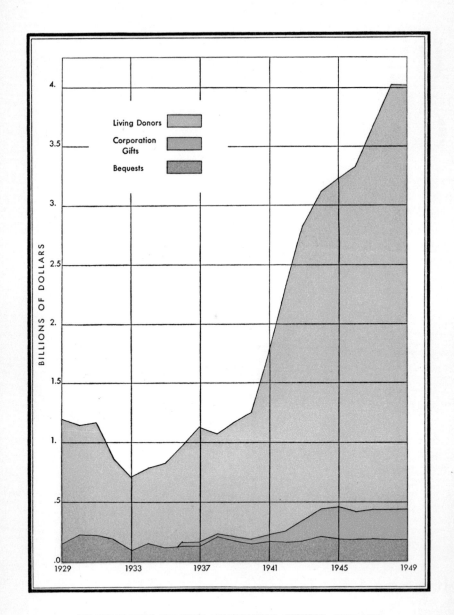

AN ESTIMATE OF PHILANTHROPIC GIVING, 1929–1949

Philanthropic Giving

By

F. Emerson Andrews

RUSSELL SAGE FOUNDATION

New York ~ ~ *1950*

Copyright, 1950, by
RUSSELL SAGE FOUNDATION
Printed in the United States
of America

Printed November, 1950
Reprinted January, 1951

WM. F. FELL CO., PRINTERS
PHILADELPHIA, PA.

Foreword

IT IS difficult to imagine what life in the United States would be like today without philanthropic giving. Private gifts supported the pioneering ventures which are now accepted as essential public services in the fields of education, health, and welfare. In all these fields philanthropy continues to give substantial aid to research designed to keep the frontiers of knowledge always advancing, to innovations in practice taking account of new knowledge and changing circumstances, and to ongoing activities. Even where government has assumed the chief burden, private agencies are still needed as a supplement, for comparisons, and to carry on experimental work.

Nearly all of us—the rich, the well-to-do, and the poor alike—accept an obligation to give from our private means for the benefit of others. But great differences of opinion exist on how much to give, to whom, and for what kinds of benefits.

Current information about giving is fragmentary and biased. Few objective students have made philanthropy their central concern, although economists, social historians, specialists in the social behavior disciplines, and others should have found it an exciting field for study. Actually, the bulk of what has been written on the subject consists of essays explaining personal points of view about giving, exhortations to generosity for a variety of purposes limited only by human imagination, and overly sympathetic accounts of the activities of philanthropic individuals and agencies. Critical analyses of the relative needs and oppor-

tunities for philanthropy, of the relative advantages of the various
ways of giving, and of the relative effectiveness of the many
proffered means for accomplishing any philanthropic purpose are
indeed rare. Not even elementary facts about donors and their
objectives are known with reasonable accuracy and complete-
ness. This seems out of character in a society which takes pride in
efficient planning in its affairs.

Perhaps giving has been too widely regarded as a private concern to permit the ready growth of an adequate body of knowledge about it. Public esteem for philanthropy is increased if it is
accomplished unostentatiously or even in secret. The wisdom of
the giver in the object and manner of his giving is hardly considered subject to public question in our culture except for
evident fraud. Recipient agencies in turn are commonly assumed
to spend their philanthropic dollars wisely, and only gross mis-
management is considered properly subject to public criticism.
And then there is the traditional attitude that giving away money
and helping people in need are best done with benevolent
motivation but with little necessity for the skills acquired through
knowledge and experience. Changes in these attitudes promise an
increasingly rational view of philanthropy, with a growing
understanding of the most useful ways of spending private dollars
for the benefit of others.

In 1946 Russell Sage Foundation published *American Foundations for Social Welfare* by Shelby M. Harrison and the author of
the present volume, F. Emerson Andrews. That publication reviewed the history, organization, resources, fields of activity, and
general trends of American foundations and included a list of 505
foundations with brief descriptive statements about each. An
annotated bibliography was included. The work followed a number of bibliographies and directories in the same field prepared
and published during the previous three decades. Staff consultation on problems of foundation organization and administration
and also with individuals and agencies needing advice about
potential sources of philanthropic aid began just about the time
Russell Sage Foundation was established in 1907 and has continued ever since. The present volume carries this interest forward

beyond the foundation field into the larger area of philanthropy in all of its common forms.

Philanthropic Giving was first proposed as a manual or handbook, but it quickly became evident that voluntary giving is not properly subject to the kind of standardized advice characteristic of such guides. There is too large an element of personal judgment both as to capacity to give and as to purpose to permit anything resembling rules of thumb. However, when questions of individual judgment have been decided the well-analyzed record of philanthropy can help donors make the most of their contributions by calling attention to comparative opportunities and likely pitfalls. Mr. Andrews' analysis of the major fields for philanthropy and of the common questions confronting potential donors avoids any pretense of finality and yet offers well-balanced, expert guidance to the less experienced donor. In words borrowed from the first chapter which are too modest but describe the author's purpose well, *Philanthropic Giving* presents "an informing picture of giving" in the United States. By doing this and more it earns its place as a valuable contribution to sense and order in the emotional and disorderly field of benevolence.

DONALD YOUNG
General Director
Russell Sage Foundation

September 20, 1950

Acknowledgments

PREPARATION of this book involved consulting more than eight thousand references, including books, pamphlets, magazines, and newspapers, and conferences with numerous persons. Also heavy correspondence marked the project from its beginning. Without exception publishers granted permission to use excerpts from their works, and their cooperation is here gratefully acknowledged. The footnote references to these documents form a useful bibliography on many of the topics discussed.

A very few individuals and agencies were unwilling, or declared themselves unable, to supply requested information. The missing data, if needed for the rounded picture, were sought elsewhere, but probably with some loss in accuracy.

The great majority of persons consulted were interested in the project, and generous with their time, opinions, and factual data. This book owes much to their deeply appreciated aid. Because of their number, it is not possible to name all these individuals, but personal acknowledgment should go at least to these: Ralph H. Blanchard, Mrs. Sallie Bright, Albert E. Brownbridge, J. Frederic Dewhurst, Miss Dorothy Ducas, Paul C. Fahrney, Arnold Gurin, Ralph Hayes, David H. Holbrook, Edward C. Jenkins, John Price Jones and his staff, Walter C. Laidlaw, Mrs. Natalie W. Linderholm, the Rt. Rev. Monsignor James J. Lynch, Walter A. Mayer, the Reverend Dr. Robert J. McCracken, Mrs. Esther M. Moore, Harry S. Myers, Earl N. Parker, D. Paul Reed, John W. Riley, Jr., C. August Sandberg, John H. Thompson, and

Miss Ellen Winston. Personnel in federal offices were most help-ful, particularly the Bureau of Internal Revenue, the Department of Commerce, and the Office of Education.

Berrien C. Eaton, Jr., was retained as legal consultant for this study. He has supplied the appendices dealing with matters of law and has reviewed the whole volume with respect to legal and tax aspects. Chapter 13 leans heavily on his advice and some of his published papers.

I acknowledge, also, a large debt to my colleagues in Russell Sage Foundation for critical reading of the manuscript and other help.

F. E. A.

Contents

Tables

Charts and Maps

CHAPTER 1

The New Era in Giving

A NOTED philanthropist, Julius Rosenwald, once declared that he found it "nearly always easier to make $1,000,000 honestly than to dispose of it wisely." Many of us have not solved the first problem, but in giving even small sums, we need to do some straight, hard thinking.

How can we give effectively under the conditions that prevail today? For we have entered a new era in giving. Many of the rules have changed, some of them within the past few years.

The Changing Conditions

Government has recently entered large areas that used to be a first charge upon our private purses. The Social Security Act, passed in 1935 and broadened by later amendment, is the greatest stride this country has made toward Cornelia J. Cannon's hoped-for day "when our philanthropic obligations will be brought to our attention, not by an appeal from boards of directors, but by a tax-bill from the properly constituted authorities." Over four million persons are receiving aid from federal, state, and local funds at a recent rate of $2 billion a year under three Social Security assistance programs: old-age assistance, aid to dependent children, and aid to the needy blind. Meanwhile, the "appeals from boards of directors" have not notably diminished, and many thoughtful givers see opportunity for more useful forms of private philanthropy now that the burden of mere relief is largely removed.

Income-tax rates, partly to meet the federal government's share in these new charges but in vastly greater measure because of the heavy costs of past and present national defense, have risen to a stratosphere undreamed a decade ago.[1] This is affecting the stream of giving in several diverse ways. It limits large fortunes, which in the past had been a source for great individual gifts. On the other hand, through the 15 per cent deduction provision on charitable gifts, these rates encourage contributions by making giving nearly costless for persons in the higher income brackets. The Collector of Internal Revenue has now taken over Viola's speech in *Twelfth Night:* "What is yours to bestow is not yours to reserve."

A sharp decline has occurred in income from most investments and in interest rates generally. Present indications are that low levels may remain for a considerable period. The effects on giving are various. Welfare and educational institutions which formerly derived much of their annual income from endowments find themselves in desperate financial straits and in need of larger current gifts. But potential givers whose income is derived chiefly from investments have less annually from which to give. Finally, contributions to endowment funds, which used to be an effective way of helping schools, hospitals, and similar institutions, are no longer very productive in terms of annual income, and need rethinking.

The arrival of instantaneous worldwide communication and the impact of two world wars have convinced many of us that we are now citizens of one planet, with the economic and social welfare of other peoples directly affecting our own welfare, and possibly our survival. A later chapter examines the extent to which giving is expanding toward this planetary horizon.

Patterns of giving are changing. Radical shifts are occurring in choices among our three important almoners, the church, the government, and private agencies. Among the agencies there is a present struggle between the advocates of federated giving—as in the community chest movement—and certain independent agencies.

---

[1] In 1939 the surtax rate applicable to a net income of $100,000 was 55 per cent; in 1949 it was 84 per cent.

A small but troublesome group of charity racketeers have taken advantage of the present confused state of giving to organize a variety of ingenious schemes to draw dollars from the pockets of the unwary. Their total "take" is probably not large, but their schemes, when discovered, receive a great deal of publicity, discourage some givers, and for the wise giver make additional checking necessary.

Toward a Science of Man

Still more important in this new era in giving is the influence of an increasingly critical and scientific attitude. There have been periods when giving has been considered chiefly from the viewpoint of effect upon the giver. "Prayer carries us halfway to God, fasting brings us to the door of his palace, and alms gains us admission," said the Moslem proverb. In the Middle Ages the Christian church promised remission of temporal punishment for sins, and even remission of purgatorial atonement, in return for stated payments. Some psychologists insist that all giving has basically selfish motivation, and it is certain that some modern giving springs from a desire to have names prominent on a contributors' list or in the hope of personal gain, here or hereafter.

But for those people who give out of a deep sympathy for their fellow man and a concern for his welfare, the effect upon the recipient has become the important concern, and that effect is increasingly measured by the methods of science. We have had surveys of foreign missions, of hospitals, of the welfare agencies of whole communities. Case studies of individuals and of families have shown us that a careless kindness is at least wasteful, and often harmful.

Nearly two decades ago family service societies coined an illuminating slogan, expressing the changing attitude: they were interested, they said, "not so much in helping people in trouble as in helping people out of trouble." If this program is broadened into also helping people to avoid trouble, and helping them to realize their own full capacities for work and play and growth, then the opportunities—and the difficulties—of the new era in giving begin to be defined.

We may someday have a science of man founded so firmly on accumulated knowledge in the social sciences that discovery will pile upon discovery, as in the physical sciences and in medicine. Then the challenge to our giving will be clear for this new science of man and his relationships. At present many of its findings are negative; we begin to know what will not work. Investigations of the results of giving, designed to make giving more effective, have sometimes served to emphasize the difficulties of giving rather than its new opportunities.

Story of the Cliff

We are like the people in the old story,[1] who lived in a village at the base of a great cliff. At the top of this cliff ran a much-used highway, and so many hapless travelers fell over the cliff that the kindly villagers were kept busy picking them up and caring for their wounds. Finally, at great expense, they bought an ambulance, which they kept ever ready at the base of the cliff, for the better care of the unfortunate wayfarers. An old man said to them, "Why do you not build a fence at the top?" But the screams of the suffering were sharp in their ears, and they were so busy helping the injured that they could not take time to climb the cliff and build the fence.

The government is now running the ambulance at the bottom of the cliff, and providing most of the necessities which used to be so heavy a charge upon our private purses. We still need to take care of its oversights and inadequacies, and handle delicate situations where person-to-person giving (and not always of money) is the only effective form giving can take. We need to continue supporting secular and religious agencies in our community, provided they are in step with the new era in giving. But now that most of the crushing burden of relieving destitution has been moved from the shoulders of the individual giver to those of society, where it belongs, the individual giver can apply some of his surplus to the promising task of building that fence at the top of the cliff—if he has the wisdom.

---

[1] One version appears in the poem "The Fence or the Ambulance" by John N. Hurty, *American Journal of Public Health*, August, 1933, p. 796; original source not certain.

The Need for Facts About Giving

There are at least 500 national voluntary agencies functioning in the field of social welfare today, nearly all of which invite contributions toward their varying programs. Local educational, health, and other agencies, together with some statewide and some international agencies, vastly increase this total. How shall the giver choose? Moreover, is it even certain that all the needed portions of that fence at the top of the cliff are in the plans of one or another of these many agencies?

The forms giving may take are not quite so numerous as the beckoning causes, but they offer considerable variety. They range from the small coin in the blind man's cup to the gift or bequest of many millions to a private foundation, incorporated with the aid of skilled lawyers and often endowed with at least legal perpetual life.

Objective facts, which might afford useful guidance to prospective givers, are seriously lacking. It is certain that some agencies are outright rackets; a considerable number, sincerely conceived, have outlived their usefulness or are inefficiently run; still others, worthy enough in themselves, are receiving too much for their needs, or at least far more than would seem a wise proportion in view of other requirements. Meanwhile, the total of American giving is probably less than two cents on the dollar of national income, and long stretches of that fence of prevention remain unbuilt.

Later chapters endeavor to present an informing picture of giving in America. Glances at history and at customs in other countries are included to lend perspective, to suggest where gaps may exist in our own conceptions of need, and as a guide to present and future trends. Statistics are held to the minimum that seemed necessary to establish proportions in a field where proportion and measurement have been too little available.

What Is Philanthropy?

Lecky distinguished between *charity*, which "alleviates individual suffering," and *philanthropy*, which "deals with large masses and is more frequently employed in preventing than in allaying calamity." Giving, obviously, may be directed toward both of these purposes, and toward ends included in neither definition. It is doubtful whether an art gallery prevents calamity or alleviates individual suffering (unless of the artists, who are usually dead before their pictures are recognized as valuable), and yet it may be a very desirable gift. The S.P.C.A. might not be "philanthropy" to the language purist, who points out that the term means "love for mankind"; but the Internal Revenue Code specifically includes "prevention of cruelty to children or animals" as among purposes entitling organizations to tax-exempt status. Lord Beveridge defines "philanthropic motive" as the "desire by one's personal action to make life happier for others."

Ideas of philanthropy have varied with the customs of peoples and with changing needs. One of the oldest records of giving is in *The Book of the Dead*, the chief monument of the religious literature of Egypt, which goes back to about 4000 B.C.

> I have given bread to the hungry man, and water to him that was athirst, and apparel to the naked man, and a ferry-boat to him that had no boat. I have made propitiatory offerings and given cakes to the gods. . . .[1]

Cakes for the gods are no longer a necessary charity. But if providing ferry service seems strange, it should be noted that more than five thousand years later, in the Statute of Charitable Uses of Queen Elizabeth in 1601, "repair of bridges, ports, havens, causeways, churches, sea-banks and highways" was included among appropriate charitable uses.

Rather recently, the Hall of Benevolence of Chefoo, China, presented in its decennial report for 1882–1891 this interesting list of its 17 fields of activity:

1. Non-interest loans to the poor
2. Burial facilities for the poor
3. Waste-paper collection
4. Assisting shipwrecked persons
5. Fire protection
6. Aid to widows
7. Reception of deserted infants
8. Free supply of books to the poor who are desirous of reading
9. Free education for poor children
10. Orphanage
11. Industrial school for poor girls
12. Refuge for the cure of opium habit
13. Refuge for the homeless sick
14. Hospital work
15. Refuge for the poor in winter
16. Free kitchen
17. Vaccination

[1] *The Papyrus of Ani*. Translated by E. A. Wallis Budge. G. P. Putnam's Sons, New York, 1913, p. 587.

We shall attempt no philosophical definition of either charity or philanthropy, recognizing that man's concept of The Good changes with his culture, with climate, and with the needs of his own time. For the practical purposes of this book, including its statistical summaries, we shall accept the definitions of the United States Treasury Department for "allowable contributions" for income-tax purposes. Section 23 (o) of the Internal Revenue Code provides the basic definitions, but the Treasury's 1949 bulletin, *How to Prepare Your U. S. Income Tax Return*, is in some details more explicit:

> . . . you can deduct gifts to religious, charitable, educational, scientific, or literary organizations, and organizations for the prevention of cruelty to children and animals, except when the organization is operated for personal profit, or to conduct propaganda or otherwise attempt to influence legislation. You can deduct gifts to fraternal organizations if they are to be used for charitable, religious, etc., purposes. You can also deduct gifts to veterans' organizations, or to a governmental agency which will use the gift for public purposes. A contribution may be made in money or property (not services), but if in property, then the amount of the contribution is measured by the fair market value of the property at the time of the contribution.

No defense for these limitations is undertaken. The welfare of mankind, certainly in this nation, sometimes depends upon vigorous efforts to influence legislation; persons may wish to advance legislative and other causes with their money, or make gifts to needy individuals, without regard to loss of tax deductibility. Their acts are philanthropic in motive, but for statistical reasons the summaries in this book are based on the Treasury's definitions.

Problems the Giver Faces

Every giver must answer for himself a number of questions, some of them simple, some of them difficult, and varying with the nature of his gift.

How large shall the gift be—with relation to his ability to give, with relation to the need to be met? If it is substantial, shall it be given in a lump sum, in annual installments, or as an endowment of which only income is to be spent?

Shall it be given to an individual (which presents tax problems), to an organization already in existence in the field, or must a new organization be set up?

Shall it be given locally, nationally, or internationally? If the money was made in a given locality, should it not be returned to that community? But if this becomes usual practice, where will the poorer communities, in which little profit is made, receive help for their greater need?

Shall it be given to relieve individual suffering; or for rehabilitation; or for research into the causes of disease and social maladjustment, and their cure? Or for general culture, education, recreation? Or for the salvation of souls?

Is it better to give for the young, who have much to contribute, or for the old, who have given much?

Finally, among a thousand beckoning causes and ten thousand beseeching agencies, to which shall the gift be given?

In 1936 a midwestern millionaire, puzzled by some of these problems, offered a thousand-dollar prize to readers of the *Atlantic Monthly* for the best proposal for spending $1,000,000 in his own city of one hundred thousand population, already possessed of good schools, parks, playgrounds, swimming pools, golf courses, and an art gallery; but no college. Even under these special conditions, the answers are an interesting indication of the vast variety of philanthropies which seemed important to one group of thoughtful people.

There were, the editors reported, 8,461 entries, "as diverse as the individuals who sent them, and in most cases [bearing] a direct relationship to the nature and occupation of the author."

The subjects of the plans fell largely into two main divisions, education and recreation, with two smaller ones of agriculture and the care of the needy. Scholarship plans of infinite variation outnumbered all the rest—traveling scholarships, exchange scholarships, music scholarships, scholarships for bright children to be leaders and average children to be followers. Also under the head of education were schemes for trade schools and vocational training, child guidance, matrimonial instruction, and civic research.

Proposals for recreation provided community centres, elaborate and complete, parks, hobby houses, gardens, forests, and swimming pools. Sanctuaries were suggested for birds, beasts, and for creative people; planetariums, aquariums, gymnasiums. There was at least one plea for a cooperative football team. Music and theatre projects were dear to many contestants, who wished for free concerts, glee clubs, community singing, drama, pantomime.

Agricultural plans included specific assistance against drought, grasshoppers and chinch bugs, as well as agricultural colleges to be operated in conjunction with a model farm or dairy.

The old are neediest, said nearly fifteen per cent of the contributors. Let the donor provide more houses where they can be together and independent. Children are needy, too—perfect orphanages and modern day nurseries were recommended, also shoes for unshod boys and girls, a year on a farm for every fifth-grade child.

Housing plans formed a large classification that embraced model communities, apartment or small house projects for special groups— the single woman in business, for example, or the unemployed over forty.

Religion dictated many of the proposals—for Bible schools and institutes, for spiritual retreats, for air-conditioning the churches, for a sectarian hospital. One competitor wished for a fund to eliminate the collection of money during church services.

More worldly plans advocated a factory to take care of the unemployed in the community, a subsidized newspaper, a fund for cancer research, a tax-free town, socialized medicine, kindergartens, libraries, psychiatric clinics. . . .

A few plans were unique—for a goats' milk dairy; a temple of poetry; one competitor wanted to buy the Parthenon and set it up in the donor's city, another to build public baths, Roman style, a third to enforce an ordinance requiring a maximum speed for all vehicles of twelve miles an hour.[1]

The prize was awarded to Howard Douglas Dozier for a plan for the further education of high-school graduates, involving the setting up of a College Savings Trust Fund Association, promoting systematic savings for college education by agreeing to match the $10-a-month contribution of the parents or friends of beneficiaries.

Personal Services

Gifts of money, or those that possess monetary value, are the concern of this book, but it needs to be said that money is not the only gift that can be made, or the most important.

[1] *Atlantic Monthly*, December, 1936, pp. 723-724.

In the older dispensation, money could buy a loaf of bread and save a man from starving. In the present era of more creative giving, money alone cannot buy the discovery of a cure for cancer, or the needed research toward a sound tax policy. All that money can do is to release for creative work a man of vision and ability, and give him tools.

The real contribution comes from the man, who must give long years of patient searchings, destined for delay, disappointment, and frequent failure, with only now and then a glimpse of a far new truth which will benefit not him, but chiefly his fellow man—if he does find it.

Even the giving of money cannot be done effectively without a personal giving of time, thought, and care to make certain that the money gift is wisely placed. "You nearly always have to do some work to be kind," said an eight-year-old girl after her class had been struggling hard to make a really useful gift. "You have to think, and find out things."

Gifts in personal service, and in "thinking and finding out things," go beyond the yardsticks of science and cannot be presented in statistical summaries. With this acknowledgment of their superior worth, we return to the forms of giving which can be measured, and which often underlie and make possible these gifts of life itself.

A Glance at History

Tحe GIVING men do is a personal thing, but some differences seem rooted in religion, nationality, or economic level, and there have been sweeping historic shifts. No attempt can be made here to present a history of philanthropy, but some of these changes and developments are worth noting briefly. Before considering the cultures from which our own philanthropic practices and institutions developed, a few examples may be taken from primitive societies and early literate peoples to suggest the range of divergent patterns which men have created to meet the problems of the poor and handicapped. They shed little direct light upon today's problems, but they do emphasize the fact that there is almost no limit to the forms of charitable activities and that the prevailing forms must be adapted to social values and institutions as a whole.

Some Primitive Examples

Giving in our present understanding of the term—donating an object or rendering a service without expectation of any personal return—seems scarcely to have existed among some primitive peoples. Malinowski said of the Trobrianders:

> It must be remembered that accidental or spontaneous gifts, such as alms or charities, do not exist, since everybody in need would be maintained by his or her family. Again, there are so many well-defined economic obligations, connected with kinship and relationship-in-law, that anyone wanting a thing or a service would know

where to go and ask for it. And then, of course, it would not be a free gift, but one imposed by some social obligation.[1]

This security based on kinship was apparently available not only to the needy, widows, the maimed, the aged, but even to an able-bodied lazy fellow. Says William Whitman concerning the Oto Indians, "If a man chose, he might refuse to work and take up residence with some close relative who would be obliged to keep and feed him. Such an aberrant would be despised . . . but he could not be denied."

Group security might extend beyond immediate kin. The Hottentot chief was expected "to have an open house and an open hand." The successful hunter among the Chukchees was met, as he came ashore, by widows and orphans to whom he threw some portions of his meat, giving "at least to the nearest door." The Indians of our Northwest added a word to the language through their curious giving-feast, the potlatch. "The final act of the potlatch," says Cornelius Osgood,[2] "is the distribution of gifts. To do this, the potlatch-giver chooses a friend of his own clan, someone of prominence whom he wishes to honor. The distributor presents the guests with the objects from the fence. These are given out with regard to the needs of the people."

The often-reported lavish "gifts" to strangers must not be confused with true giving. They are a primitive form of barter, with gifts of equal value expected in return. But the traveler in need of food and shelter may usually expect these. Among the Mongols, for example, milk is the most valuable food, so highly prized, according to Larson, that it can never be sold, there being nothing of equal value to give for it. But "it must be freely given to a hungry traveler."

Generally speaking, almsgiving was not common among primitive peoples because there was little need for it. There were no "poor" in the modern sense; needs were the elemental ones for food, clothing, and shelter, and these were supplied through the

---

[1] Malinowski, Bronislaw, *Argonauts of the Western Pacific*. E. P. Dutton and Co., New York, 1922, p. 177.

[2] *Contributions to the Ethnography of the Kutchin*. Yale University Publications in Anthropology, No. 14. Yale University Press, New Haven, 1936, p. 127.

family or the clan—unless all went hungry or shelterless. To belong to a numerous family was to have aid to dependent children, maternity benefits, unemployment insurance, home relief, what medical care was available, fire insurance, an old-age annuity, and free burial.

Family Responsibility in the Orient

In the Orient this sense of the family not only existed from the times of the earliest records, but survives today with a strength not general in western civilizations. Because of the security the family afforded, only those who lacked the usual family ties could be called "the most forlorn of Heaven's people," though a few others with obvious handicaps might need aid. At the time of the Five Rulers (2255–2205 B.C.) we find it written:

> One who, while quite young, lost his father was called an orphan; an old man who had lost his sons was called a solitary. An old man who had lost his wife was called a pitiable widower; an old woman who had lost her husband was called a poor widow. These four classes were the most forlorn of Heaven's people, and had none to whom to tell their wants; they all received regular allowances.
>
> The dumb, the deaf, the lame, such as had lost a member, pigmies and mechanics, were all fed according to what work they were able to do.[1]

The whole village might function as an expanded family, as in many respects it often was, and support its members. Said Paul Ibis of the people of Taiwan:

> You do not see any beggars, for each village takes care of its poor people and those who are too old to work any more. For each wealthy man feels that it is his responsibility, and there are voluntary gifts of clothing, food, medicine, even coffins, which are kept in the temple and given to every person who really suffers from poverty.[2]

No attempt can be made here even to outline the spirit of Oriental philanthropy, but the key difference with the West, this strong reliance upon the family, deserves emphasis.

[1] *The Lî Kî:* A Collection of Treatises on the Rules of Propriety or Ceremonial Usages. Translated by James Legge, in *The Sacred Books of the East* edited by F. Max Muller. Clarendon Press, Oxford, 1885, vol. 27, pp. 243–244.

[2] "Auf Formosa," Ethnographische Wanderungen, *Globus*, vol. 31, 1877.

Examples of Charity in Egypt

Many centuries before the Christian era, Egyptian civilization developed a philanthropy which corresponds to many modern practices. *The Book of the Dead* has already been cited. A record of giving and right action motivated by a desire to improve one's lot after death is inscribed on the tomb of Harkhuf, a nobleman of the Sixth Dynasty, about 2500 B.C., reporting that he acted as he did because "I desired that it might be well with me in the great god's presence."[1]

Modern foundations were dimly foreshadowed in the capital funds set up by Egyptian noblemen, the income of which was to ensure perpetual maintenance of their soul cult; but these "foundations" were simply memorials, without charitable or social purposes.

Amenophis, the son of Kanakht, included in his *Teaching Concerning Life* an admonition on collecting taxes from the poor:

> If thou findest a large debt against a poor man, make it into three parts: forgive two, let one remain; thou wilt find it a path of life; thou wilt lie down at night and sleep soundly. On the morrow thou wilt find it like good news.[2]

Bolkestein cites many epitaphs of the Saitic (eighth century) and later periods which refer to a wide variety of charitable deeds, but he correctly warns that epitaphs, then as now, may tell us less about actual deeds than the impression the deceased or his friends wished to leave. Say some of these epitaphs:

> "He was the healer of the sick." "He was the eye of the blind man and the foot of the lame."[3] "His doors were open to those who came from abroad and he offered what they needed for the sustenance of life; he was the refuge of him who came from afar." "He gave grain to the widow and her son . . . was the husband of the widow . . .

---

[1] Breasted, James Henry, *Ancient Records of Egypt*. University of Chicago Press, Chicago, 1927, vol. 1, pp. 151–152.

[2] Griffith, F. L., "The Teaching of Amenophis, the Son of Kanakht," Papyrus B. M., 10474, *Journal of Egyptian Archaeology*, vol. 12, 1926, p. 213.

[3] Compare with Job 29:15–17, which may be older: "I was eyes to the blind, and feet was I to the lame. I was a father to the poor: and the cause which I knew not I searched out. And I brake the jaws of the wicked, and plucked the spoil out of his teeth."

the refuge of the orphan . . . the robe of him who has no mother
. . . the support of old men." "I am the unshakable support of him
who is in need, whom everyone mourns; I am the well-born benefactor; I am he whose hand is always open to him who has nothing;
never has my heart said, 'I have already given.' "[1]

The emphasis in ancient Egypt was upon meeting the needs of
the destitute, with pity the strong motive and without sharp
limitation to family and clan.

Greek and Roman Concepts

The Greek and the early Roman concept of philanthropy was
radically different; it consisted in kindly acts "toward people,"
not toward the poor. It was not almsgiving, it had little or no
connection with poverty, it was seldom motivated by pity. One
of its earliest expressions is in Homer's lines:

> And greatly was he loved, for courteously
> He welcomed to his house beside the way
> All comers.[2]

Demosthenes cites the charitable acts of one citizen as "fitting
out triremes [war vessels] for the public service, defraying the
cost of public choruses, payment of property taxes, ransoming
prisoners of war." Cimon the Athenian, son of Miltiades, "by
keeping open house for his fellow-citizens, and giving travelers
liberty to eat the fruits which the several seasons produced in his
land, seemed to restore to the world that community of goods,
which mythology says existed in the reign of Saturn."[3] It was
Cimon, also, who converted the Academy into a well-watered
grove, with shady alleys to walk in—appropriate teaching center
for Socrates and Plato.

Every year in ancient Athens, at the beginning of the sowing
season, a priest stood at the foot of the Acropolis and pronounced

---

[1] Bolkestein, Hendrik, *Wohltätigkeit und Armenpflege im Vorchristlichen Altertum.* A.
Oosthoek, Verlag, A. G., Utrecht, 1939.

[2] *The Iliad of Homer.* Translated by William Cullen Bryant. Houghton, Mifflin and
Co., Boston, 1870, p. 151.

[3] Plutarch, *Lives:* Cimon.

curses upon those who transgressed the maxims of Bouzyges. Ancient writers considered these Bouzygian Curses a key to man's proper behavior toward his fellow man. Unfortunately, no complete list has come down, but the partial list cited by Bolkestein illustrates again the Greek ethic of general kindliness rather than duties to special classes of the unfortunate: do not overlook an unburied body; kindle a fire; give a share of water; tell the way; advise truthfully.

Xenophon set up a "foundation" in Scillus dedicating land and building a temple to Artemis, and providing for an annual festival at which all citizens and neighbors, men and women, should receive "barley meal and loaves of bread, wine and sweetmeats, and a portion of the sacrificial victims from the sacred herd as well as the victims taken in the chase." This was like its modern, and dubious, counterpart, the Christmas basket, in supplying food for a day without considering the recipient's continuing problem, but unlike it in offering the food to all comers, without respect to need.

Pre-Christian Rome followed the Greek pattern of giving for the benefit of the state or of any worthy citizen rather than to the needy, out of pity. Bolkestein goes so far as to assert that there is no record that Rome made any provision for the sick, widows, or orphans. Cicero suggests as gifts walls, ships, ports, aqueducts; and of lesser value, theaters, colonnades, and new temples. However, the soldiers of Pompey who had three or more living children were given free land, in one of the rarer examples of consideration of the economic situation of the recipient. The famed "bread and circuses" were not charity, but political measures to prevent insurrection.

In later centuries giving in Rome was more often directed toward needy persons or classes, but to what extent this was due to the Christian influence is in doubt. Faustina, wife of Antoninus (second century after Christ) gave grain "for the poor of the city," an action which Bolkestein calls probably the first example of this sense of that phrase in the western world. In the first centuries A.D. private associations bearing some resemblance to foundations increased in number. Many municipalities had foundations for *alimentarii*, to aid in feeding, clothing, and educating needy legitimate children. The Theodosian Code, a compilation under the Christian emperors made in A.D. 438, mentions four kinds of charitable institutions: xenodochia (guest houses for strangers and wayfarers), poorhouses, orphanages, and foundling asylums. The Justinian Code (A.D. 529) continues these institutions and adds decrees concerning hospitals and old people's homes.

Judaeo-Christian Influences

The Hebrews, like their neighbors the Egyptians, have a tradition of generous giving to God and to the poor extending back to the oldest records. Jacob saw a vision at Bethel and promised to give a tenth "of all that thou shalt give me" to his Lord. The Mosaic Code required that the land be left fallow every seventh year; the crops that grew of themselves were for the poor. In normal years the corners of the field should be left unreaped, and the gleanings of the vineyard, also, were "for the poor and stranger." Hospitality, even for outlanders, was an obligation: "And if thy brother be waxen poor, and fallen in decay with thee; then thou shalt relieve him; yea, though he be a stranger, or a sojourner; that he may live with thee." To give was a religious duty, and to withhold might have serious consequences: "He that giveth unto the poor shall not lack; but he that hideth his eyes shall have many a curse."

The principle of giving the tithe, or tenth, was firmly established among the Hebrews, beginning with Abram's gift of the tithe to priestly Melchizedek. It was ordinarily a religious offering, paid in kind or in money, but sometimes it was a gift to the poor:

> At the end of three years thou shalt bring forth all the tithe of thine increase the same year, and shalt lay it up within thy gates: and the Levite (because he hath no part nor inheritance with thee,) and the stranger, and the fatherless, and the widow, which are within thy gates, shall come, and shall eat and be satisfied: that the Lord thy God may bless thee in all the work of thine hand which thou doest.[1]

[1] Deuteronomy 14:28–29.

Tithing was by no means limited to the Hebrews. It was common among many ancient peoples but frequently it was a general tax, rather than a religiously sanctioned gift to God and the poor.

The teachings of Jesus set up a new and lofty personal ethic for givers, which became the most important single influence on the philanthropy of the western world. Some of these teachings had been foreshadowed in the Hebrew prophets, in Egypt, or in other religions; some are concepts so far above men's thinking, then or now, that they remain more admired than followed. They included such principles as these:

The spirit of the giver is more important than the size of the gift:

> Woe unto you, scribes and Pharisees, hypocrites! for ye pay tithe of mint and anise and cummin, and have omitted the weightier matters of the law, judgment, mercy, and faith: these ought ye to have done, and not to leave the other undone.[1]

Value of the gift is determined by the sacrifice of the giver: "This poor widow hath cast more in, than all they which have cast into the treasury; for all they did cast in of their abundance; but she of her want did cast in all that she had, even all her living." The mere tithe might not be enough; the rich young ruler was advised to "sell all that thou hast, and distribute unto the poor, and thou shalt have treasure in heaven."

Giving has its rewards, for through alms one lays up "a treasure in the heavens that faileth not" and "it is more blessed to give than to receive." Giving should not be limited to family and friends, but extended even to the despised Samaritan who has fallen among thieves. Finally, the gift should be made in secret, and not for public credit: "Take heed that ye do not your alms before men, to be seen of them; otherwise ye have no reward of your Father which is in heaven."

These precepts set up a high personal ethic for givers, emphasizing the virtues of complete unselfishness and sacrificial giving. They dealt only incidentally, however, with the problem of suiting the gift to the recipient.

[1] Matthew 23:23.

Many centuries later, about 1180, Rabbi Moses ben Maimon, better known as Maimonides, dealt with this problem in his *Mishneh Torah:*

> There are eight degrees in the giving of charity, one higher than the other.
>
> The highest degree, than which there is nothing higher, is to take hold of a Jew who has been crushed and to give him a gift or a loan, or to enter into partnership with him, or to find work for him, and thus to put him on his feet so that he will not be dependent on his fellow-men. . . .
>
> Lower in degree to this is the one who gives charity to the poor, but does not know to whom he gives it, nor does the poor man know from whom he receives it. This is an unselfish meritorious act comparable to what was done in the Chamber of the Secret in the Temple where the charitable would deposit [alms] secretly and the poor of better family would help themselves secretly. Related to this degree is the giving to the [public] alms-chest. . . .
>
> Lower in degree to this is when the giver knows to whom he gives, but the poor does not know from whom he receives. An example of this is the great scholars who used to go about in secret and leave their money at the door of the poor. This is proper practice, particularly meritorious when the officers in charge of charity are not administering properly.
>
> Lower in degree to this is when the poor knows from whom he receives but the giver does not know to whom he gives. An example of this is the great scholars who used to tie up their money in [the corner of] their cloaks and throw them back over their shoulders. The poor would then come and take it without being put to shame.
>
> Lower in degree to this is when one gives even before he is asked.
>
> Lower in degree to this is when one gives after he has been asked.
>
> Lower in degree to this is when one gives less than he should but graciously.
>
> Lower in degree to this is when one gives grudgingly.[1]

The Medieval Church

In Europe, through the Middle Ages, the church was the chief almoner. Gifts to the church, or the income from its own substantial holdings and the free services of its growing religious

[1] Marcus, Jacob R., *The Jew in the Medieval World*. The Sinai Press, Cincinnati, 1938, pp. 364–365.

orders, supported not only the church and its religious activities, but a widening circle of general charities. These often included care of the parish poor, widows, the aged, the infirm; orphanages; guest rooms or guest houses for travelers; and gradually, hospitals and schools.

Voluntary giving to religion for support of these activities was seldom adequate; it was often bolstered by strong inducements and even compulsions from church and state. Councils of the church urged and tried to enforce the payment of tithes. The earliest state enactment appears to have been about 800, when Capitularies of Charlemagne commanded that tithes be applied to the maintenance of the bishop and clergy, the poor, and the general purposes of the church.

The church began to encourage contributions by granting *indulgences*, which were remissions of temporal punishment, often including severe penances, for certain sins under strict conditions of contrition and confession. But these qualifications were soon forgotten, and people believed they could buy forgiveness for any sin for trifling sums. "Fie, penny-preacher!" said Berthold of Regensburg. "Thou dost promise so much remission of sins for a mere halfpenny or penny, that thousands now trust thereto, and fondly dream to have atoned for all their sins with the halfpenny or penny, and thus go to hell."

The worst of these abuses were corrected, but the idea persists that salvation can be bought. In more recent years a Scotsman is said to have summoned his minister to his deathbed, asking, "Should I be placed among the elect if I left ten thousand for Free Kirk sustentation?" The minister wanted the money, but he was more cautious than the "penny-preachers" of the medieval church. "It is," he said, "an experiment well worth trying."

Secular Giving

As the position of the church grew less commanding at the close of the Middle Ages, and the power and wealth of the state and of individuals within the state grew stronger, the church ceased to be almost the exclusive almoner. Sometimes the king or the nobles made substantial gifts. In 1225 Louis VIII gave

100 sous each to the two thousand houses for lepers within his realm. (There were then 19,000 leper houses in western Christendom.)

Wealthy individuals, too, were beginning to make their own gifts, for purposes of their own devising. As the individual became philanthropist, giving took on individuality—sometimes constructive, sometimes merely amusing.

In England endowments for schools or sums set aside for poor scholars were frequent charities. There were numerous endowments for sermons; at Coventry, at the not excessive remuneration of 6s. 8d. apiece. In the parish of Shoreditch a woman, Joan Smales, carried the churchly idea in a new direction; she set up a fund out of which those who had to listen to the sermon would be paid 20s. for their labor, while the preacher was given 10s.

This new wave of philanthropy springing neither from the church nor from the state but from the rising middle class required legislative definition and recognition. In England an act was passed under Queen Elizabeth in 1601 for the creation, control, and protection of such funds, and has become the cornerstone of Anglo-Saxon law concerning philanthropies. Commonly called the Statute of Charitable Uses (43 Elizabeth, cap. 4), its preamble is worth quoting for the variety of purposes it describes as charitable:

> Some for relief of aged, impotent and poor people, some for maintenance of sick and maimed soldiers and mariners, schools of learning, free schools, and scholars in universities, some for repair of bridges, ports, havens, causeways, churches, sea-banks and highways, some for education and preferment of orphans, some for or towards relief, stock or maintenance for houses of correction, some for marriages of poor maids, some for supportation, aid and help of young tradesmen, handicraftsmen and persons decayed, and others for relief or redemption of prisoners or captives, and for aid or ease of any poor inhabitants concerning payments of . . . taxes.[1]

Many of the gifts of this period were in the form of permanent funds—permanent so far as the giver could foresee. They were

[1] Pickering, Danby, *The Statutes at Large*, from the Thirty-ninth of Q. Elizabeth, to the Twelfth of K. Charles II inclusive. Printed at Cambridge University, 1763, vol. 7, p. 43.

often called "foundations" and are, indeed, forerunners of the American foundations described in a later chapter, but they lacked one important ingredient of the American device—wide freedom of action. They were more nearly relief societies than research and educational foundations of the modern type.

Most of these intended perpetuities sooner or later dissolved in financial crises or other disasters, but great numbers of them survived long enough to outlive their usefulness. Cases in which the narrow purposes of the donors could no longer be carried out, and cases of abuse in administration, became so numerous that in 1837 a Royal Commission of Inquiry reported on 28,840 "foundations" then in existence, and made many recommendations, one of which resulted in the establishment by the British Parliament of a regulatory commission having "the duty of superintendence and control of all property devoted to charitable uses, with an accounting and power to summon all parties concerned in management, to appoint and remove trustees, and to take care that no sale, mortgage, or exchange of charity property be effected without concurrence, and that all funds applicable be invested upon real or government security."

Quite aside from insecurity of their funds, some of these experiments in giving ran into other disasters, making worse the very conditions they set out to improve. One example, cited by Sir Arthur Hobhouse and, more recently, Lord Beveridge, illustrates several of the underlying problems.

Sir John Port, dying in 1556, settled his property upon two philanthropies, a school in Repton and Etwall Hospital. The latter was not a hospital in the modern sense, but an almshouse, and his will specified that this almshouse was to care for six of the poorest of Etwall parish, who were to have weekly forever 1s. 8d. apiece. Sir John died believing, doubtless, that he had solved the problem of poverty for Etwall; all but those poorest six, probably, would be able to support themselves, and the other residents of Etwall would bless his name for relieving them forever from all, or nearly all, costs of relief.

What happened? In this case the principal grew, so that by 1869 the annual income approached $15,000 (£3,000). Meanwhile, the fame of Etwall's six free livings attracted into the parish many shiftless persons, who established residence in the hope that sooner or later they would fall heir to one of those favored places. Etwall had a higher poor rate than its neighboring parishes!

This intolerable situation, created by Sir John's well-meant gift of nearly four centuries ago, has been partially relieved by a series of changes made in 1874, 1908, and 1923. A large part of the income of the almshouse has been transferred to the school. The almshouse was permitted to admit 16 alms-people from Etwall parish, and contribute to a number of out-pensioners, men or women from the whole county of Derby.

The Poor Law in England

Some light is shed on even the current problems of giving for "relief" by examining its gradual development in the English poor laws.

In 1014 King Ethelred decreed that one-third of the tithe of the church was to be given to "God's poor and needy men in thraldom." But it was not until the sixteenth century that extensive legislation was passed for relief of the poor. The City of London appears to have been first, with collections by the aldermen at church doors for relief of the poor under decree of the Court of Aldermen in 1532.

About three years later Act 27 of Henry VIII made each local parish responsible for its poor, and ordered clergy and local officials to obtain charitable offerings for their poor "with boxes every Sunday and holiday or otherwise," to be administered as a common fund for the whole parish. The Act also forbade private alms (in modern version, giving to panhandlers or tramps) upon pain of forfeiting ten times the amount given.[1]

If this penalty for giving to beggars seems severe, it is explained by an account of the times:

> Discharged serving men, old soldiers, ruined smallholders, out-of-work agricultural labourers, masterless men of all kinds helped to

[1] Aschrott's *The English Poor Law System* (Knight and Co., London, 1902) and Gray's *History of English Philanthropy* (P. S. King and Son, London, 1905) have been followed for most of this section.

make up an almost unbelievably numerous crew of rascals, who swarmed over the whole country-side. . . .

The most fantastic and horrible of these creatures to be met on the high road were the Palliards, the Abraham-Men, and the Counterfeit Cranks. The Palliard, who was also known in the canting tongue as a Clappendudgeon, was the kind of beggar who deliberately covered his limbs with loathsome running sores to rouse compassion and elicit alms. To make these raw and bleeding places they would tie arsenic or ratsbane on an ankle or an arm. When it had produced its corrosive effect they would then leave the sore exposed, and surround it with bloody and filthy rags, and so take their way from fair to fair and market to market.[1]

Attempts to put down these sturdy beggars resulted in even severer penalties against the beggars themselves. For some twenty-one years during the reign of Queen Elizabeth a vagrant's ear was bored the first time he was caught, and for a second offense the penalty was death.

But punishments, whether upon beggars or givers or both, did not abolish need, and aldermen standing in front of church doors did not collect enough in their boxes to meet it. The Act of 1551–1552 ordered appointment of two or more "collectors of alms" by whom the parishioners were to be "gently exhorted and admonished to contribute according to their means." If exhortation failed, the person was brought before the bishop, who might take measures to reform his obstinacy. By 1563 it was found necessary to add a provision that the person refusing the bishop could be haled before the magistrate, who was first to try to "move and persuade" him to contribute, but failing that, could assess him for the sum judged reasonable. From this it was no long step to outright taxation, established as the Poor Rate in the Act of 1601.

This Act for the Relief of the Poor divided persons to be relieved into three classes: children, able-bodied, and the infirm. Assistance to these classes consisted, in the case of children, in apprenticing them till their twenty-first or twenty-fourth year; the able-bodied, in setting them to work, with penalty for refusal;

---

[1] Byrne, M. St. Clare, *Elizabethan Life in Town and Country.* 2d ed., rev. Methuen and Co., London, 1934, pp. 87–88.

the infirm, in maintaining them, with power to place them in poorhouses.

Even the scanty provisions of this Poor Law, amended from time to time, met with objections. As late as 1786 the Reverend Joseph Townsend, a "well-wisher of mankind" according to his description of himself on the title page of his *Dissertation on the Poor Laws*, delivered these opinions. There must be hunger, for only hunger can goad the poor to work. It would be unfortunate if the poor lost their improvidence, for then there would be no one left to do the most sordid and ignoble jobs. But compulsory provision of relief under the poor laws, by promoting idleness, produced more improvidence than was needed for these purposes, and kept wages from falling as low as they were in Scotland. Legal aid for the poor should therefore be abolished.

The Organization of Charity

Thoughtful men and women saw broader needs than could be met by workhouses, doles from the poor rate, almshouses, hospitals, and schools. The joint stock company was beginning to build great businesses out of the small investments of many members; charity also might gain strength for these new tasks from numbers. They banded themselves together in associations.

Interesting experiments were tried. Health insurance had perhaps its beginnings in a Roman Catholic sick club, organized in Norwich, England, in 1782. It had honorary (benefactor) members, and ordinary members, who paid 1s a month if men and 6d if women. They received certain benefits when certified by their priest to be sick.

In 1796 Sir Thomas Bernard founded The Society for Bettering the Conditions and Increasing the Comforts of the Poor. Its method was to search for and "disseminate useful and practical knowledge with regard to the poor," soliciting reports from correspondents in various parts of the country.

Societies and associations of various types multiplied rapidly, particularly after the industrial revolution brought its added complications of crowded cities, child labor, long hours, periods of unemployment, low wages, disease, and other maladjustments.

The individual, or the individual family, the leaders were recognizing, should be treated in his or its individual setting. Sometimes only advice and guidance would be necessary, but these should be directed toward rehabilitation and prevention of future difficulties, with less emphasis upon meeting merely immediate need.

Family social work, the name now applied to this sort of program, had its beginnings in England in 1869, with the founding in London of the Society for Organising Charitable Relief and Repressing Mendicity—speedily renamed the Charity Organisation Society, and now the London Family Welfare Association. In the United States, Buffalo was the first to set up a society of this kind, in 1877. The movement spread rapidly here, and soon there were a multitude of associations organized to deal with not only family maladjustments but many of our civilization's more specialized "dis-eases." The voluntary "friendly visitors" of the first such societies were largely replaced by trained, professional staffs.

Germany (under Bismarck), France, and other countries have also done important pioneering in social legislation, and more recently New Zealand, Australia, the U.S.S.R. But traditionally Great Britain had been, and in many respects remains, the proving ground for the United States for experiments in relief and philanthropy in general. In a few respects, however, the United States has proceeded more rapidly or along different lines. One of these was the establishment of great foundations, not of the type of the earlier British "foundations" devoted to limited, closely defined purposes, but as exploratory and research agencies, providing much of philanthropy's "venture capital."

More recent developments in voluntary philanthropy are discussed in later chapters devoted to individual fields.

Expansion of Government Services

W̅E IN AMERICA are in a period of transition in the auspices of charitable care. The vast expansion of government services in the past two decades has changed conditions and vitally affected needs in nearly every field of voluntary philanthropy. The ratio between government and voluntary spending for welfare purposes will differ with definitions of "welfare purposes," but it is estimated that government expenditure (including federal, state, and local) is now about nine times voluntary giving for purposes which a generation or two ago would have been deemed to lie wholly within the field of private "charity."

Education

Education was one of the first areas to be extensively financed by government. A bitter controversy was being waged only a hundred years ago over free public elementary education in the United States. One Rhode Island farmer even threatened to shoot educator Henry Barnard if he ever caught him on his land advocating "such heresy as the partial confiscation of one man's property to educate another man's child." But this heresy became law, and a cornerstone of American democracy. In many communities approximately half of the local tax bill goes to support of the public schools. The United States Office of Education reported total expenditures for public elementary and secondary schools at $4.3 billion for the school year 1946–1947, which is more than all of us together gave to all charitable causes in that period.

As to higher education, in addition to that provided by state and municipal universities and state and federal support of special programs in other universities and colleges, the "GI Bill of Rights"[1] has resulted in the federal government's meeting about half the budget of most colleges in recent years. The Hoover Commission's special task force on federal educational activities reported federal funds for education at $3,400 million in 1949, as compared with $100 million in 1940. But $2,888 million of this was spent by the Veterans Administration, chiefly for GI's, and this item is being radically reduced.

Social Security

The greatest single stride ever made in bringing into the orbit of government the services that were formerly first charges upon our philanthropies was the Social Security Act, enacted in 1935 but broadened by later amendment and still needing considerable improvement. Where it touches most closely the traditional

TABLE 1. EXPENDITURES FOR ASSISTANCE UNDER THREE CATEGORIES OF THE SOCIAL SECURITY ACT AND FOR GENERAL ASSISTANCE IN UNITED STATES, JANUARY, 1950

Category	Beneficiaries	Amount
Old-age assistance	2,749,049 recipients	$122,786,247
Aid to dependent children	1,550,203 children (in 610,443 families)	44,785,459
Aid to the blind	93,109 recipients	4,300,971
General assistance	598,000 cases	29,199,000
Total		$201,071,677

SOURCE: *Social Security Bulletin*, April, 1950, p. 30.

fields of "charity" is in its provisions, in which the states participate, for the needy aged, dependent children, and the needy blind. Table 1 details expenditures in these three "categories," together with general assistance in which the federal government does not participate. Heavy federal expenditures were made for

[1] Servicemen's Readjustment Act, Public Law 346, 78th Congress.

general assistance—"relief"—during the depression, but the states and localities now carry this expenditure.

We shall not discuss whether these amounts were adequate at 1950 prices, whether a few dubious cases slipped through, or how numerous were the other cases which should have had help but failed to get it. The big fact is that in these four programs alone more than five million persons (the number of persons involved in the 598,000 general assistance "cases" is not given but must have exceeded a million) received from state and federal funds in one month $201 million. Here we are giving at a rate of more than $2.4 billion a year to just those distress cases which would otherwise pull strongest at our heartstrings and our private purses—needy old folk, fatherless children, the needy blind, and families which have run into hard luck.

The need for relief should also be much reduced through the vast social insurance programs now in effect and being expanded, even if not all prove to be actuarially sound. Under the Social Security Act are unemployment insurance and old-age and survivors' insurance, with benefit payments to some 2,077,000 beneficiaries under the former program and 2,781,000 under the latter in January, 1950. Retirement plans financed by employers or jointly by employers and employes have become common in many industries. "Health and welfare funds," a part of an increasing number of recent union contracts, are too late a development for appraisal. A vast national health insurance program has been proposed; meanwhile, voluntary hospital and medical plans of various types cover some of the medical emergencies of millions of citizens. These insurance programs are a means of spreading the risk of many of the major disasters which in the past have brought heavy demands upon voluntary charitable agencies.

The Federal Budget

The insurance programs under government auspices are in theory paid by the individuals insured and their employers, but the funds are not segregated and may need supplementation from other tax funds. The recent growth in direct federal expenditures for welfare purposes is shown in Table 2, which compares welfare expenditures of the federal government in 1941 with the President's budget estimates for 1950 and 1951. The table includes only items with a substantial relation to projects which might otherwise appeal to private philanthropy.

TABLE 2. CERTAIN WELFARE EXPENDITURES OF THE FEDERAL GOVERNMENT IN FISCAL YEAR 1941 COMPARED WITH PROPOSED EXPENDITURES FOR YEARS 1950 AND 1951

In millions

Budget number	Description	Fiscal years ending June 30		
		1941 actual	1950 estimate	1951 estimate
103.	Veterans' readjustment benefits	$ 10	$ 3,038	$ 2,687
104.	Veterans' hospitals, other services, and administrative costs	104	1,107	1,117
152.	International recovery and relief	16	5,060	3,654
153.	Foreign economic development	100	82	81
155.	Philippine war damage and rehabilitation . . .	..	221	91
201.	Retirement and dependents' insurance	143	613	601
202.	Accident compensation	5	25	28
203.	Assistance to the aged and other special groups .	725	1,257	1,515
204.	Work relief and direct relief	1,575	29	39
205.	Social security administration	8	..	..
206.	Promotion of public health	53	280	432
207.	Crime control and correction	39	93	99
251.	Public housing programs	333	117	133
252.	Aids to private housing	*198*a	833	1,027
253.	Research and other housing aids . . :	..	7	8
254.	Provision of community facilities	*4*a	38	103
255.	Urban development and redevelopment . . .	..	11	58
301.	Promotion of education	26	41	358
302.	Educational aid to special groups	12	7	12
303.	Library and museum services	5	11	12
304.	General purpose research	24	65	52
405.	Recreational use of natural resources	14	29	40
	Total	$2,990	$12,964	$12,147

a Italicized figures represent credits, repayments in this year exceeding expenditures.

SOURCE: President Truman's proposed Budget of the United States for the Fiscal Year Ending June 30, 1951, Appendix 5, and earlier data.

If the 1951 estimates are reasonably accurate, federal expenditures on these items will have jumped in a decade from about $3 billion to more than $12 billion, an increase of nearly $9.2 billion. But much of this increase ($7.4 billion, in fact) is in the first five items—services for veterans and relief and reconstruction abroad —all war related. Indeed, the seven items 201–207, subclassified in the President's budget as "social welfare, health, and security," have collectively increased only $166 million, or 6.5 per cent, which is meager in view of the population increase and the decreased value of the dollar.

As compared with our total giving for all charitable purposes, the taxes we pay to the federal government for welfare purposes seem very large, even if we deduct the first five items as war related and call the amount $4.5 billion. But as compared with some of our other expenditures, they seem less impressive. For direct national defense we were proposing to spend even before the outbreak of the war in Korea some $14.5 billion, and for interest on our debt, $5.6 billion. During World War II we were spending for war purposes alone some $8 billion in single months.[1]

State and Local Welfare Budgets

Emphasis has been laid on expansion of federal expenditures for welfare purposes, though states and localities participate in some of the programs mentioned. Because of the many state and local jurisdictions, and the wide differences among them, it is not possible briefly to present a picture of their welfare activities.

In general, it may be said that the states contribute heavily, under complicated formulas for matching funds with the federal government, for three public assistance programs—old-age assistance, aid to dependent children, and aid to the needy blind. In the year ending June 30, 1949 benefits and administration in these programs totaled $1,812 million, of which $940 million were federal funds and $872 million state and local funds. General assistance—"relief"—has now become entirely a state and local responsibility. Elementary public education is paid largely from local taxes, with some aid from state revenues. The considerable sums involved in these and similar programs on the state level are suggested by the budget of one state for 1949–1950, in Table 3.

Welfare expenditures of some of our larger cities are also considerable. The Welfare Department of New York City had a budget of $169 million for the fiscal year 1948–1949, and asked

[1] War Production Board Release 6106.

$175 million for 1950. A special bill passed the state legislature in 1949 to permit New York City to expend $150 million for hospital construction beyond the City's permitted debt limit.

TABLE 3. CERTAIN WELFARE APPROPRIATIONS OF NEW
YORK STATE FOR THE FISCAL YEAR 1949–1950

In millions

Purpose	State programs	Local programs	Total
Correction	$ 23	..	$ 23
Education	44	$236	280
Health	13	20	33
Mental hygiene	102	..	102
Social welfare	5	137	142
Youth Commission	..	2	2
Total	$187	$395	$582

The Road Ahead?

Clearly, we are now in a period of change, and one of the most significant elements in that change is the extent to which many basic needs of man are being met by government. Said Lord Beveridge of the present situation in England:

> The State has undertaken to see that, irrespective of the means of his parents, every child shall have education fitted to his abilities. The State has set out to ensure freedom from want by ensuring that at all times, of earning and not earning alike, the income of each family shall be enough for its basic needs. The State has set out to ensure freedom from avoidable disease, so far as this can be attained by providing that every sick person irrespective of means shall be able to get the treatment needed to make him well.[1]

We have not proceeded that far in the United States; here, the "welfare state" is both defended and opposed. Much of the opposition is economic—the fear we cannot afford what the people may demand. Some of it is political—the danger of concentration in government of so much power. Others argue that too much security will weaken the work incentive and moral fiber

[1] Beveridge, Lord, *Voluntary Action.* The Macmillan Co., New York, 1948, p. 225.

of recipients—and at least one churchman recently complained that governmental invasion of the field of child welfare was bad for givers. "How can we maintain our spirit of Christian charity, our spirit of brotherhood," he asked the House of Representatives Ways and Means Committee, "without the appeal of the great charitable institutions for the care of children?"

Chapters that follow deal with many important fields in which needs vastly outrun resources, even if government should further extend its services. But the changed conditions do require rethinking, so that giving, relieved from some burdens, may become more effective and creative.

CHAPTER 4

Who Gives and How Much?

IT HAS been pointed out that a considerable shift in patterns of personal giving has been taking place in recent years. In appraising these changes, it is unfortunate that accurate information on total giving in the United States does not exist. Unmapped areas trouble the explorer whether he examines the records of givers or the balance sheets of recipients.

Sources of Information

The main sources of information supplied by givers are these:

a. Contributions of persons as reported on individual income-tax returns
b. Gifts for charitable purposes as reported (since 1932) on gift-tax returns
c. Corporation contributions as reported (since 1936) on corporate income-tax returns
d. Bequests reported on estate-tax returns
e. Foundation reports of grants

Unfortunately, the extensive reports published by the Bureau of Internal Revenue cannot be used as an index of philanthropy, particularly in recent years. In 1944 a standard deduction provision permitted persons with total incomes of less than $5,000 to deduct approximately 10 per cent without itemizing, and persons with larger incomes could deduct a maximum $500 without itemizing. From that year on, fewer than one taxpayer in five itemized contributions. Most of those who did itemize had either very large incomes or had in that year unusually heavy deductible items, among which may have been contributions. It had become manifestly unsafe to use these reported contributions, either in their totals or in proportion to income, as an index of giving.[1]

However, available income-tax data reach a very substantial total, the amount of income on which contributions are not itemized can be calculated, and informed guesses can be made as to the rate of charitable contribution. These informed guesses must take into account, however, the probability that not all income-tax reports are reliable either as to the gross income reported—the government is collecting data on what is politely called "understatement of income"—or as to contributions.

As a check on these crude estimates, an attempt can be made to discover the income of philanthropic organizations. The main sources of such income are:

a. Contributions for current purposes from individuals, corporations, or a central fund-raising agency such as a community chest
b. Contributions for endowment, building, or other permanent funds
c. Bequests, which may be for current or permanent funds
d. Grants from foundations
e. Appropriations from local, state, or federal government
f. Income from invested funds
g. Fees charged for services
h. Income from business operations

The equivalent of further income is represented by possession of buildings (saving rent) and exemption from taxation.

Most national and many local agencies issue financial reports, but troublesome gaps exist. In religion, for example, few statistics on giving are available from the Roman Catholic Church, the Church of Christ, Scientist, or the Jewish congregations. Thousands of local welfare organizations issue no reports, or if they do, their reports are not centrally collected. Among available reports, some are difficult to interpret or fail to reveal significant items.

[1] See Appendix H for a detailed discussion of this point.

Enough remains, however, to be highly illuminating as to the directions current giving is taking.

The Low-Income Giver

Some years ago the writer was walking through the Great Smoky Mountains in Tennessee. The depression was in its blackest depths, and a government program was making small allotments to impoverished farmers for seed, stock, or needed improvements. He met a government agent who had just asked a mountain woman, scratching a bare living from two poor acres, what she would do "if the government could allot you two hundred dollars?"

The woman thought a moment. Her cabin had no floor but the packed earth, and light came through chinks in its walls. Finally she said:

"Reckon I'd give it to the poor."

The generosity of the very poor, in proportion to their resources, has been proverbial, one famous example being Jesus' parable of the poor widow with her two mites.

Many people assume that though some of the poor give a large proportion of their earnings, their total contribution remains a small part of philanthropic income; that most of this income is received in relatively large amounts from wealthy persons.

This is far from the truth. Newspapers dramatize the large contributions, which have been the main resource of professionally directed campaigns for endowments, new buildings, and similar major philanthropic collections, though even here the lower-income contributor is recently taking a larger part. But the whole of philanthropy, which includes giving to churches, rests most heavily upon low-income givers.

Exact statistical demonstration is difficult. Until 1941 the income-tax filing provisions did not dip low enough to include many low-income givers, and from 1944 on, a large proportion from nearly all income classes took the newly permitted standard deduction. Table 4, however, presents some extremely interesting data for 1943, when contribution records represent the highest proportion of total personal income.

In that year nearly 44 million individual income-tax reports were filed, showing total income of nearly $107 billion. More than half of this income, $62 billion, was reported by taxpayers in the "below-$3,000" class. In that year all net-income classes

TABLE 4. INCOME-TAX DATA ON CONTRIBUTIONS AS RELATED TO NET INCOME CLASS, 1943

Net income class	Returns (thousands)	Total income (millions)	Contributions (millions)	Per cent
Under $3,000 reporting contributions:				
No net income	215.4	$ 170.9	$ 5.7	3.3
Under $1,000	3,052.3	2,457.4	88.7	3.6
$1,000 under $2,000	6,090.3	10,539.8	338.7	3.2
$2,000 under $3,000	6,333.2	17,704.7	430.1	2.4
Subtotal	15,691.2	$ 30,872.8	$ 863.2	2.8
Under $3,000 using form 1040A	20,341.5	31,086.5	621.7a	2.0a
Total under $3,000	36,032.7	$ 61,959.3	$1,484.9a	2.4a
$3,000 under $4,000	4,676.3	$ 17,339.2	$ 382.3	2.2
$4,000 under $5,000	1,411.3	6,735.2	143.1	2.1
Total $3,000 under $5,000	6,087.6	$ 24,074.4	$ 525.4	2.2
$5,000 under $6,000	469.3	$ 2,797.7	$ 58.1	2.1
$6,000 under $7,000	249.5	1,769.4	37.2	2.1
$7,000 under $8,000	166.0	1,360.7	28.0	2.1
$8,000 under $9,000	119.6	1,116.4	23.1	2.1
$9,000 under $10,000	95.2	989.1	20.4	2.0
Total $5,000 under $10,000	1,099.6	$ 8,033.3	$ 166.8	2.1
$10,000 under $20,000	330.3	$ 4,949.1	$ 95.9	1.9
$20,000 under $50,000	138.4	4,429.1	89.3	2.0
$50,000 under $100,000	24.8	1,813.7	43.4	2.4
$100,000 under $250,000	6.4	995.7	30.1	3.0
$250,000 under $500,000	.7	275.0	9.3	3.4
$500,000 under $1,000,000	.3	161.2	7.6	4.7
$1,000,000 under $5,000,000	..	86.0	3.8	4.4
$5,000,000 and over	..	8.3	1.0	12.0
Total $10,000 and over	500.9	$ 12,718.1	$ 280.4	2.2
Total reporting contributionsb	23,379.3	$ 75,698.6	$1,835.8	2.4
Total including group using form 1040A	43,720.8	$106,785.1	$2,457.5a	2.3a

a Estimate.　b Omits group under $3,000 using form 1040A.
SOURCE: Compiled from *Individual and Taxable Fiduciary Income Tax Returns for 1943*, Treasury Department, June, 1947. Estimate on 1040A contributions by author.

were required to report contributions except the "below-$3,000" group, and more than 15 million of that group, with approximately half the income of the group, elected to do so.

Among all income classes reporting contributions, the lowest rate was for the group with net incomes between $10,000 and

$20,000—1.9 per cent of total income. The rate rose gradually for wealthier individuals, topping 4 per cent after $500,000 and reaching 12 per cent for the single individual with an income of $8 million in that year.

The rate also rose as income declined from the $10,000 level. At $9,000 to $10,000 the rate became 2 per cent. For all income classes from $4,000 to $9,000 the rate was a consistent 2.1 per cent. It was somewhat higher for the $3,000 to $4,000 class, 2.2 per cent.

For the under-$3,000 groups the picture is less clear. Contributions were itemized for only half the income represented, and by fewer than half the taxpayers. For those who did report contributions, the rate rose quite sharply, reaching 3.6 per cent for those with income below $1,000, and standing at 3.3 per cent even for those whose deductions were greater than their total income, giving them no net income.

Were those who filed on 1040A mostly nongivers or small givers, and those who took the trouble to make out the longer report nontypical heavy contributors? The question is important because the 1040A group is so large. Table 5 bears on this question.

It is obvious from this table that contributions were not the major factor in inducing this "under-$3,000" group to trouble with the longer, itemized form. Contributions were less than a quarter of their total deductions. Deductible taxes alone were greater; indeed, this poorest group paid a higher percentage of their total income in such taxes (which do not include the federal income tax itself, of course) than the wealthier groups. From this showing it seems unlikely that in the two "under-$3,000" groups there is any wide difference in contribution rates. Generous charitable contributions, coupled with high other deductions, may have pushed a few taxpayers into the group for whom itemized reports became desirable; but many equally generous contributors must have remained in the 1040A group either because their total deductions were not above 10 per cent or were so near that figure that the added effort of the longer form was not worthwhile.

TABLE 5. DEDUCTIONS CLAIMED ON 1943 INCOME-TAX RETURNS
WHICH ITEMIZED DEDUCTIONS FOR TWO NET INCOME
GROUPS

Amounts in millions

Item	Net income under $3,000		Net income $3,000 and over	
	Amount	Per cent of total income	Amount	Per cent of total income
Total income	$30,872.8	100.0	$44,825.8	100.0
Deductions:				
Business-type[a]	467.8	1.5	287.8	0.6
Interest paid	528.1	1.7	528.0	1.2
Taxes paid	959.8	3.1	1,169.4	2.6
Loss from fire, storm	90.8	0.3	49.2	0.1
Medical, dental, etc.	582.3	1.9	217.3	0.5
Contributions	863.0	2.8	973.0	2.2
Other deductions	578.3	1.9	506.2	1.1
Total deductions	$ 4,070.1	13.2	$ 3,730.9	8.3

[a] Net loss from sales of capital assets and other property, business loss, partnership loss.

SOURCE: *Individual and Taxable Fiduciary Income Tax Returns for 1943.*

A contribution rate of 2 per cent has therefore been estimated for the 1040A group, as compared with the 2.8 per cent reported by those "under-$3,000" taxpayers who did itemize deductions. This estimate, which includes an allowance for overstatement of contributions on the part of those who included that item, is probably too conservative. Nevertheless, if we count on no more than this amount, surprising conclusions emerge:

The lowest-income groups (under $3,000) supply more than half the contributions philanthropy receives from living donors.

The lowest-income groups contribute at a rate higher than the average for all groups.

In the 1943 sample, the "under-$3,000" group appears to have contributed slightly more than 60 per cent of the total, and to their $1.5 billion should be added the unknown contributions of the numerous persons having incomes too small to require income-tax returns. The only other years offering extensive contribution data, 1941 and 1942, closely correspond with 1943.

Fragmentary data on contributions from more recent income-tax reports show no contrary evidence, but must be used with caution. For example, the 1946 report[1] indicates that in the

[1] See Table 45, p. 290.

"under-$5,000" class only one taxpayer in seven itemized his contributions, while nearly half (47 per cent) of the higher-income groups found it worthwhile to do so. But this seventh of the "under-$5,000" group reported contributions of $843 million, while all remaining groups reported only $796 million.

It is probable also that within the low-income group there is an unusually large amount of person-to-person giving to meet immediate emergencies. Such giving falls outside the definition of philanthropy of the Bureau of Internal Revenue and the statistical summaries of this volume, but it is a widespread practice which should not be overlooked. It reached very large proportions in the form of cash remittances and parcel-post packages sent overseas, usually to relatives, just after the war.

Other Income Groups

Although more than half of all philanthropic giving appears to come from the low-income groups, a large proportion of this giving goes to a single agency, the church. Colleges, hospitals, voluntary welfare agencies—particularly where these are supported by organized campaigns, which cannot deal economically with small gifts—still receive a large part of their support from higher-income groups. Even the National War Fund reported:

> In cities with population of 25,000 or more, it was found that about a third of the money comes from the 100 largest givers, individuals and corporations, with almost half of this amount from the 10 largest givers. About another third comes from the 1,000 next largest givers, and the rest from everybody else. . . . In smaller cities and non-chest towns and rural areas, the best yardstick we found was to seek 60 per cent of the money from about 2 per cent of the population, with the 2 per cent group including those who were thought to be able and willing to give $25 or more.[1]

For all except the very low-income groups, already discussed, income-tax returns furnish fairly complete reports on contributions from 1922 until 1944, when the new standard deduction

[1] Seymour, Harold J., *Design for Giving:* The Story of the National War Fund. Harper and Bros., New York, 1947, p. 52.

began to be taken by many taxpayers. It would be naïve to assume that no falsification exists in these reported contributions. However, this source of error is probably not large in relation to total, and is at least partly offset by legitimate contributions forgotten by conscientious taxpayers. In comparing giving trends for the various income groups a more serious problem is the changing value of money. A $3,000 income in 1940, for example, was almost equivalent in purchasing power to a $5,000 income in 1950.

Generally speaking, gifts rise with income in absolute amount. But the lowest rate in giving appears to be somewhere around the $10,000 level. In 1943 the rate was only 1.9 per cent of total income in the $10,000 to $20,000 class. In 1947 the lowest rate of contribution to total income of those who reported on this item was 3.0 per cent, for the $20,000 to $25,000 class. All other income groups reported higher rates—the poorest (those with less than $1,000) 6.5 per cent; the 6 persons with incomes above $5 million, 9.7 per cent. Not much reliance, however, can be placed on such comparisons in 1947 because of the varying proportions of taxpayers who reported contributions in the different income groups.

Table 6 compares, for selected years, the average gifts of persons in certain income classes. The data of this table correspond more nearly with popular impressions of philanthropy. Large sums are given out of current income only by the very wealthy. The rate of giving based on total income is low for all income classes, but ascends in the highest groups where high-bracket taxes result in tax reductions offsetting an increasing portion of the gift.

In the time span shown, no long-term trends can be discerned, unless 1946 marks a genuine increase. This is somewhat doubtful, because of the partial nature of the 1946 data, as has been indicated. Disregarding 1946, contribution rates were lower in 1942 than in 1922 for all these groups except the million-dollar incomes, which show a pronounced upward trend; and even in their case the 1946 figures are comparable, for all but one of the 94 taxpayers in this group did itemize deductions.

For reasons clear from this table, many agencies seeking funds concentrate on the higher-income groups. They cannot afford intensive cultivation of persons whose gifts are small.

TABLE 6. AVERAGE TOTAL INCOME,[a] CONTRIBUTION, AND RATIO OF CONTRIBUTION TO INCOME FOR SELECTED INCOME CLASSES[b] AT FOUR-YEAR INTERVALS, 1922–1946

Year	Average income	Average contribution	Rate	Average income	Average contribution	Rate	Average income	Average contribution	Rate
	$5,000–$10,000			$10,000–$25,000			$50,000–$100,000		
1922	$7,990	$167	2.1	$17,757	$340	1.9	$80,922	$2,079	2.6
1926	8,012	135	1.7	17,326	312	1.8	77,966	1,910	2.5
1930	8,192	137	1.7	18,701	339	1.8	87,520	2,258	2.6
1934	8,054	143	1.8	17,741	336	1.9	79,683	2,216	2.8
1938	7,870	149	1.9	17,617	349	2.0	81,836	2,353	2.9
1942	7,498	149	2.0	16,576	317	1.9	74,242	1,769	2.4
1946[c]	6,695	263	3.9	15,291	498	3.3	66,544	2,356	3.5
	$300,000–$500,000			$1,000,000 and over					
1922	$458,311	$15,631	3.4	$2,508,881	$77,045	3.1			
1926	402,753	12,852	3.2	2,391,879	86,359	3.6			
1930	480,654	16,357	3.4	2,859,053	164,500	5.8			
1934	451,759	19,362	4.3	2,137,152	126,788	5.9			
1938	467,203	23,808	5.1	2,214,040	79,660	3.6			
1942	420,940	13,927	3.3	2,386,605	110,263	4.6			
1946[c]	372,888	21,022	5.6	1,968,699	159,699	8.1			

[a] Adjusted gross income in 1946.

[b] Net income classes, except in 1946; in that year adjusted gross income classes.

[c] In 1946 use of the standard deduction by 61 per cent of taxpayers in the $5,000 to $10,000 class and 40 per cent in the $10,000 to $25,000 class makes it probable that the contribution percentage, derived from the remaining itemized reports, is too high for these classes.

SOURCE: *Statistics of Income* for the years indicated, Bureau of Internal Revenue, Treasury Department.

But Table 6 needs the corrective of wider perspective. The small giver is more liberal, within his means, than many of the larger givers, and there are very many more of him. Consider in Table 7 the picture of national giving developed from the fairly complete 1943 data, accepting the assumed 2 per cent contribution rate of the 1040A taxpayers, which is believed conservative.

In 1943 the group with incomes above $10,000 constituted only 1 per cent of the income-tax filers, and contributed only 11.4 per cent of the estimated total. Yet from this small group must come the support of many specialized agencies and welfare activities.

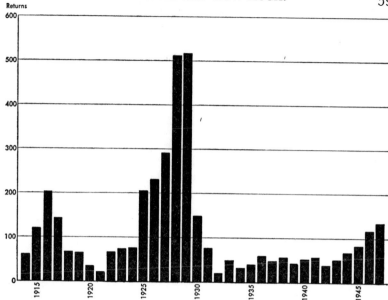

CHART 1. NUMBER OF FEDERAL INCOME-TAX RETURNS WITH
NET INCOME OF $1,000,000 OR OVER, BY YEARS, 1914–1947

NOTE: Individual and fiduciary returns are included in all years. Because of
changes in classification procedure, the "income" is net income through 1943,
adjusted gross income thereafter.

Taxation policies and other factors have sharply reduced the
number of persons with very large incomes, as is indicated by
Chart 1, showing by year the number of million-dollar incomes
since 1914. In both 1928 and 1929 these exceeded 500; even in
recent years of inflated prices they have only recently passed 100.

TABLE 7. CONTRIBUTIONS BY INCOME CLASSES, 1943

Net income class	Returns (thousands)	Contributions	
		Amount (millions)	Per cent of total
Under $3,000	36,032.7	$1,484.9[a]	60.4
$3,000 under $5,000	6,087.6	525.4	21.4
$5,000 under $10,000	1,099.6	166.8	6.8
$10,000 under $50,000	468.7	185.2	7.5
$50,000 under $100,000	24.8	43.4	1.8
$100,000 under $1,000,000	7.4	47.0	1.9
$1,000,000 and over	..	4.8	0.2
Total	43,720.8	$2,457.5	100.0

[a] Assuming a 2 per cent rate for 1040A reports.

SOURCE: Compiled from *Individual and Taxable Fiduciary Income Tax Returns for 1943*.

Nevertheless, the alleged "drying up" of gifts from persons of very large incomes has been overstated. It seems unlikely that family fortunes comparable with those of the Rockefellers and the Fords are now accumulating, or are likely to accumulate under present tax policies. The Rockefeller family benefactions were recently estimated at approximately $1 billion, of which Mr. Rockefeller, Sr. gave more than $530 million. But recipients of very large incomes (over $300,000 adjusted gross income) numbered over one thousand in 1947. As Table 8 indicates, their income was only half that of the similar group in 1925 and less than a quarter that of lush 1929, but—perhaps stimulated by high

TABLE 8. INCOME AND CONTRIBUTIONS OF PERSONS WITH INCOME[a] ABOVE $300,000, IN SELECTED YEARS

Year	Persons reporting	Income (millions)	Contributions	
			Amount (millions)	Per cent of income
1925	1,578	$1,221	$38	3.2
1929	2,730	2,890	84	2.9
1933	272	242	8	3.2
1937	523	394	22	5.7
1941	550	390	20	5.1
1945	857	495	34	6.9
1947	1,056	658	48	7.3

[a] Net income except in 1945 and 1947; in those years adjusted gross income.

SOURCE: *Statistics of Income* for the years indicated.

taxes in their bracket—their rate of giving had notably increased. Charitable and welfare agencies therefore received from this group in 1947 more than half as much as in peak 1929, and six times as much as in depressed 1933.

Geographical Differences

Giving varies not only with income group, but with geography. It is not merely that income is concentrated in certain areas; the rate of contribution itself shows marked sectional differences. As Table 9 and the accompanying map demonstrate, the West and Middle West, except Utah, tend toward low rates; the South is intermediate; relatively high rates are confined to the industrial East and a few southern states. These data are from income-tax

TABLE 9. CHARITABLE CONTRIBUTIONS OF PERSONS BY STATES IN 1942 WITH RELATION TO GROSS INCOME AND NATIONAL TOTAL, AND COMPARED WITH QUOTAS PROPOSED BY THE NATIONAL QUOTA COMMITTEE

Dollar figures in millions

State	Gross income	Contributions[a]		Per cent of national total	
		Amount	Per cent of gross income	Actual contributions	Proposed quotas
Alabama	$ 858	$ 18.5	2.2	0.9	1.1
Arizona	307	5.2	1.7	0.3	0.4
Arkansas	418	9.7	2.3	0.5	0.7
California	6,902	118.9	1.7	6.1	8.8
Colorado	640	11.5	1.8	0.6	0.9
Connecticut	1,968	43.2	2.2	2.2	1.6
Delaware	260	6.2	2.4	0.3	0.3
Dist. of Columbia	860	17.9	2.1	0.9	0.9
Florida	962	20.6	2.1	1.1	1.5
Georgia	943	22.3	2.4	1.1	1.4
Idaho	258	4.1	1.6	0.2	0.3
Illinois	6,472	144.0	2.2	7.4	7.5
Indiana	2,221	44.9	2.0	2.3	2.6
Iowa	1,350	24.4	1.8	1.3	1.9
Kansas	950	17.2	1.8	0.9	1.3
Kentucky	892	22.1	2.5	1.1	1.2
Louisiana	808	16.2	2.0	0.8	1.2
Maine	479	10.3	2.2	0.5	0.5
Maryland	1,737	37.5	2.2	1.9	1.5
Massachusetts	3,548	86.3	2.4	4.4	3.6
Michigan	4,814	95.0	2.0	4.9	4.4
Minnesota	1,481	30.4	2.1	1.6	2.0
Mississippi	382	8.7	2.3	0.4	0.6
Missouri	2,022	46.5	2.3	2.4	2.8
Montana	329	4.8	1.5	0.2	0.4
Nebraska	660	11.7	1.8	0.6	1.0
Nevada	148	2.4	1.6	0.1	0.1
New Hampshire	302	6.3	2.1	0.3	0.3
New Jersey	3,690	106.2	2.9	5.4	3.5
New Mexico	180	2.7	1.5	0.1	0.2
New York	11,306	351.9	3.1	18.0	14.2
North Carolina	1,027	28.4	2.8	1.5	1.5
North Dakota	239	4.2	1.8	0.2	0.3
Ohio	5,501	117.3	2.1	6.0	5.7
Oklahoma	742	15.8	2.1	0.8	1.1
Oregon	989	15.4	1.6	0.8	1.0
Pennsylvania	7,128	180.2	2.5	9.2	7.1
Rhode Island	625	14.6	2.3	0.7	0.6
South Carolina	510	14.3	2.8	0.7	0.7
South Dakota	232	3.9	1.7	0.2	0.4
Tennessee	1,001	24.5	2.4	1.3	1.4
Texas	2,961	58.7	2.0	3.0	4.4
Utah	344	8.9	2.6	0.5	0.4
Vermont	163	3.4	2.1	0.2	0.2
Virginia	1,366	35.4	2.6	1.8	1.5
Washington	1,667	26.4	1.6	1.4	1.7
West Virginia	798	16.2	2.0	0.8	0.9
Wisconsin	1,931	39.2	2.0	2.0	2.2
Wyoming	152	2.5	1.6	0.1	0.2
Total	$85,523	$1,956.9	2.3	100.0	100.0

[a] Includes 1040A contributions estimated at 2 per cent of gross income.

SOURCES: *Statistics of Income for 1942*, Part 1; National Quota Committee *Recommendations* dated May, 1949.

records for 1942, one of the few years when contributions were extensively reported.

Because some of the higher rates are concentrated in states of considerable wealth, sectional differences in total amount of giving from personal income are even more pronounced. A compact block of three states, New York, New Jersey, and Pennsylvania, accounted for nearly a third (32.6 per cent) of the giving in this sample year, although they had less than 26 per cent of the gross individual income. The final column in the table represents the

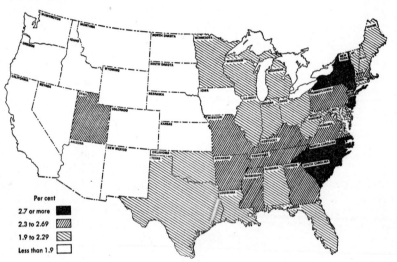

Per cent
2.7 or more
2.3 to 2.69
1.9 to 2.29
Less than 1.9

MAP 1. CONTRIBUTIONS AS PER CENT OF GROSS PERSONAL INCOME BY STATES, 1942

National Quota Committee's 1949 recommendations on uniform state quotas for national appeals. The chief bases for these quotas are described on page 151. The quotas correspond fairly closely with the actual averages in 1942.

Labor Contributions

Recently Matthew Woll, American Federation of Labor vice-president, wrote, "Community fund-raisers must make room for new comers. The new comers are labor."

The contributions of wage-earners have always been an important part of philanthropy in America. Solicitation of employe groups within plants dates back at least to World War I. What is relatively new is organized participation of labor-union groups.

This participation may take a variety of forms. A single union may contribute, either through a collection among its members or a contribution from the union treasury itself. The members of the International Ladies Garment Workers Union make contributions to a variety of causes. In Linden, New Jersey, members of the Coopers International Union, AFL, worked by agreement on a holiday and donated their earnings to the local community chest. The American Federation of Musicians, AFL, has distributed in three years $4.5 million to provide free public music programs, the contribution coming from royalties on records paid in to the union's welfare fund; of course, these free public performances offer considerable additional employment for musicians.

Both the CIO and the AFL maintain special subsidiaries to coordinate their relations with community chests and other fund-raising organizations, activities in foreign relief, and their community relations in general. The CIO subsidiary is the National CIO Community Services ,Committee; for the AFL it is the Labor League for Human Rights. They not only cooperate in fund-raising drives; they see to it that organized labor's viewpoint is represented on the boards and committees of the disbursing and service agencies.

The increased willingness of employers in recent years to make payroll deductions for welfare contributions, sometimes even on a weekly basis, has facilitated larger gifts from employe groups. The employes of the Ford Motor Company in the Detroit area pledged $840,000 in 1949 to Detroit's Torch Drive, a sum called "the largest amount ever subscribed by workers of a single firm to any health and community services campaign." The contributions from employe groups to community chest campaigns in recent years has been averaging about 25 per cent of total amounts raised. For the 1950 chest year, this contribution was $46.5 million out of a total of $193 million, or 24 per cent.

Corporations as Donors

Corporation giving began on a substantial scale in World War I, and after that war was continued on a more modest scale in behalf of community chests, the Salvation Army, and other agencies. When corporations were allowed a 5 per cent deduction for charitable contributions in the Revenue Act of 1935, they began again to be more substantial contributors.

The law in this field has not yet been wholly clarified. The federal provision[1] establishes deductibility of such gifts, but does not grant the right so to use the stockholders' money. A few states have permissive legislation, but most do not. Nevertheless, no successful stockholder's suit to restrain such giving is recorded, and in most large corporations it has become standard practice.

Not all corporation contributions toward philanthropy are recorded as such in corporation income-tax returns. For some types it is possible to claim full deduction as a business expense, rather than a contribution, without regard to the 5 per cent limitation.[2] On the other hand, a few items reported as contributions are not philanthropy in its usual definition. But the growth in corporation "contributions or gifts" as recorded in tax reports is impressive.

CORPORATION CONTRIBUTIONS, IN MILLIONS

1936	$30	1940	$38	1944	$234
1937	33	1941	58	1945	266
1938	27	1942	98	1946	214
1939	31	1943	159	1947	241

It is surely more than coincidence that the amount rose sharply with high wartime taxation rates, reaching a peak of $266 million in 1945. On January 1, 1946 the excess-profits tax was repealed, though the 38 per cent tax on corporation income remained.[3] The year 1946 saw a decline in corporation contributions, though not so severe as some of the benefiting agencies had feared; 1947 showed an increase over 1946. What might happen in a depres-

1 Internal Revenue Code, Section 23, q. See p. 271.   2 See p. 235.
3 It became 45 per cent in 1950.

sion, with stockholders conscious of reduced or omitted dividends, has not yet been tested.

The present important position of the corporation as a donor is indicated by the fact that since 1942 recorded contributions from corporations have been about equal to the contributions of all individuals with incomes above $25,000; they have also closely paralleled total contributions to community chests; of those contributions, indeed, they themselves constituted 40 per cent for 1950.

We have already seen that announcement of the demise of the big-income giver has been premature; but the decline in such givers that has taken place is probably being compensated for by the new large donor, business. Henry Ford II said recently, on establishment of the Ford Motor Company Fund:

> It is our observation that traditional sources of financial support of private institutions operating in these fields are tending to disappear. We do not like the consequences inherent in the alternative facing such private institutions—that of having to turn to government for much-needed financial aid. In our opinion, this situation places an increasing responsibility upon American businesses in their role of industrial citizens.

Aside from questions of policy, the amount of a corporation's gifts varies with its size, type, and current financial position. Efforts have been made to arrive at standard formulas for different types of business. For example, the Greater New York Fund reports in 1950 these formulas for solicitations:

> Department stores, $1 for each $2,500 of sales
> Advertising agencies, $65 for each $1 million of business volume
> Hotels, 60 cents per room
> Savings banks, $25 per million in deposits
> Commercial banks, $50 per million in deposits, or $25 per employe, or 0.88 per cent of net earnings
> Miscellaneous companies, chiefly local, $5 to $30 per employe
> National companies, for New York, 0.1 per cent of earnings

The community chest in Rockford, Illinois, suggested for company quotas an average of three factors: one day's payroll, 0.1 per cent of annual sales, and 1 per cent of annual profits before taxes. Chain stores are said usually to budget 0.1 per cent of gross sales to be contributed through division or unit managers.

Table 10 compares by industrial classifications the corporation contributions reported for the peak year 1945 and for the last prewar year, 1941.

TABLE 10. CORPORATION CONTRIBUTIONS AND GIFTS IN COMPARISON WITH COMPILED NET PROFITS, 1941 AND 1945

Industrial groups	Returns (thousands)		Compiled net profit (millions)		Contributions (millions)		Contributions as per cent of profits	
	1941	1945	1941	1945	1941	1945	1941	1945
Mining and quarrying	10	7	$ 380	$ 243	$ .9	$ 3.1	0.2	1.3
Manufacturing	84	79	10,439	10,257	28.9	149.7	0.3	1.5
Public utilities	22	20	1,929	2,940	5.0	23.6	0.3	0.8
Trade	139	121	2,082	3,364	14.0	55.6	0.7	1.7
Service	40	35	184	602	1.7	8.1	0.9	1.3
Finance, insurance, real estate, lessors of real property	144	136	1,438	3,689	6.9	22.1	0.5	0.6
Construction	15	14	178	113	.9	1.9	0.5	1.7
Agriculture, forestry, and fishery	8	7	63	134	.1	1.4	0.2	1.0
Not allocable	7	2	19ᵃ	4	.1	.2	..	3.9
Total	469	421	$16,674	$21,346	$58.5	$265.7	0.4	1.2

ᵃ Loss.

SOURCES: *Statistics of Income for 1941*, Part 2; *Press Release No. S-782*, Treasury Department.

As this table suggests, and the data for years not included confirm, about half the corporation contribution may be expected from manufacturing with its gigantic companies; another quarter from the numerous small companies engaged in wholesale and retail trade; and from all other industrial groups, the remaining quarter. The ratio of contribution to net profit is not high. It climbed slowly from less than 0.4 per cent in 1936 through 1938 to the indicated peak of 1.2 per cent in 1945 under stimulus of the excess-profits tax, and then dropped to 0.8 in 1946.

Where corporation gifts go is not fully known. The decision may vary all the way from the highly personal choice of the president of a privately owned corporation, acting perhaps under local pressures—"corporations dealing directly with the consumer are subject to a certain amount of 'legalized blackmail' and must contribute to charity drives to avoid local criticism," writes one of them[1]—to the very careful screening processes of some of the larger companies. The Standard Oil Company of New Jersey, for

[1] "Postwar Trends in Corporate Giving," *Business Record*, National Industrial Conference Board, May, 1947, p. 7.

example, employs a budget expert full time to consider the 50-odd appeals received in an average week. After his investigations a five-man committee screens those remaining, and the board of directors finally acts on the residue.

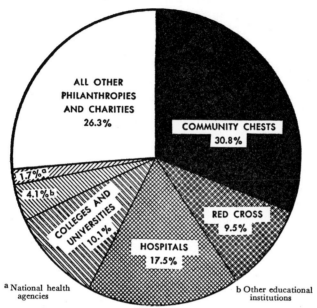

CHART 2. CHARITABLE CONTRIBUTIONS OF 79 LARGE
MANUFACTURING CORPORATIONS, 1948
Source: *Business Record*, National Industrial Conference Board, January, 1950.

Community chests are usually the largest beneficiaries. Indeed, corporation gifts appear to have totaled from a fifth to about a third of the total receipts of community chests in the 1920's and 1930's, and by 1950 they were 40 per cent of the aggregate raised by chests which reported on this subject. In the special case of the Greater New York Fund, corporation contributions have risen fairly steadily from $2.8 million in 1938 to $4.4 million in 1949, representing for the latter year about 11 per cent of the "need" of the included agencies and 85 per cent of the $5.2 million raised by the Fund itself.

After community chests, the next most favored beneficiaries are hospitals, the Red Cross, and a varying list of local agencies. Chart 2 represents the 1948 division of corporation contributions of $16.1 million made by 79 out of the hundred largest manufacturing corporations in the United States, as reported to the National Industrial Conference Board. Community chests and the Red Cross declined somewhat from the record of the previous year, hospitals and higher education increased their percentages. But since this sample represents only very large companies from one industrial classification, these proportions cannot safely be applied to all corporation giving.

As a convenient channel for their welfare contributions, many corporations in recent years have organized foundations, which are discussed in Chapter 6.

Bequests

In addition to the gifts of living donors, funds reach philanthropy every year through bequests. Such bequests are exempt from the federal estate tax[1] but if the estate is of substantial size (the amount has varied; it was $40,000 in 1935, and is now $60,000) a full report has to be filed; statistics on all larger estates are therefore available.

No comprehensive figures appear to exist for the much more numerous smaller estates. However, an analysis of the detailed federal reports filed during 1944 suggests that the omitted amounts are not very large. Filings in 1944 included all estates of a gross value of $60,000 or more and a few estates as low as $40,000 from decedents of earlier years. Reported "charitable, public, and similar bequests," excluding those of nonresident aliens, totaled $202 million. Of this amount, $128 million came from estates of $1 million or more, which contributed 17 per cent of their gross amount. Estates from $100,000 to $1 million contributed $63.5 million at a rate of 4 per cent. The estates below $100,000 accounted for slightly more than $10 million in contributions, at a rate of 2 per cent.

Clearly, philanthropic contributions from estates present an entirely different pattern from that of contributions from income. The large charitable bequests, both in total amount and in percentage of the estates involved, are made by the very wealthy.

---

[1] But not always from taxes within the states. See p. 245.

Close to two-thirds of the total recorded contributions actually come from estates of $1 million or more; only 5 per cent from those below $100,000. It may safely be concluded that the persons who leave estates below the taxing level, though they are exceedingly numerous, do not bequeath a very large aggregate amount to philanthropy. Many of them make no will, and doubtless nearly all feel responsibilities to family and near relatives that outweigh their modest resources and leave little or no margin for final philanthropy. Moreover, they are not under the persuasions of the 77 per cent federal tax levy on noncharitable bequests which affects estates in excess of $10 million.

TABLE 11. FEDERAL ESTATE-TAX RETURNS FILED IN 1944 SHOW-
ING CHARITABLE BEQUESTS, BY GROSS ESTATE CLASSES

	$40,000 and under $100,000	$100,000 and under $1,000,000	$1,000,000 and over	Total
Number of returns	6,587	7,376	309	14,272
Gross estate (millions)	$500	$1,645	$758	$2,903
Charitable bequests (millions)	$10.4	$63.5	$128.0	$201.9
Charitable bequests as per cent of gross estate	2.1	3.9	16.9	7.0
Per cent of total	5.1	31.5	63.4	100.0

SOURCE: *Statistics of Income for 1943*, Part 1.

Neglecting unreported estates, Table 13 reports charitable contributions from bequests varying in recent years from $223 million in 1930 to $96 million in 1933, with the 17-year average for 1929 through 1945 standing at $166 million. The wide annual variations are due in part to changes in the law concerning filing, but in greater degree to the filing in particular years of huge estates, the bequests from which—sometimes devoted to setting up a foundation—may represent a large percentage of the total charitable bequests of those years. The general average of 7 per cent of the gross estate devoted to charitable contributions, indicated for 1944 in Table 11, holds roughly for other years; but very large estates tend greatly to exceed this ratio.

Foundations

Grants from foundations are a source of philanthropic funds more significant for the nature of the gifts than their amount.

This subject is given extended discussion in Chapter 6. Foundation expenditures were estimated at $72 million in 1944[1]; in 1949
a re-estimate for this study places the figure at $133 million. But
some of these expenditures are for administration and direct
operations; grants to other agencies or to individuals were estimated in 1949 at $81 million. These sums represent principally
income from endowment, though increasingly foundations are
becoming channels for the current giving of corporations and
some individuals.

Income from Endowment

Foundations are only one example of income currently available from gifts and bequests of the past. Income from endowment
or other invested funds, and savings in rent from occupancy of
buildings paid off in the past, represent a large part of the "working capital" of many institutions in the welfare field, particularly
in higher education and religion.

TABLE 12. ESTIMATED   VALUE   OF   PHILANTHROPIC
PROPERTY AND ENDOWMENT IN THE UNITED
STATES, 1949

Category	Property and endowment
Religion	$10,000,000,000
Higher education, private	4,005,000,000
Foundations	2,574,000,000
Hospitals, private	5,369,000,000
Other welfare organizations	1,000,000,000
Total	$22,948,000,000

SOURCES: Religion: *Census of Religious Bodies: 1936* and data from
Chapter 10; higher education: U. S. Office of Education report;
foundations: Chapter 6, Table 18; hospitals: *American Hospital Directory*,
1950.

Only the roughest approximations can be made of total philanthropic property and endowment. Information is nowhere centrally available except for a few special fields, and in several

[1] Harrison, Shelby M. and F. Emerson Andrews, *American Foundations for Social
Welfare*. Russell Sage Foundation, New York, 1946, p. 58.

important areas the facts are held confidential. Further problems include a lack of consistent valuations for either securities or real estate. Many organizations list their securities at cost rather than market value, and this may bear little relation to present realities. In the case of real estate, appraisals may use original cost, or cost less depreciation, or present market value, or replacement value at present high construction costs. Table 12 presents a rough estimate of probable value of property and endowment now at the service of voluntary philanthropic agencies, including churches and colleges.

If this $22.9 billion in property and endowment is presumed to yield a conservative 3 per cent per year in money or its rent equivalent, the effective income of welfare institutions in the United States is increased by some $688 million from this source.

Total Philanthropic Giving

An attempt to set up an estimate of total philanthropic giving is of value only in lending perspective within the field and relating it to other consumer expenditures; it cannot be accurate in detail.

Table 13 estimates contributions by living donors, from bequests, and from corporations for 1929 through 1949.[1] It is based on Treasury Department statistics where these are available, supplemented with estimates for the portions of personal income not covered by such reports. Appendix H discusses the reliability and varying coverage of the income-tax data and details the additional estimates from which the first column of this table was derived.

The high record of the past several years, when giving has been at $4 billion a year, does not represent the great increase in generosity that the raw figures suggest. The price level rose from 100.2 in 1940 to 171.2 in 1948. We were giving more dollars out of our much larger income, but those dollars bought less in goods and services for the charitable institutions to which they went. However, if our estimates are reasonably accurate, some genuine increase in rate of giving has occurred, but that rate remains less than 2 per cent of gross personal income for the

[1] See also frontispiece.

country as a whole. In comparison with other expenditures charitable contributions are even less impressive. In 1948, when we have estimated charitable giving at $4,052 million, the Department of Commerce estimates expenditures for tobacco at $4,147 million, and for alcoholic beverages at over $8 billion.

TABLE 13. ESTIMATED CONTRIBUTIONS TO PHILANTHROPY FROM LIVING DONORS, THROUGH BEQUESTS, AND FROM CORPORATIONS, 1929–1949

In millions

Year	Gifts of living donors	Charitable bequests	Corporation gifts	Total
1929	$1,052	$154	..a	$1,206
1930	931	223	..a	1,154
1931	961	220	..a	1,181
1932	678	191	..a	869
1933	619	96	..a	715
1934	650	146	..a	796
1935	715	106	..a	821
1936	821	128	$ 30	979
1937	955	127	33	1,115
1938	858	200	27	1,085
1939	977	179	31	1,187
1940	1,068	143	38	1,249
1941	1,536	175	58	1,769
1942	2,087	155	98	2,340
1943	2,504	186	159	2,849
1944	2,678	202	234	3,114
1945	2,771	192	266	3,229
1946	2,914	182b	214	3,310
1947	3,269	186	241	3,696
1948	3,629	182b	241c	4,052
1949	3,609	182b	241c	4,032

a Data not available.   b Average 1941–1945.   c From last recorded year.

SOURCES: Reports from the Treasury Department, supplemented (in column 1) from estimates as described in Appendix H.

Religious, educational, and welfare agencies also received some income from such other sources as foundations, their own investments, and the use of buildings. Table 14 presents an estimate of total current receipts, with figures for the various items taken from recent averages or actual years.

The other side of the picture—receipts of known agencies in the field—must be based on reports which are even more fragmentary.

TABLE 14. ESTIMATE OF RECENT ANNUAL RECEIPTS OF PRIVATE PHILANTHROPY IN THE UNITED STATES, BY SOURCE

Amounts in millions

Source	Amount	Per cent
Contributions from individuals	$3,304	74
Charitable bequests	182	4
Contributions from corporations	241	5
Foundations	133	3
Income from capital (except foundations)	611	14
Total	$4,471	100

SOURCES: Individuals, average of estimates 1946–1949; bequests, average 1941–1945; corporations, actual 1947; foundations, estimate 1949; other endowment, from Table 12.

However, some indication of the relative distribution of philanthropy's dollar may be gained from the estimates of Table 15, which correspond in total with Table 14, if the nongrant portion ($52 million) of the foundations item and receipts from agency property and endowment ($611 million) are omitted.

TABLE 15. ESTIMATE OF CURRENT ANNUAL GIVING TO PRIVATE PHILANTHROPY, BY OBJECT

Amounts in millions

Category	Amount	Per cent
1. Religion	$1,894	50
2. Higher education	326	8
3. Health and welfare agencies[a]	561	15
4. Foundations	151	4
5. United Jewish Appeal	112	3
6. Charity rackets	100	3
7. American National Red Cross	67	2
8. Foreign relief, except religious	40	1
9. Museums and libraries	18	..
10. Miscellaneous and unallocated	539	14
Total	$3,808	100

[a] Excluding such agencies individually listed.

SOURCES: Item 1: Chapter 10 and Table 38. 2: Adapted from Chapter 11 and Table 41. 3: Chapters 7 and 8. 4: Chapter 6 and Table 18; represents average annual difference between 1944 and 1949 estimates of capitalization. 5: Chapter 10, p. 177. 6: Chapter 9, a rough guess. 7: Report for 1949, p. 122. 8: Chapter 5 and Table 17. 9: Department of Commerce 1948 estimate. 10: Miscellaneous.

The "miscellaneous and unallocated" sum of $539 million includes, among others, these items. Several large national agencies report their receipts as net, making no accounting of costs of the campaigns which in some cases are believed to run to as much as 40 per cent of gross receipts; but the contributor has "given" both the net receipts and the cost of the campaign. The nine listed categories fail to cover many small items, such as direct contributions to the Boy Scouts, Girl Scouts, special building funds, fraternal and service club funds, and the like, which do not pass through the records of community chests or other central reporting agencies. Many organizations, because they fear it may discourage other contributions, avoid reporting their receipts.

Under all these considerations, a "miscellaneous" item of 14 per cent seems not unduly large, and tends to confirm a total approaching $4 billion as private philanthropy's annual receipts in recent years, exclusive of income from its own property.

CHAPTER 5

Bread Upon the Waters

As A RESULT of World War II, the needs of the peoples of Europe and of other parts of the world have been desperate. We have realized that the most critical of these needs must be met, not only as a humanitarian service, but to make order and safety possible for ourselves.

Aid to other peoples is not a new idea. In 1812 the Congress of the United States appropriated $50,000 to relieve earthquake victims in Venezuela. Private contributions for foreign missions— which often included in their program health services and instruction in agriculture—have been a part of religious giving since colonial days. During and just after World War I so many agencies sprang up to aid the starving peoples of Europe, the Armenians, and others, that many communities organized war chests to bring order into the growing chaos of appeals, local and foreign. The Congress in 1919 appropriated $100 million for European food relief, an additional $600,000 for the Near East, advanced relief "loans" (of which about 6 per cent were later repaid) to European countries to a total of approximately $1 billion, and in 1922 gave $20 million for famine victims in Russia. In 1923 the Japanese earthquake prompted $6 million in a congressional appropriation, and many private gifts.

Foundations have been the channel for some of the larger private gifts going abroad. In some instances American donors have set up foreign foundations. Andrew Carnegie endowed his Scottish Universities Trust with $10 million in 1901; his Dun-

75

fermline Trust with $3.75 million in 1903; the Palace of Peace at The Hague with $1.5 million also in 1903; and the Carnegie United Kingdom Trust with $10 million in 1913. Edward S. Harkness of New York set up in 1930 the Pilgrim Trust, with an endowment of $10 million for charitable purposes within Great Britain and Northern Ireland.

Foundations incorporated in the United States sometimes use substantial portions of their income for enterprises abroad. The most notable example is the Rockefeller Foundation, established "to promote the well-being of mankind throughout the world." Its expenditures for projects in other countries totaled not less than $161 million by the end of 1949. Of this sum, $13.4 million was for foreign fellowships administered by the Foundation and extended to 5,768 individuals. The international migration of scholars and others, whether financed by foundations, by the government, or by various educational agencies, may prove one of our most rewarding foreign investments.

But at no previous period in history have gifts sent abroad for both relief and reconstruction approached the mountainous totals of the past few years. The share of government in these gifts has been overwhelmingly great; but doubtless this should be partly charged to self-interest and national security.

In comparison with the government program, private contributions for needs abroad, proceeding through numerous voluntary agencies and on a person-to-person basis, may seem small, but have formed a considerable part of our total charitable giving. A government committee called them "negligible" as a drain on American supplies; the same committee, however, pointed to their considerable importance:

> Private relief ventures abroad have adapted their resources to the meeting of particular needs in local areas. In this they have demonstrated an elasticity that is not found in the over-all programs carried on under public authority. They have shown a capacity for immediate response to emergency situations, demonstrating a speed of action not obtainable in the carefully planned and meticulously controlled programs based upon legislative grants.

> Private relief programs, furthermore, are a means of bringing Americans into personal contact with the needs of other countries.

They present an opportunity for the individual to do something on his own initiative, and to know the precise purposes for which his particular dollars are spent in relieving needs around the world. The obverse of this is that the recipient abroad knows that the assistance he receives is based upon the personal response of some individual American to his needs. The result is a harvest of good will to the American people.[1]

GOVERNMENT GIVING ABROAD

Although our government's gifts to other nations are not private philanthropy, and many of them are not even philanthropy under its broadest definition, their amount and character need to be stated to lend perspective to private giving.

The War Period

In World War II our first large outpouring of funds for other nations was in the euphemistically named Lend-Lease Program, which began some months before the United States entered the war and ended some years after Japan was defeated. Total lend-lease shipments to 38 Allies cost the United States $47.3 billion from March 11, 1941 through 1946. Most of these shipments consisted of actual war supplies, some of which were either returned or offset by reverse lend-lease. However, such items as "agricultural . . . and other commodities" might in some cases be regarded as relief contributions. These items amounted to $15.5 billion.

Supplies given civilians abroad out of Army and Navy stores during military operations, and later under the American Military Government (AMG) in both liberated and occupied enemy territory cannot be accurately totaled. The military was responsible for assuring civilian food supplies, supervising public welfare operations, and caring for displaced persons and refugees. Without including many properly chargeable items, Army and Navy grants are reported as $813 million for the war period, $744 million in 1946, $667 million in 1947, $1,181 million in 1948, and $1,068 million in 1949, with a total of $4.5 billion.

[1] *Voluntary Foreign Aid:* A Study by a Special Subcommittee of the Committee on Foreign Affairs. Government Printing Office, Washington, 1948, p. 7.

UNRRA

The United Nations Relief and Rehabilitation Administration (UNRRA) was established in 1943 by 44 governments and was finally liquidated on March 31, 1949; at that time its total expenditures were $3,968 million, 92.8 per cent of which represented commodities distributed. The original financing plan called for the contribution of 1 per cent of one year's national income by uninvaded countries; later each was asked to give an additional 1 per cent. Not all countries fulfilled their obligations. However, this first large experiment in international cooperation for relief did dispatch to the countries in which it operated some 25 million long tons (6,000 shiploads) of relief and rehabilitation goods. The government of the United States contributed a total of $2.7 billion; all other nations, $1.3 billion.

In addition to contributions from member governments, UNRRA was authorized to receive other gifts. The largest nongovernmental contribution was $37 million worth of clothing contributed through the Victory Clothing Drive in the United States.

At the conclusion of UNRRA's program, a variety of special organizations were set up under United Nations auspices to carry on work left uncompleted. Among the more important were the International Refugee Organization (IRO) and the United Nations International Children's Emergency Fund (UNICEF).

Children's Emergency Fund

The vicissitudes of the United Nations International Children's Emergency Fund illustrate some of the problems encountered in governmental and international giving. The Fund was organized on December 11, 1946 under United Nations auspices with an estimated first-year need of $200 million to assist some 20 million children in Europe and twice that number in the Far East. The United States government agreed to contribute $72 for every $28 contributed by all other governments combined, up to a total of $75 million, which the Congress appropriated. The enthusiasm of governments for creating this agency did not, in many cases, carry over into appropriating funds for it. By April, 1949 the British government had contributed only $403,000, and shortly thereafter announced abandonment of further contributions in favor of direct aid to Arab refugees. Argentina, Brazil, Ireland, and the Soviet Union were reported to have made no contributions. By late 1949 only $22 million had been contributed by all other governments, so that the United States, on the agreed matching formula, contributed only $58 million of the $75 million appropriated.

In an attempt to offset this severe disappointment the Fund tried to organize campaigns for voluntary contributions in all countries. Here it was the United States that fell down badly. Our campaign was set up to include not only the Children's Fund but some 25 other overseas agencies; it was called American Overseas Aid—United Nations Appeal for Children, and set its goal at $60 million. Collections appear to have been $4 million, of which about $1 million went for campaign expenses, with the Children's Fund receiving finally $618,000. Other countries did better, collecting some $33.5 million for various children's agencies, with about $10 million allocated to the Children's Emergency Fund. The people of Iceland gave an average contribution of $4.31 per person.

By its third anniversary the Fund was reaching some 6 million of the 60 million children estimated to be in urgent need of food. In other programs, shoes and medical aid were being furnished. The Fund accomplished useful work, but has met only a small fraction of the need.

The Marshall Plan

On June 5, 1947 George C. Marshall, then Secretary of State, suggested in an address at Harvard University that the United States embark upon an extensive program of foreign aid in an attempt to meet the critical situation existing in Europe. His speech inspired the largest program of governmental foreign aid in history. The Congress created the Economic Cooperation Administration (ECA) and for the twenty-seven months ending June 30, 1950, this agency spent $9.5 billion. In late September,

1949 a new foreign aid bill was passed totaling $5.8 billion, the chief items of which were $4.7 billion for European recovery and $912 million for government and relief in Army-occupied areas.

The European Recovery Program has been costing the American people some $30 per person per year, or about $120 per family. This program has been promoted, not so much as needed relief and aid to other peoples in deep trouble, but as a matter of national policy and even as "the greatest bargain the American people ever had." Paul G. Hoffman, while ECA administrator, declared in an address that United States defense costs would reach $30 billion a year in place of the present $15 billion if Western Europe should go communist, but that such conquests could be blocked by strengthening the free nations of Europe.[1]

Nevertheless, many of the operations of ECA are measures which private charity would undertake if it had funds large enough for both "relief" and reconstruction. "In undertaking the European Recovery Program," reported the ECA early in 1949,[2] "we abandoned piecemeal attempts to restore economic health, and rejected mere relief for the concept of recovery." More than half of its expenditures have gone to stimulate industrial production, but one encounters also such items as these: $9 million for streptomycin to combat tuberculosis, particularly in France and Italy; $15 million per year to pay the ocean freight on relief packages sent to ECA-benefiting countries by nonprofit relief agencies or by individuals within the United States.

Expenditures for the ECA program have been so monumental that they presently dwarf other governmental operations, even "the bold new program" for aid to underdeveloped areas, which apparently will chiefly involve technical rather than financial assistance.

A Summation

Total grants for foreign aid of the United States government from the beginning of the war period to the close of the fiscal

[1] By September, 1950 defense appropriations for the current fiscal year reached approximately $30 billion as a result of the outbreak of war in Korea.

[2] *A Report on Recovery Progress and United States Aid.* Economic Cooperation Administration, Washington, February, 1949, p. 2.

year 1949 amounted to $60.7 billion; however, the larger part ($47 billion) represented lend-lease—almost wholly war supplies. Reverse grants of $8.1 billion during the same period reduced our net grants abroad to $52.6 billion. In addition, our government extended net credits during the same period totaling $9.8 billion, a considerable portion of which may not be repaid.

Table 16 summarizes these grants by program and by period. It will be noted that if the lend-lease expenditures of 1946 are excluded, grants have risen steadily since the end of the war period.

TABLE 16. GRANTS FOR AID OF FOREIGN COUNTRIES BY THE UNITED STATES GOVERNMENT, FISCAL YEARS 1941–1949

In millions

Purpose or agency	War period 1941–1945ᵃ	1946	1947	1948	1949	Total
Lend-lease	$46,074	$1,213	..	..	..	$47,287
Civilian supplies, Army, Navy, etc.	813	744	$ 667	$1,181	$1,068	4,473
UNRRA	83	1,184	1,377	16	..	2,660
Post-UNRRA	..	..	..	296	3	299
Interim aid	..	..	..	534	24	558
American National Red Cross	62	10	..	..	..	72
Chinese aid, including military assistance	380	120	..	1	283	784
Korean aid	..	..	..	..	11	11
Greek-Turkish assistance	..	..	..	260	258	518
Philippine rehabilitation	..	..	61	92	193	346
Inter-American aid	53	11	7	6	5	82
Refugee assistance	3	..	4	71	79	157
International Children's Emergency Fund	..	..	..	33	25	58
European recovery	..	..	..	204	3,221	3,425
Total	$47,468	$3,282	$2,116	$2,694	$5,170	$60,730

ᵃ Government fiscal years ending June 30.

SOURCE: *Foreign Transactions of the U. S. Government.* Department of Commerce, Washington, 1949, p. A-8.

VOLUNTARY FOREIGN AID

American nongovernmental aid to Europe began on a substantial scale before the war actually opened, chiefly as relief to refugees from Nazi Germany. Upon passage of the Neutrality Act in 1939, all American voluntary agencies engaging in relief in belligerent countries, except the American National Red Cross, were required to register and submit monthly reports to the Department of State. The record of the value of cash and goods received by registered foreign relief agencies from September 1939 through 1945 follows[1]:

1939	$ 2,900,000
1940	20,600,000
1941	39,000,000
1942	37,100,000
1943	62,100,000
1944	109,100,000
1945	233,900,000
Total	$504,700,000

As the record shows, contributions grew rapidly after 1939, and with their growth came many complications. A committee set up to examine the situation found, for example, that in 1941 more than 70 organizations, with scores of local branches, were soliciting contributions for Britain during the blitz. Costs of collection mounted, due to overlapping, inexperience, and some outright racketeering. On July 25, 1942 the President appointed a War Relief Control Board with broad powers to license, coordinate, and regulate agencies engaging in "foreign and domestic relief, rehabilitation, reconstruction, and welfare arising from war-created needs." When the National War Fund[2] was created in 1943, it became possible to combine nearly all the appeals for overseas aid in one vast campaign, and to exercise considerable control over budgets.

With the end of active hostilities on August 14, 1945 the picture began to change. The National War Fund conducted its final campaign in the fall of that year. The President's War Relief Control Board was dissolved on May 14, 1946. It was recognized, however, that relief for the sufferers from war would not end for many years, and therefore an Advisory Committee on Voluntary Foreign Aid of the United States Government was set up in the Department of State. It continued some of the functions

---

[1] *Voluntary War Relief During World War II:* A Report to the President by the President's War Relief Control Board. Government Printing Office, Washington, 1946, p. 8.

[2] See p. 149.

of registration and coordination of the Control Board, but lacked its compulsive powers.

From the invasion of Poland through 1947, American voluntary agencies which were registered with the Control Board and its successor committee reported foreign relief expenditures totaling more than $950 million.

American National Red Cross

During and immediately after the war, the American National Red Cross conducted a wide-scale generalized relief program in war-torn countries. Supplies included clothing, food, and medical equipment. From September, 1939 through 1949, its contributions to relief abroad and in specialized assistance to Red Cross societies totaled over $100 million.

In addition, the United States government, by congressional appropriation, furnished supplies for foreign relief valued at about $72 million, which were distributed through the American Red Cross.

Private Parcels

As soon as war restrictions on private parcels sent abroad were removed, country by country, a flood of food and clothing and a considerable amount of cash began to flow from Americans to friends and relatives abroad. No complete record of such gifts exists, and in the strict sense most of them, as gifts to individuals, were not tax-deductible philanthropy. Their volume, however, was tremendous, and their total effect in relieving need quite important.

A government committee reported that parcel-post packages to Europe alone in the fifteen months from July, 1946 through September, 1947 represented a value exceeding $241 million.[1] Relief packages to Europe cost almost the same amount of money as we were contributing in the same period to all community chests for their 14,000 participating agencies. This contribution seems insignificant only in comparison with government expendi-

[1] *Voluntary Foreign Aid*, p. 2.

tures for relief abroad, and even here the reporting government committee said of it:

> The receipt of a personal gift from the United States, a gift appropriate to individual needs of the receiver and representing a personal bond with the donor, has a good-will value that is beyond the capacity of impersonal, Government-furnished assistance to inspire.[1]

CARE

The difficulties individuals encountered in assembling packages and arranging for their shipment, together with problems in delivery abroad, resulted in the organization of the Cooperative for American Remittances to Europe, Inc. (CARE) in November, 1945 by 22 relief and welfare agencies, with government and UNRRA sanction. CARE began by distributing Army ration packages, speedily available; its first shipment reached Le Havre, France, in May, 1946. Soon its assembly lines were processing a variety of standardized packages of food, clothing, and other needed supplies which Americans could purchase at a stated price and send to any named individual in the countries in which CARE operated, or simply to "a French widow," "a Greek orphanage," "an Italian teacher."

By the close of its fourth year, in November, 1949, CARE had shipped overseas nine million packages valued at $88 million; 94 per cent of these contained food. However, CARE was beginning a new program of supplying "food for hungry minds" which it estimated would bring $1 million worth of books to devastated libraries in 1950.

The Changing Picture

The picture of present giving abroad is a complicated one. It includes spectacular single efforts like the 1947 Friendship Train which on its transcontinental journey picked up 270 railroad cars of food for Europe, and much less noticed efforts like the Girl Scouts' Clothes for Friendship drive, which in fifteen months provided clothing for 150,000 destitute children in Europe and Asia.

[1] *Voluntary Foreign Aid*, p. 89.

It includes the continuing efforts of many voluntary agencies, some of them organized specifically for relief abroad, others simply including that special function among their regular activities.

A later chapter is devoted to giving through religious agencies, but mention should be made here of the large sums these agencies have sent abroad to meet war-induced needs. One of the most remarkable developments in American philanthropy is the giving of the Jewish people, first to aid sufferers from the Nazi persecutions, lately to meet the needs of newly established Israel and its many immigrants. Amounts received by the United Jewish Appeal rose from $15 million in 1939 to $150 million in 1948; not all of these funds have gone overseas, but late in 1949 the United Palestine Appeal, major beneficiary of the United Jewish Appeal, reported that $150 million would be spent in Israel in 1949 for immigration, rehabilitation, and resettlement.

Many Protestant and Eastern Orthodox churches with their relief organizations cooperatively created Church World Service in 1946 "to collect money and supplies with which to carry on a church relief and reconstruction program for war devastated people overseas." It also assists in the resettlement of displaced persons. In 1948 Church World Service shipped to 36 countries in Europe, Asia, and Africa and to the World Council of Churches in Geneva about 33 million pounds of supplies valued at $11 million; additional cash disbursements raised the total for the year to $15.3 million.

The American Friends Service Committee has conducted a substantial program overseas, with a 1949 budget of about $4 million. In addition to food and clothing shipments, it establishes neighborhood centers and work camps, where American young people share work and food and ideas with those they help. The National Catholic Welfare Conference maintains a War Relief Service. Its total receipts from inception of the program in April, 1943 to the close of 1949 amounted to $24.4 million in cash and 300 million pounds of food, clothing, and other supplies valued at over $100 million.

Table 17 summarizes the relief expenditures for 1948 of the 43 voluntary agencies which were then reporting to the Advisory

Committee on Voluntary Foreign Aid, with some detail on all those spending $1 million or more.

TABLE 17. EXPENDITURES FOR RELIEF ABROAD OF 43 VOLUNTARY AGENCIES IN 1948

In thousands

Agency	Relief distributed			Total
	In cash	In purchased goods	In contributed goods	
American Friends Service Committee	$ 1,217	$ 891	$ 2,478	$ 4,586
American Jewish Joint Distribution Committee	49,797	15,940	3,226	68,963
American ORT Federation	2,232	..	..	2,232
American Relief for Italy	222	..	1,421	1,643
American Relief for Poland	255	256	582	1,093
CARE, Inc.	3,018	22,575	..	25,593
Church World Service, Inc.	4,423	..	10,913	15,336
Foster Parents' Plan for War Children	712	168	476	1,356
Greek War Relief Association	820	1,230	441	2,491
Hebrew Sheltering and Immigrant Aid Society	2,132	..	..	2,132
Lutheran World Relief, Inc.	337	63	2,738	3,138
Mennonite Central Committee	618	40	1,387	2,045
Save the Children Federation, Inc.	408	87	892	1,387
War Relief Services, National Catholic Welfare Conference	2,826	1,739	10,939	15,504
29 other agencies	3,962	1,433	3,267	8,662
Total	$72,979	$44,422	$38,760	$156,161

SOURCE: Adapted from Circular 26, Advisory Committee on Voluntary Foreign Aid of the United States Government.

No one year can be regarded as typical, since substantial changes were taking place. The dollar value of relief sent abroad by voluntary agencies reporting to the Advisory Committee totaled $133 million in 1947; $156 million in 1948, with $69 million of that sum representing the American Jewish Joint Distribution Committee; and $51 million for the first eight months of 1949.

In addition to amount and destination, relief abroad has been changing in character. In 1947 food represented about 34 per cent of total contributions; cash transfers, 29 per cent; clothing, 27 per cent; the remaining 10 per cent consisted of medical and surgical supplies, hospital, school, and health center equipment, some industrial and agricultural equipment, and miscellaneous items. More recently, direct relief items such as food and clothing have been diminishing; a larger proportion of aid has gone into facilities for health, recreation, reconstruction, and rehabilitation, with emphasis upon helping local leadership carry out programs.

During 1949 American relief agencies, and some international agencies without American personnel, found themselves no longer welcome in certain satellite countries of the Soviet Union, and their operations were closed down. Difficulties were also encountered at various times with other governments; seven thousand gift packages were impounded by Greece when CARE refused to divulge the names of recipients, but were released upon CARE's threat to withdraw entirely from Greece.

Foreign Missions

A form of giving abroad that has continued for many generations and is not subject to such violent fluctuations is contributing through the various churches for missionary enterprises. Not all such giving can be identified; some churches make no public financial reports, and others do not separate foreign from home missions. These problems are discussed in more detail in Chapter 10.

That substantial sums are sent abroad through these channels is sufficiently indicated, perhaps, by presenting recent figures of the Foreign Missions Conference of North America. This Conference includes 55 religious denominations with a combined membership of 37 million persons, some of whom are in Canada. Omitting Canadian contributions, the various boards in the Foreign Missions Conference spent in 1948 for regular overseas work $34.3 million; for relief and certain special projects, $10.8 million. Only a few small items in this $45 million are also reported to the Advisory Committee on Voluntary Foreign Aid, and therefore represent a duplication with those figures. Indeed, the distribution of the missionary funds is radically at variance with the war-relief contributions. For instance, Africa south of the Sahara, negligible in the Advisory Committee tabulations, received over $4 million from the missionary boards; India, Pakistan, and Ceylon received nearly $6 million.

Programs of the various mission boards differ widely, many of them including in their efforts agricultural and medical aid, and education, broadly conceived. The contributors of these millions, if the Foreign Missions Conference speaks for them, frequently have in mind broader objectives than the salvation of individual souls or the advancement of a particular creed. A recent circular says:

> We of the Foreign Missions Conference are convinced that the secret of permanent peace and security is One World in Christ— a world united through a common faith in God through Christ and so thoroughly "in Christ" that His commandment to love one another is fulfilled in all human relationships.

Return Gifts

Sometimes gifts cross the seas in the opposite direction. France sent a Gratitude Train to the United States. In October, 1949 the American Diabetes Association announced a gift from Denmark of $56,000 for diabetes research. Diplomatic Washington gasped when the Children's Aid Society in that city received six crates of clothing for needy Washington children from a foundation headed by Señora Doña María Eva Duarte de Perón, the wife of Argentina's President.

The mixed feelings with which we ourselves have received some of these gifts should warn us against expecting marked gratitude for our own gifts across the seas, particularly where they have been motivated in part by national or self-interest. The final chapter of this book discusses the delicate problem of attitudes of recipients.

Accomplishments

It needs to be emphasized, however, that our gifts to the peoples of other lands, particularly gifts from individuals rather than from government, may turn out an unexpectedly shining chapter in philanthropy. Beyond the dollar figures are the individuals who have received needed food, or clothing, or perhaps hospitality in some of the exchange programs, from someone whose face they know, or with whom they at least feel an acquaintance. At the same time we the givers have broadened our own horizon to the needs and problems of a whole planet.

In a world that desperately needs friendship and understanding across national boundaries, this bread cast upon the waters may do more than satisfy the immediate hungers of those to whom it is sent. A generation may pass before we can appraise its full accomplishments and realize all its benefits.

CHAPTER 6

Foundations and Community Trusts

THE FOUNDATION is an effective instrument for giving large sums. In such newer forms as the community trust and the family foundation, most of its advantages are also available for more modest contributions, or for annual gifts which are expected to grow into a large final amount.

A foundation may be defined as a nongovernmental, nonprofit organization having a principal fund of its own and established to maintain or aid social, educational, charitable, or other activities serving the common welfare. Its predecessors, which were usually endowments for limited purposes, existed from earliest history, at some periods in considerable numbers.[1] The special ingredient which distinguishes the foundation in the American understanding of the name is wide freedom of action. With a very few exceptions, such organizations have arisen only in the United States and nearly all of them within a half century.

Some legitimate foundations call themselves endowments, trusts, funds, institutions, boards. On the other hand, because "foundation" has acquired an aura of substance and respectability, many organizations use this title with little or no justification. These include agencies which solicit contributions instead of disbursing from an established fund, and some which are trade associations, pressure groups, or outright rackets. For example,

[1] See p. 38.

the American War Heroes Foundation, Inc., which sponsored the Park Avenue Canteen, had its charter revoked in 1942 by New York Supreme Court Justice William T. Collins, who called it "avarice masquerading as patriotism."

Their Number and Size

No exact figure can be given on the number of existing foundations. They may be incorporated under the laws of any of the 48 states[1] or of the federal government, or they can be set up as unincorporated charitable trusts, with the result that complete listings are nowhere available. The United States Treasury Department reports some ten thousand organizations which might be called foundations under broad definition. The Rich and Deardorff report[2] lists 899, including 435 which declined information or failed to answer inquiries. Under the tighter definition given above, and requiring endowment of at least $50,000, Shelby M. Harrison and the author of this volume, in a survey[3] published by Russell Sage Foundation in 1946, culled 505 foundations from lists totaling 5,000.

The vast majority of "foundations" in the longer lists are too small to be of any significance. They would not have been organized as separate entities except for certain taxation advantages, or the pride men have in perpetuating their own names. One in Wilmington, Delaware, soberly reports its capital assets as $849.61 and its total expenditures for 1947–1948 as $1.51. It is questionable whether foundations should be set up unless their disbursements will reach at least $100,000 annually; smaller funds find it difficult to attract trustees (who usually serve without pay) of proper caliber or to hire the needed administrative staff. Even for considerably larger sums other devices possessing most of the advantages of the separate foundation, but avoiding its complications and costs, may be more desirable.

---

[1] See pp. 282–283 for references to this legislation.

[2] Rich, Wilmer Shields and Neva R. Deardorff, editors, *American Foundations and Their Fields*. Raymond Rich Associates, New York, 1949.

[3] Harrison, Shelby M. and F. Emerson Andrews, *American Foundations for Social Welfare*. Russell Sage Foundation, New York, 1946.

The largest five foundations and the assets they report[1] are these:

Ford Foundation	$238,000,000
Carnegie Corporation of New York	173,013,520
Rockefeller Foundation	153,000,000
Duke Endowment	135,000,000
Kresge Foundation	75,041,237

The new giant, the Ford Foundation, will receive additional stock assets when the estate of Henry Ford is settled, and the Treasury Department has been contending that the valuation of all its stock should be considerably increased. Whatever the final figure, the Ford Foundation is the largest private fund devoted to charitable purposes the world has seen. Possibly the new Hugh Roy Cullen Foundation belongs in this list; but its reported assets of $150 million appear to represent estimated eventual yield of oil lands rather than current assets.

Thirty-five foundations report assets above $10 million and at least 13 which decline to report are believed to fall within this range, making a total of probably 48 foundations in the "large" category of $10 million or more. Some foundations with smaller endowment are doing work of nationwide significance, but their ability to continue costly projects will depend upon unusual yield on investments, invasion of capital, or receipt of additional funds.

The popular impression that foundations are a reservoir of almost unlimited wealth, able to undertake vast projects at will, is quite mistaken. The Russell Sage Foundation study indicated that for the year 1944 total resources of all included foundations approximated $1,818 million and their expenditures were about $72 million. Additional foundations have since been established, but most of them are small. Table 18 details a new approximation, bringing the 1944 information to date wherever possible, and adding foundations from the Rich and Deardorff directory, reports in the press, and other sources. Total endowment appears now to approximate $2.6 billion, with an annual expenditure in the neighborhood of $133 million.

---

[1] Estimated for the Duke Endowment, which lists assets but without dollar values.

Because of the miscellaneous sources from which these data are drawn, great reliability must not be assumed. The B Estimates are particularly suspect. Many of these 509 foundations on which no financial information was available are family foundations, serving simply as corporate channels for individual or family giving. Since some of them function as immediate dispensers of charitable gifts, their expenditure total, estimated at 3 per cent of assumed capitalization, is probably too small; but in a discussion of endowed foundations it seemed inappropriate to attempt to include the additional sums which represent purely current giving that happened to pass through their books.

TABLE 18. ESTIMATED   CURRENT   CAPITAL   ASSETS,   ANNUAL
GRANTS AND EXPENDITURES OF 1,007 FOUNDATIONS
Amounts in thousands

Nature of data	Capital assets		Grants		Expenditures[a]	
	Founda-tions	Amount	Founda-tions	Amount	Founda-tions	Amount
Reported for publication	395	$1,908,486	291	$53,758	361	$ 98,281
A Estimates[b]	103	615,057	207	25,930	137	33,469
B Estimates[c]	509	50,900	509	1,527	509	1,527
Total	1,007	$2,574,443	1,007	$81,215	1,007	$133,277

[a] Includes grants.

[b] Based on newspaper reports, confidential information, and miscellaneous other sources.

[c] No information available. Arbitrarily estimated that capitalization averages $100,000; expenditures, all in form of grants, are 3 per cent of capital.

SOURCES: *American Foundations for Social Welfare*, 1946; *American Foundations and Their Fields*, 1949; newspaper reports; correspondence.

In perspective, foundation assets and annual expenditures are small. Americans exhale in tobacco smoke every year more dollars than the accumulated wealth of all the foundations together. Many foundations can spend income only, and that income has recently been much reduced both in dollars and in purchasing power. In terms of meeting relief needs, which some foundations still attempt to do, their $133 million a year would be negligible. We are now paying out of tax funds about $1.47 billion a year[1] for old-age assistance benefits; it would take all the income of all

[1] See Table 1, p. 44.

the foundations eleven years just to meet one year's bill for the needy aged alone.

Even in the smaller field of private philanthropy, where many persons have assumed foundations play a major financial role, they have in fact only about 3 cents of the private philanthropic dollar to spend. Some single agencies have annual budgets closely approaching the total available to all the foundations together. The American National Red Cross raised $118 million in 1946 with a war budget; $67 million in 1949.

In view of their limited funds, most experienced foundation administrators have felt that they should not contribute to individual relief or other causes which can be met by general charitable contributions or from tax funds, but should reserve what might be called the "venture capital" of philanthropy for longer-range, more difficult projects, which would not usually appeal to individual givers. Their enviable record of accomplishment and leadership in their first half-century has been in large part the result of careful choices of this sort, and their growing experience in giving.

Setting Up a Foundation

Foundations are a special form of charity, and as such fall under the classic legal definition of Justice Gray in a Massachusetts case of 1867, as a gift to be administered "consistently with existing laws, for the benefit of an indefinite number of persons, either by . . . education or religion, or by relieving their bodies from disease, . . . or by assisting them to establish themselves in life; or by creating or maintaining public buildings or works; or by otherwise lessening the burdens of government."[1]

A variety of legal procedures are available. Some of the earliest foundations were set up by special acts of Congress; among these were the Carnegie Institution of Washington, the Carnegie Foundation for the Advancement of Teaching, and the General Education Board. A few foundations, among them most community trusts, are not incorporated, but operate as charitable trusts under a will, resolution, or instrument of trust.

[1] Jackson v. Phillips, 14 Allen 539, 556 (Mass. 1867).

By far the commonest form of organization, however, is incorporation under the laws of a particular state. The laws of incorporation for charitable organizations differ somewhat in the various jurisdictions. The incorporators are usually the original members of the board of trustees (or a part of that board, to be filled out later), and usually include the founder. The statement of purpose may be quite specific, or as broad as "the welfare of mankind." In view of many unfortunate past experiences with highly restricted perpetuities, the modern tendency has been toward broad statements of purpose, or at least the granting of substantial powers to the trustees for effecting changes. In many cases perpetuity is made discretional, and in some a policy compelling liquidation within a set term of years has been adopted.

Many corporate charters, usually to avoid possible question as to their tax-exempt status, follow closely the wording of Section 101 of the Internal Revenue Code[1] or similar sections in the laws of their state defining a charitable corporation. Appendix E[2] presents a sample charter, and the charters and other basic documents of 18 foundations are reprinted in *Charters of Philanthropies.*[3] An extended discussion of legal and tax aspects of foundations has been presented elsewhere[4] by Berrien C. Eaton, Jr., legal consultant for this book.

The specific purposes of the founder, and his general desires, may be set forth in nonbinding language in a letter of gift, or even an instrument of trust, thereby avoiding the dangerous rigidity and binding restrictions which might follow inclusion of such purposes in an instrument of incorporation.

To establish tax exemption for a foundation, its officers file with the Collector of Internal Revenue for its district an affidavit or questionnaire, together with a copy of the articles of incorporation, declaration of trust, or other similar instrument, and the latest financial statements. The Treasury Department, if satisfied,

---

[1] Presented in Appendix A, p. 263.

[2] See p. 279.

[3] Chambers, M. M., *Charters of Philanthropies.* Carnegie Foundation for the Advancement of Teaching, New York, 1948.

[4] Eaton, Berrien C., Jr., "Charitable Foundations, Tax Avoidance and Business Expediency," *Virginia Law Review,* vol. 35, November and December, 1949.

will confirm by letter the tax-exempt status. Usually such a ruling is obtainable after twelve full months of actual operation.

The Board of Trustees

Entire responsibility for management of a foundation rests usually with the board of trustees, who may also be called directors, managers, or members of the corporation.

The original board of trustees is in most cases selected by the donor, with power in this board to fill vacancies and possibly to expand the board membership. Election may be for life, though stated terms, often of three years with times of election arranged to overlap, are more usual. Re-election has proved highly probable. The number of trustees varies from 3 to 50; many foundations find that from 7 to 12 members provide needed variety of viewpoint without being too many for efficiency. Several have recognized the dangers of rising age levels on their boards: the General Education Board and the Rockefeller Foundation provide that persons above the age of sixty-five shall not be eligible as trustees, and the Research Corporation—a nonprofit corporation with some foundation characteristics—provides that, given certain circumstances, new trustees must be under forty-five years of age.

As a general rule trustees are not paid, except for traveling and other expenses incident to meetings. The practices of some of the small foundations are not known, but among the larger foundations we have found only five exceptions to this rule. The Carnegie Corporation of New York in its earliest period paid $5,000 a year to each trustee, but the trustees themselves soon voted to abandon this payment. The Board of Managers of the Buhl Foundation is authorized "to fix the compensation each shall receive from time to time." The Harry C. and Mary M. Trexler Estates, functioning still as an estate but with power to incorporate, is understood to pay its trustees the fees usual in estate management. The Duke Endowment sets aside 3 per cent of income for payment of its trustees, of whom there are 15. The Rhode Island Charities Trust, established by Royal Little, is reported to pay its trustees, of whom there are three, 1 per cent of the corpus a year.

Such payment is generally frowned upon as not necessary and not in the public interest. Foundations with challenging programs have experienced no difficulty in obtaining without pay the services of able persons. Board membership in such bodies, whether corporate or trust, does not ordinarily involve personal liability for the actions of the organization or for the safety of its funds. Specific protection is sometimes provided in the charter or other legal document; the trust agreement creating the Twentieth Century Fund provides that "no trustee hereunder shall be liable for anything except his own personal and wilful default or misfeasance."

Many family foundations begin with a board made up of members of the donor's immediate family or close business associates, and some of the large general foundations started with a similar pattern. But in addition to management of the funds, trustees have the still more important duties of selecting the fields and methods of operation, and professional personnel. Careful choice of trustees is therefore of the first importance. An effective board should include members with sound business judgment, with experience in varied fields, and with social vision.

One foundation endeavors to maintain on its board at least one trustee possessing specialized knowledge in each of the major fields of its current interest. Heavy professional representation on the board, however, is not recommended; lay members of broad experience and sound judgment are also needed. The Milbank Memorial Fund endeavors to meet this dual need by obtaining eminent specialists as paid advisers to the board.

Financial Management

General problems of investment are beyond the scope of this book, but certain questions of investment policy peculiar to foundations and other charitable endowments require discussion. Low interest rates and inflated costs make the choice between safety and better income newly critical; problems involved in tax-exempt organizations operating a business for profit are treated in Chapter 13.

Investment by foundations may need to be considered from still other aspects. For example, should a foundation make investments for social betterment which themselves produce income (perhaps a housing development) in distinction from investments selected solely for maximum safe income? Mrs. Russell Sage gave specific permission to her trustees to invest not more than one-half the principal of the fund in enterprises "for social betterment," even though such investments "may not produce a percentage as large as that produced by bonds or like securities," but they must be "likely to produce an annual income of not less than three per cent." The Lavanburg Foundation includes among its assets two model housing units. Student loans on which interest is charged and a substantial effort is made to secure the return of the principal, may be regarded as a very common example of combining philanthropy and investment. But the Rockefeller Foundation "has consistently adhered to the policy of declining . . . to invest in securities which have a philanthropic rather than a business basis."[1]

Certain types of investment are unwise because of effects on the foundation program or reputation. Obviously, no investment will be made in an enterprise generally regarded as antisocial. Also, any operating foundation having investments in, or whose executives have investments in or derive profits from, a business which is a subject of its surveys is in serious danger of having the objectivity of its findings challenged.

Finally, as foundations increase common-stock holdings, which involve voting rights, the question will arise as to their responsibility for the personnel and social policies of the companies in which they have substantial, and sometimes controlling, power.

The Question of Perpetuity

A donor may establish his foundation in any of four patterns: an accumulating foundation where none of the principal and not all the income is spent, at least for a stated period; a perpetuity, which may spend income but not principal; a discretionary per-

---

[1] Vincent, George E., *A Review for 1922.* Rockefeller Foundation, New York, 1922, p. 51.

petuity, which is permitted to spend part or all of its principal, but is not enjoined to do so; or a liquidating fund, whose complete liquidation is compulsory, usually within a stated term. Sometimes the donor unwittingly sets up a perpetuity; Edward A. Filene in presenting certain securities to what is now the Twentieth Century Fund stated in his letter of gift that "the income . . . shall be applied . . ."; in a later letter he emphasized that it was not his desire to make the Fund perpetual and gave the trustees power, after 1947, "at their discretion to use the principal as well as the income."

Accumulating Foundations. The theoretical possibilities of compound interest have attracted a few donors, including Benjamin Franklin who set up funds in Boston and Philadelphia, portions of which were to accumulate for 200 years, until 1991.[1] But compound interest over long terms becomes a mathematical absurdity. One dollar at 5 per cent interest compounded annually becomes $131.50 in 100 years, more than $39 billion in 500 years, and in 1,000 years its value could be expressed only by a figure 22 digits long.

With the exception of the Duke Endowment, which was required to accumulate 20 per cent of income until the corpus had been increased by $40 million, substantially all the large foundations spend at least their income.[2] This is not necessarily so in any one fiscal year, for appropriation dates vary, reserves against capital losses are sometimes set up, or early expenditures from capital in an emergency period are later recouped. But the weight of practice and of social thinking is clearly against suspension of present activities in behalf of problematical future needs. The Revenue Act of 1950 forbids certain accumulations.[3]

Perpetuities. Originally, the intention of perpetuity was the almost universal characteristic of foundations. Experience has shown perpetuity to be a relative term, and where this perpetuity has been applied not only to the organization but to narrowly

[1] See *American Foundations for Social Welfare* (pp. 66–70) for examples and a more detailed discussion of these various types of foundations.

[2] "Income," in this sense, does not include additions to the corpus by later gifts from the donor, or others, or appreciation in the market value of assets.

[3] See p. 300.

defined purposes, inevitable changes in conditions and human needs have sometimes rendered such perpetuities useless or even harmful. Recent founders of perpetuities have usually taken warning, and have allowed great freedom to governing boards to permit them to adjust program from time to time to changing needs.

Discretionary Perpetuities. In setting up the $2,000,000 Peabody Education Fund in 1867, George Peabody gave his board "the power, in case two-thirds of the Trustees shall at any time, after the lapse of thirty years, deem it expedient, to close this Trust." His example was followed in the Rockefeller benefactions and in many others, particularly in recent years when the devalued dollar and declining interest rates have severely reduced the effectiveness of rigid perpetuities.

Liquidating Funds. Some donors have gone further than merely to grant discretion to their boards in spending from capital. Julius Rosenwald declared that he was "not in sympathy with this policy of perpetual endowment" and set up the Rosenwald Fund "with the understanding that the entire fund in the hands of the Board, both income and principal, be expended within twenty-five years of the time of my death." The Fund came to an end in June, 1948. Work remained in various fields of its interest, which it hoped other foundations or agencies would carry on; but during the period of its active life it was able to spend considerably more than could a perpetuity with the same endowment.

No final agreement has been reached on the relative merits of the perpetuity with its greater stability, contributing to both the present and the future but in danger of obsolescence or ineffectiveness, and the policy of liquidation, making larger sums available for a brief term. The purely mathematical relationship is indicated in Table 19.

With its principal returning 3 per cent interest, which is more than many funds were receiving in 1949, a fund liquidating in twenty-five years could spend during that period nearly twice as much as a perpetuity of the same amount. If rates rise to 4 per cent, the relative position of the perpetuity would improve; if they should decline much below 3 per cent, the perpetuity might find its income too small for any effective program. At the close of the quarter century, however, the perpetuity would have its capital intact, but possibly impaired by a severe inflation or other catastrophe. The liquidating fund would have no dollars left, but it might bring benefits to that later generation by the "social increment" of its larger initial spending.

TABLE 19. $1,000,000 TREATED AS A PERPETUITY AND AS A LIQUI-
DATING FUND DURING A 25-YEAR PERIOD

Type of fund	With interest at 3 per cent		With interest at 4 per cent		Remaining at end of 25 years
	Available each year	Aggregate available in 25 years	Available each year	Aggregate available in 25 years	
Perpetuity—principal remaining intact	$30,000	$ 750,000	$40,000	$1,000,000	$1,000,000
Liquidating fund—expenditure level over 25 years	57,428	1,435,697	64,012	1,600,299	..

Method of Operation

At least three well-defined methods of operation are open to foundations. They may confine their program to the making of grants; they may set up temporary research staffs or experimental projects; or they may maintain a permanent staff for research or service.

A program confined to making grants is relatively simple, and requires a minimum of staff. Some of the smaller foundations attempt such programs without any paid workers. For effective distribution of substantial sums, however, a larger staff is desirable, to conduct necessary investigations into the merits of the appeals, handle correspondence, appraise accomplishment, and be the eyes of the foundation, seeking out new opportunities for service. Most foundations are of the grant-giving type. A few of these also conduct some direct work, but administrative problems in mixing the two types are severe. Some suggestions on relations with grantees are included in Chapter 14.

Some foundations build and disband operating staffs on a project basis, keeping permanently only a small central staff.

This plan is suitable for research projects, as in the case of the Twentieth Century Fund, or for demonstration projects, as for example the rural hospital demonstrations of the Commonwealth Fund.

A few foundations set up full, permanent staffs to conduct studies or furnish services in particular fields This form of organization ensures effective follow-up in the chosen field, and a high degree of stability. However, original research tends to become submerged under increasing demands for conferences, lectures, and committee memberships, and there is some danger of continuing a service after the need has passed.

Each of these patterns—limitation to grants, *ad hoc* staff, permanent staff—is well adapted to certain kinds of work. A choice should be made after consideration of the advantages and limitations of each for the particular goals which have been chosen.

Fields of Work

The humanly appealing causes of direct relief—orphans, widows, crippled children, impoverished age—still attract the funds of many small foundations, and a few larger ones. But most experienced administrators reserve their limited funds for exploratory work directed toward prevention or cure rather than treatment or relief. Discovery is the keynote of their programs—discovery in the physical sciences, discovery in the social sciences, discovery in the application of knowledge already won.

In the Russell Sage Foundation study, 335 foundations, including nearly all the larger ones, reported their fields of substantial interest. For 1944, nearly half indicated education as a field of major interest, and nearly as many social welfare, which included relief projects. Health, under which were medical research and medical education, ranked third in number of foundations concentrating in the field, but was probably second in terms of funds expended.

All other spheres of activity received far less attention. Recreation was a major interest with 51 foundations, many of which are community trusts. Thirty-seven specified religion as a major interest, and 26 named international relations and the promotion of peace. Race relations also claimed attention from 26. Only 19 were substantially concerned with problems of government and public administration, and the same number—less than 6 per cent—with the whole broad field of economics.

Both this classification and a more detailed examination of projects reveal that there was some concentration on noncontroversial fields. "The average man," said Frederick P. Keppel when president of the Carnegie Corporation, "is far from comfortable in the presence of any deep-lying social problems, and in no mood to contribute towards their solution by supporting the very steps he extols when they are applied to problems in the natural sciences." Foundation boards apparently are not immune to this discomfort, though a few of them do courageously undertake controversial studies. Several of the larger foundations have turned increased attention to these areas in the past few years.

The world in which foundations operate has now considerably changed. As Chapter 12 indicates, large sums are becoming available from other sources for research in nearly all of the noncontroversial fields. Neither government nor business, however, is likely to undertake research into the really controversial problems of the social sciences. Foundations are the "venture capital" of philanthropy. They are the only important agencies in America free from the political controls of legislative appropriations and pressure groups, and free from the lay controls of needing to temper programs to the judgments and the prejudices of current contributors. Because of this position of unusual freedom, they have an opportunity, and perhaps a special responsibility, for helping push forward today's most important frontier—the study of man himself and his relationships.

Family Foundations

For the person not wealthy enough to donate, at least at one time, the multiple millions required for an efficiently operating general foundation, there are two other possibilities in the foundation field—the family foundation or a fund within a community trust.

Parenthetically, it should be said that general foundations, like community trusts, may legally receive gifts from any persons who are in sympathy with their programs and wish to contribute to such programs without the expense of setting up a new organization. A few such gifts are on the record. The Rosenwald Fund, for example, received $20,195 from the estate of Theodore Max Troy of Jacksonville, and "small gifts . . . from individuals who were interested in one or another of the activities of the Fund." The Field Foundation recently reported generous contributions of cash and securities from "interested friends, wholly unconnected with Field interests," some of whom have also named it as a beneficiary in their wills. However, few general foundations—we exclude the collecting agencies which sometimes call themselves foundations—have ever received substantial gifts from others than the donor or his family. Most donors prefer to establish a fund bearing their own name or that of a person whose memory they desire to honor.

Family foundations, typically, are set up by a living person or persons rather than by bequest. The same high tax rates in the upper income brackets which now tend to prevent large accumulations of wealth have encouraged, through the provision for a charitable deduction, the formation of family foundations built up by annual contributions. Generally they are initially small, and have no administrative organization or headquarters other than the office of the donor or of a law firm. They serve as a buffer between the giver and the numerous appeals directed to him, and as a channel through which he and his family can give from varying income, at periods financially convenient. They permit greater leisure for the distribution of gifts, after more adequate investigation and in accordance with a continuing plan. Some of them have served as a means for keeping within a family the control of a tightly held corporation by reducing the founder's taxable estate.

Such foundations are entirely legal and for the most part seem a socially desirable channel for giving. Unfortunately, the secrecy which has surrounded the operations and even the existence of most of these foundations, and several examples of undoubted abuse, have cast some shadow upon them, and upon foundations in general. The Revenue Act of 1950, however, requires these and various other tax-exempt organizations to furnish annually full financial information to the Treasury Department, this information to be "made available to the public at such times and in such places as the Secretary may prescribe." Certain "prohibited transactions" are spelled out in the new act, which may correct some abuses of the past.[1]

Since most family foundations are controlled by the donor and close associates, much of their giving will probably center upon local welfare agencies, not following the pattern of research, prevention, and exploration of many of the older and larger foundations. Where substantial assets are not in sight, programs of spending from capital, with relatively speedy liquidation, would seem more desirable than the setting up of many small independent perpetuities with too little income for significant work in any year. However, some of them may be built up by annual gifts from one or more individuals and larger death bequests until they become foundations comparable in size with the older giants, and capable of programs of national as well as community significance.

Community Trusts

A giver may secure most of the advantages of a foundation without the costs and inefficiencies of maintaining a small separate fund. Community trusts have been set up for just that purpose; at least 76 are now active in as many different cities in the United States,[2] with combined assets totaling $100 million.

Community trusts are a special class of foundations concerned with problems of social welfare but acting under community control in a sense seldom found in the usual philanthropic endowment. Most such trusts are organized within a single city, a few bear the name of a county, and several are statewide. Their funds may often be used more widely than their names would suggest; some are applied to international purposes.

[1] See pp. 298–301 for a summary of these provisions.
[2] A geographical list of community trusts in the United States reporting assets of at least $50,000 appears in Appendix G.

These trusts admit separate, named funds, designated for specific purposes. In practically all such trusts, capital gifts or bequests are received and administered as to principal through the trust departments of qualified local banks and trust companies. The income is distributed, together with such portions of the principal as may be authorized in any trust, under supervision and control of a distribution committee of citizens selected for representative character and knowledge of charitable affairs. An important provision is the reservation of power to the distribution committee to transfer to other purposes any funds which can no longer be effectively used for the ends originally designed, thereby avoiding the dangers of rigid perpetuities.

The first such community trust was the Cleveland Foundation established in January, 1914 by Frederick H. Goff, who believed "that better results and greater efficiency could be secured if the management and control of the property dedicated to charitable use in each community could be centralized in one or at most a few governing bodies."

Typically, the contribution is made through any trust company the donor chooses which has membership in the community trust. The fund is invested and managed by the trust company, which turns over to the community trust the interest received, together with portions of capital if that is specified. For this service the trust company receives a fee, which varies in different states, with the size of the fund, whether or not it is a perpetuity, and sometimes by special arrangement. For example, in New York State the permissive fee (which may be altered by individual agreement) on a perpetual trust is 7 per cent on the first $2,000 of income collected yearly, and 5 per cent on the balance of income collected yearly, with no fee on the principal.[1] For a fund of $200,000 yielding 3 per cent the annual fee would be, therefore, $340, which is approximately one-sixth of 1 per cent on the principal or 5.67 per cent of the income.

Members of the distribution committee are unpaid, but usually the community trust requires a small executive staff. This is an additional expense which is sometimes met, in whole or in part,

[1] Effective April 1, 1948.

(1) by a proportionate levy on the sums distributed, (2) by contributions from the trust companies out of their income, or (3) by a special fund contributed to take care of administrative costs. Efficient and economical administration is best assured by a fairly substantial accumulation.

Funds within the community trust maintain their separate identity. The New York Community Trust, for example, was administering more than 100 separate funds at the beginning of 1950. The largest single such fund now known is the James Longley Estate in the Permanent Charity Fund of Boston, amounting to $4,238,080, but at least 18 others exceed $1,000,000. Some community trusts decline small funds because of the costs of administration; others have developed pools for their receipt, called combined, united, or composite funds.

Policies of Community Trusts

The distribution committee of the community trust, acting with the advice of the executive staff, is the effective policy-making body. Selection of its members is usually arranged by constitutional provision to represent a wide variety of interests. For example, the Resolution and Declaration of Trust of the New Haven Foundation provides that its distribution committee shall consist of seven members each appointed for seven years, no more than two of whom may belong to the same religious sect or denomination, and none of whom may hold a salaried public office. Each of the following officials appoints one member: the chief executive of the city of New Haven, the president or other executive officer of the chamber of commerce, the chief judge of the probate court, the president of Yale University, the president of the county bar association; two are appointed by the trustees' committee.

Policies of distribution committees differ, but the funds of local foundations of the community trust type go more largely to specific local charities and for relieving individual need than to broad social research, as might be expected from their local character and the expressed wishes of many of the donors. However, research does enter into many programs. The Cleveland

Foundation in its early years financed the extensive Cleveland Surveys in the fields of education, recreation, and crime; the Buffalo Foundation continuously maintains a Bureau of Studies and Social Statistics; the New York Community Trust administers several funds in such general fields as agricultural research and international scholarships.

Because of their community character, some of these trusts have assumed responsibilities for planning or coordinating welfare, recreation, and similar activities in their localities, or for financing such planning. They would seem to have a close relation to the community chests, which collect and administer funds on an annual basis for many of the agencies also assisted by the community trust. In Rochester, New York, and more recently in several other cities, this relationship has taken specific form; there the community chest organized a trust department in which 60 separate funds are now combined, functioning in this respect as a local foundation of the community trust type.

Growth and Distribution

The idea of the community trust was accepted enthusiastically, especially by officers of trust companies, and organizations were set up at the initiative of banks in many towns and cities. Some have never attracted any funds, and exist only as paper organizations. Some control only negligible amounts, and their future is uncertain. Growth has been steady, however, though not spectacular, as indicated in Table 20.

Three community trusts have assets in 1950 exceeding $10 million:

	Capital assets	Disbursements in 1949
New York Community Trust	$19,258,489	$1,065,065
Chicago Community Trust	14,533,977	416,680
Cleveland Foundation	11,294,011	412,151

These larger organizations are the equivalent in assets and in annual disbursements of many of the larger foundations. The total of $100 million for all community trusts is a philanthropic endowment which is already substantial, and which may be expected to grow since most of the funds involved are perpetuities and additions are constantly being made.

TABLE 20. AGGREGATE CAPITAL ASSETS AND DISBURSE-
MENTS OF COMMUNITY TRUSTS, 1921–1949
Dollar figures in thousands

Year	Capital assets	Disbursements	Disbursements as per cent of assets
1921	$ 7,000	$ 375	5.4
1922	7,500	350	4.7
1923	10,000	350	3.5
1924	12,000	400	3.3
1925	13,500	500	3.7
1926	15,000	550	3.7
1927	16,000	600	3.7
1928	24,000	700	2.9
1929	30,298	852	2.8
1930	35,390	941	2.7
1931	37,100	1,002	2.7
1932	37,500	1,107	3.0
1933	39,250	1,026	2.6
1934	40,818	1,060	2.6
1935	45,137	1,129	2.5
1936	46,329	1,109	2.4
1937	48,020	1,150	2.4
1938	48,503	1,757	3.6
1939	51,804	1,278	2.5
1940	52,473	2,225	4.2
1941	54,273	1,606	3.0
1942	56,036	1,725	3.1
1943	57,135	1,740	3.0
1944	67,042	1,918	2.9
1945	75,092	2,022	2.7
1946	77,835	2,205	2.7
1947	81,362	2,250	2.8
1948	91,402	3,362	3.6
1949	100,136	3,855	3.8
Total, 29 years		$39,144	..
Average, 29 years		..	3.1

SOURCES: Data on capital assets and disbursements for 1921–1929 from *Community Trusts in the United States and Canada,* American Bankers Association, New York, 1931, p. 31. Data for 1930–1949 from *The First Ten Million:* Report for 1941, New York Community Trust, and later releases of this Trust.

Map 2 indicates the very high concentration of these trusts in the large cities of the East, with a few on the West Coast. But this device has taken little root in the Mountain or Prairie States. A renewed effort to direct capital gifts and bequests into useful welfare channels, particularly through the device of the community trust, began in 1949 through organization of a National Committee on Foundations and Trusts for Community Welfare, which includes representatives of Community Chests and Councils, community trusts, and the National Social Welfare Assembly. A large field for future development lies open.

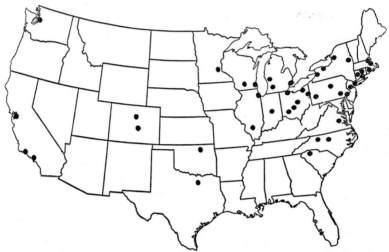

MAP 2. GEOGRAPHICAL DISTRIBUTION OF THE 43 LARGER COMMUNITY TRUSTS IN THE UNITED STATES, 1950

An interesting parallel to the community trust in the United States is the organization of Common Good funds in Britain. As early as the Middle Ages Scottish kings set up a few such funds through grants of land to the Royal Burghs. These were greatly extended by bequests, gifts, and additional grants. In the House of Lords in 1949 it was proposed that such funds be set up locally in towns and counties throughout the British Isles "to subsidise any kind of public amenity for which money is not otherwise available," attracting "gifts and bequests from many quarters, generation after generation" and being the beneficiaries of unclaimed funds in banks, estates of people with no near relatives who die intestate, and the funds of trusts and foundations whose original purposes can no longer be fulfilled.

CHAPTER 7

Voluntary Welfare Agencies

WE TURN from givers—individuals, business corporations, labor unions, foundations—to a consideration of the organizations that solicit and receive gifts. Their number and variety are astounding. Anyone who desires to contribute to a cause, from the treatment of alcoholics to the maintenance of zoos, can usually find at least one organization operating in that field. This multiplicity presents both advantages and dangers to givers. The advantages can be achieved only through some knowledge of various types of agencies and what they do.

Public and Voluntary Agencies

With the government increasingly operating in various fields of health and welfare, it became necessary to distinguish between agencies run by the government and those supported by individual initiative—and contributions. At first these were respectively called "public agencies" and "private agencies." But "private" seemed an unfortunate word for describing agencies which in many cases offered services to the public. For want of a better term, "voluntary" is now in general use. A voluntary welfare agency is one organized by private initiative and usually supported by voluntary contributions. It may or may not have "volunteer" (unpaid) workers.

We have examined elsewhere[1] the recent growth in government participation in education, health, and welfare, and the fact that our contributions to such purposes through taxes far exceed all private giving. But since giving through taxes is a matter over which the individual has very little personal control, the important work of the tax-supported agencies is beyond the scope of this chapter, except for its bearing upon the voluntary agencies.

In broad generalization, public agencies undertake to meet, more or less adequately, basic economic, health, and educational needs; in some cases for the whole population, in others for only certain specific classes of the disadvantaged. To voluntary agencies remain the important tasks of filling in gaps and inadequacies in these fields, of establishing standards and checking the work of public agencies, of covering many additional needs not now met by government, and of doing most of the exploratory, experimental, and research work in building that important fence of prevention above the dangerous cliff.

Some of these differences in emphasis by area of service are reflected in the chart below:

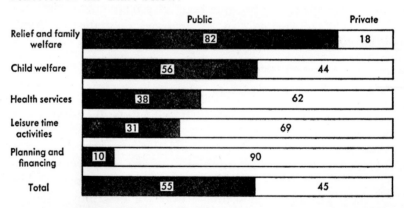

CHART 3. PERCENTAGE OF WELFARE EXPENDITURES IN 18 URBAN
    AREAS FROM PUBLIC AND FROM PRIVATE FUNDS, BY
    FIELD OF SERVICE, 1946

SOURCE: *Expenditures for Community Health and Welfare in Thirty-One Urban Areas, 1946.* Community Chests and Councils, adapted from Table 6, p. 7.
    [1] See Chapter 3.

As the final bar in Chart 3 makes clear, this comparison by field of service gives no picture of relative actual expenditures. The per capita expenditures in the relief category were $9.84 from public and $2.10 from private funds; in the planning category, where private funds had so large a percentage advantage, the per capita expenditures were only 4 cents from public and 36 cents from private funds.

National Agencies

Many welfare services are organized on a national, and sometimes an international, basis. The *Social Work Year Book* list,[1] limited to "organized activities in social work and in related fields," includes 430 national voluntary organizations in the United States. Some hint is given of the breadth of activities involved by a glance at the agencies described on the first page of this list:

Alcoholics Anonymous
Alliance for Guidance of Rural Youth
Amateur Athletic Union of the United States
American Academy of Political and Social Science, Inc.
American Arbitration Association, Inc.

The giver need not wander hopelessly in this maze of nearly half a thousand agencies. Many do not seek his gift, and a classified index will lead him directly to the agencies specializing in the field of his interest. Within such groups some unnecessary duplication undoubtedly exists, but usually quite diverse aspects of a common problem are attacked. The first agency, for example, deals with alcoholism; below are descriptions, condensed from the *Year Book*, of this agency and three others in the same field:

Alcoholics Anonymous. *Purpose:* To help the sick alcoholic if he so wishes. The organization is made up of members who have recovered from alcoholism, and who have banded together to help others.

National Committee for Education on Alcoholism, Inc. *Purpose:* Distributes literature, maintains a free lecture service, and provides

[1] Hodges, Margaret B., editor, *Social Work Year Book, 1949*. Russell Sage Foundation, New York, 1949, pp. 573–654.

general and specific information on alcoholism and the facilities for treatment of alcoholics.

National Committee on Alcohol Hygiene, Inc. *Purpose:* To disseminate scientific information to the public through various educators (teachers, clergymen, physicians, and others) regarding the problem of alcoholism, which must be clearly distinguished from social drinking, so that they may help to educate individuals and the community about the significance of this public health problem in the contemporary social setting.

Research Council on Problems of Alcohol, Inc. *Purpose:* To help bring about a continuing reduction in problem drinking and other conditions associated with the excessive use of alcohol through research, education, and the establishment of model alcoholic centers. [This agency was recently discontinued.]

Of these 430 national voluntary agencies, 131 call themselves "national," 130 "American" or "of America," and 15 more include "United States" in their official title. But however "national" they may be in name, these agencies have their roots in local soil and must usually get their financial support from individuals in local communities, either directly or through chapters. One commentator[1] declares that "one of the best moves national agencies could make would be to stop calling themselves national agencies. . . . Acceptance for national programs must come from the grass-roots, and must have unity all the way."

Organizationally, national agencies are of three main types. Some are very loose associations, created by local agencies to perform certain advisory, research, and coordinating functions, with the national office closely controlled by the local member agencies.

Others, usually organized before their local members, retain strong control in the national office, dictating program and policy to local chapters chartered by the national organization. These local chapters may participate in policy formation through annual conventions or councils.

Finally, a few national agencies have no local affiliates. They may be study or planning groups, operating only on the national level, or not yet large enough for local chapters. In some cases

[1] Seymour, Harold J., *Design for Giving:* The Story of the National War Fund. Harper and Bros., New York, 1947, p. 134.

they are organizations of national organizations. For instance, a number of national agencies in the health field found among themselves so many common problems that in 1921 they formed the National Health Council.

Indeed, the need for central consultation and planning in the whole field of social welfare resulted in the formation in 1922 of the National Social Work Council, reorganized and broadened in 1945 as the National Social Welfare Assembly. This Assembly has 56 affiliated national organizations and 4 associate groups, and expresses its purposes as the following: to facilitate more effective operation of organized social welfare; to study and define social welfare problems and human needs and develop plans of action to meet those problems and needs; and to act in behalf of social welfare where representation of its interests is indicated.

For their financial support, some organizations run nationwide campaigns, and are known to all givers. Others appeal to selected groups, or are supported by dues or service fees of member organizations; the giver at the grass-roots does support them in the final analysis, but he may do so by indirection and not even know their names. Some national agencies have endowments or other sources of income adequate for their needs, and make no appeals for funds.

Budgets of various types of these organizations are examined later. Collectively, national agencies represent a wide range of choice for givers, with usually more emphasis upon research, policy formulation, and administration than on meeting individual needs.

Local Agencies

The local agencies, however, are insistently on the doorstep and in the mail basket of most givers. Their number is large, as indeed it must be, since it is through the local agencies that services reach the people. The New York directory currently includes almost 1,100 organizations. It "lists primarily welfare and health agencies, public and voluntary, serving New York City. Civic, educational and religious organizations are included only if they offer services in the field of social welfare or in closely related fields. National agencies with offices in New York City, whose work is in the social field, are also included."[1]

The Chicago *Social Service Directory* lists some 700 agencies. All the larger cities have a hundred or more; even in cities with less than 200,000 population, usually from 50 to 100 agencies are active in the fields of health and welfare.

Obviously, the roster differs considerably from community to community, and no attempt can be made to name or list these local organizations. The 28 headings under which New York's agencies are classified indicate something of the breadth of activities: they range from child health services to care of the aged; from mental hygiene to legal aid; from employment and vocational guidance to recreation and vacation services.

This multiplicity of agencies reflects the growing complexity of modern life. Undoubtedly greater efficiency would sometimes result through amalgamation of related agencies, and some mergers have recently occurred. But persons trying to find their way to a particular service in this labyrinth must often wish for one more agency—which would tell them where to go. For people on the move, Travelers Aid Societies largely fill this need, and for the stationary citizen in any community some central agency or worker can supply the information, but may not be easy to find. The British are meeting this problem with Citizens' Advice Bureaus, which by 1946 numbered 639.

> A Citizens' Advice Bureau is an office to which any citizen can go in person to seek information and advice as to his rights and duties as a citizen, as to the bearing on him of laws and regulations, as to any problem of his relation to other citizens. . . . The inquiries coming to the bureaux have been and are extremely varied. They are classified under twenty-one heads ranging from rationing, social insurance, income tax and employment to housing, travel, and family and personal problems.[2]

The American contributor besieged by appeals, and wishing to sort out the dubious ones, will find in many cities, under a variety of names, bureaus to assist him.[3]

---

[1] *Directory of Social Agencies of the City of New York, 1948–1949.* Columbia University Press, New York, 1948.

[2] Beveridge, Lord, *Voluntary Action.* The Macmillan Co., New York, 1948, pp. 277–279.   [3] These are described in Chapter 9.

Decline of the Relief Function

The most notable change in the activities of many voluntary agencies has been the shift from direct relief activities to various kinds of services. The extent to which public agencies have taken over responsibility for meeting most of the primary needs has already been noted. How voluntary agencies have changed their programs is dramatically illustrated by the dates on excerpts from one of the most famous of the Christmas appeals, *The New York Times* "Hundred Neediest":

December 16, 1928 (A prosperous year)

Case 46. ANNA STRICKEN SEEKING WORK

The employment manager reported the case when Anna fainted at the agency while looking for work. There was only some dry bread in the cold, bare room overlooking the railroad tracks where she lived with her mother. Both of them had been starving slowly . . .

December 11, 1932 (Depression, before Social Security)

Case 66. AN AGED SISTER AND BROTHER

Recently he has been fortunate when he earned as much as $1.25 or $1.50 a week. For many months they tried to live on that until some one discovered that they were close to starvation and asked help. . . .

December 5, 1948 (Editorial)

THE NEEDIEST

True it is that many who are not eligible for public assistance must have supplemental material aid to buy essential basic comforts . . . but by far the greater number, trapped in the dark recesses of confused and hopeless thoughts, are desperate for the encouragement, wise planning and sober counseling that cannot be measured by dollars. By far the greater number need help out of their psychological sickness if they are to help themselves.

December 5, 1948

Case 14. SINGLE-HANDED

To provide for her children—Wendy, 4; Patty, 3; and Boyd, 2—Mrs. L., an experienced librarian, has been working at two jobs. Recently she suffered a heart attack, and, forced to rest for several months, she is receiving a $32 weekly allowance from the Department of Welfare. Talks with the social worker have helped her to see that hope for her children's future depends on taking care of her health now. Bewildered by all that has happened during the past two years, she asks, "Can I really look forward to anything when I've lost so much?" With the agency's help, Mrs. L. shows promise of changing her answer from a "no" to a "yes," and continued guidance will strengthen her belief in a future for herself and her children. . . .

The final case illustrates both the opportunities and the problems which stem from this change. The voluntary agency to which Mrs. L. turned for help after her heart attack did not have to supply food for a starving family—the Department of Welfare's $32 a week took care of that first necessity. It asked for $300 for other services, to put this family on its feet. However, many givers will open their purses generously to a plea of starvation, but find little appeal in these other "services." The record of contributions to the "Hundred Neediest," now hovering around the level of twenty years ago, may reflect this difficulty.

TABLE 21. CONTRIBUTIONS TO THE NEW YORK TIMES "HUNDRED NEEDIEST" IN SELECTED YEARS

Year	Number of contributors	Amount
1912	117	$ 3,631
1916	2,716	55,792
1920	6,187	111,126
1924	11,424	233,525
1928	12,574	338,111
1932	10,808	265,400
1936	9,742	271,497
1940	9,785	245,920
1944	12,437	326,397
1948	11,574	347,147
1949	11,263	307,266

SOURCE: *The New York Times.*

In nearly every city there is a family welfare society, under that or a similar name, and often a child welfare society as well, taking care of maladjustments among families which are not covered by the services of public welfare agencies. In recent years many of these societies have added marriage counseling to their special services. These local societies often are served by national organizations. Twenty-one national organizations are represented in the Social Casework Council affiliated with the National Social Welfare Assembly, including such agencies as the American Association of Medical Social Workers, Child Welfare League of America, Family Service Association of America, National Conference of Catholic Charities, and National Travelers Aid Association.

"Overhead" and Services

Many contributors assume that the essence of wise giving is seeing to it that the whole of their gift reaches the person or persons in need, avoiding charges for "overhead," "service," and any but a minimum of staff salaries. Let us consider this matter a moment.

It might seem a commendable act (and would show up irreproachably on the annual report) for an agency to give a breadwinner who has lost his arm $20 a week toward support of his needy family. Instead, this agency may interview the man, his friends, his former employer; take the facts discovered to a specialist in employment for the handicapped; and send him to a school to be fitted for a job where his handicap will not seriously interfere with his ability to earn. Soon he may again be supporting his family, with self-respect and interest in living revived. All of this is service and "overhead," but in the end it will cost vastly less even in cold cash than continuing weekly aid, and do vastly more for the man and his family.

Overhead does need to be examined. A later chapter, dealing with charity rackets, points out instances where agencies were organized for the private profit of the promoters, who pocketed substantially all the income; in other cases inefficient agencies, through costly fund-collecting procedures or poor organization, devote so small a portion of their receipts to their announced purposes that it is doubtful whether givers should longer support them. But most modern agencies are in the position of the example cited, where skilled staff services are more needed than direct relief. Such services require highly trained and adequately paid personnel. A danger exists that, because of traditional contributor attitudes, this sort of overhead may be kept too low.

Health Agencies

Health is at present one of the largest fields for voluntary giving. Medicine, it has been said, has made as much progress in the past seventy-five years as in the previous three thousand. But the resulting specialized treatment and continuing research are costly; they are financed in part by contributions to voluntary organizations. Most of the health agencies are now in the National Health Council, which has the following members:

Active

American Association of Medical Social Workers, Inc.
American Cancer Society, Inc.
American Dental Association
American Hearing Society
American Heart Association, Inc.
American Hospital Association
American Medical Association
American National Red Cross
American Nurses' Association, Inc.
American Pharmaceutical Association
American Public Health Association
American Social Hygiene Association, Inc.
Association of American Medical Colleges
Association of State and Territorial Health Officers
Conference for Health Council Work
Maternity Center Association
National Association for Mental Health, Inc.
National Epilepsy League, Inc.
National Foundation for Infantile Paralysis, Inc.
National Organization for Public Health Nursing, Inc.
National Safety Council
National Society for Crippled Children and Adults, Inc.
National Society for the Prevention of Blindness, Inc.
National Tuberculosis Association

Advisory
United States Children's Bureau
United States Public Health Service

Associate
American Diabetes Association, Inc.
American Eugenics Society, Inc.
American Physical Therapy Association
National Multiple Sclerosis Society
Planned Parenthood Federation of America, Inc.

In addition to the national agencies, and a few international, operating in the field of health, there are many local agencies, of which the hospital is the most common. While 78 per cent of all hospital beds are operated by federal, state, or local government, most of these hospitals are restricted to special groups (such as veterans) or to patients hospitalized for particular diseases, such as mental illness or tuberculosis. The voluntary hospital usually finds itself supported only in part by patients' fees, and needing to appeal to community chests or individual givers to make up its deficits. Such support amounted to at least $37 million one recent year according to a report to the American Hospital Association from 2,846 hospitals.

Building costs range from $9,000 to $15,000 or more per bed; operating costs run from $2,000 to $3,000 per bed per year. Single hospitals may have operating budgets exceeding $1,000,000 per year; the New York University-Bellevue Medical Center reported that its budget for the fiscal year beginning in 1949 would be $6,434,000, excluding the costs of operating Bellevue Hospital, owned by the City of New York.

Health services in the United States in 1947 cost an astronomical $8.4 billion, divided roughly as follows[1]:

Personal medical care	$6,500,000,000
Governmental health services	1,500,000,000
Health expenditures by industry	125,000,000
Philanthropic contributions	300,000,000
Total	$8,425,000,000

[1] Clark, Dean A. and Katharine G., "Medical Care," *Social Work Year Book, 1949*, p. 302.

We are here concerned primarily with the $300 million raised through philanthropic contributions. This is a small fraction (3.6 per cent) of the whole health expenditure, but it is an important fraction, since out of this sum comes much of the support for research in the health field, and for exploratory programs.

A large proportion of this $300 million goes to the big national agencies in the health field. The giver is acutely conscious of this fact, for most of them make individual appeals of one sort or another, beginning just before Christmas with the seal campaign of the National Tuberculosis Association, with a 1949 campaign budget of $21 million; it raised $20.2 million. In January comes the National Foundation for Infantile Paralysis, with a 1949 budget of $30 million as "amount required"; its March of Dimes raised $25.7 million, and a supplementary campaign was conducted in the fall. The American Heart Association uses St. Valentine's Day to start its National Heart Week; 1949 goal, $5 million; raised, $2.9 million. March is the dating for the largest campaign of all, the American National Red Cross, which asks contributions in the form of memberships; 1949 goal, $60 million; amount raised, $67.1 million. The National Society for Crippled Children and Adults conducts an Easter seal campaign; 1949 tentative goal, $7 million; raised, $5.8 million. In April the American Cancer Society campaigns, with a 1949 goal of $14.5 million; raised, $13.7 million. Numerous other agencies in the health field, national and local, also make appeals, either independently or in connection with community chest campaigns.[1]

The results of these fund-raising methods in the health field have been criticized. While the total raised in all the fields is much less than could usefully be spent, it is also clear that the amount raised in any particular campaign is more nearly related to the "heart appeal" of the cause and the technical skill of the fund-raisers than to proportional need. Said the Gunn-Platt report:

> It is not irrelevant to raise the question, Can the whole private health movement be well served when two voluntary health move-

[1] The controversy over individual versus federated campaigns is discussed in the chapter following.

ments [National Foundation for Infantile Paralysis and National Tuberculosis Association], fighting two diseases, obtain from the public $26,000,000 in one year, while very many other public health dangers of greater individual or collective importance must be combated by all the other voluntary health movements with only a small fraction of this amount?[1]

More recently, organizations fighting several additional diseases have moved into the big-collection category, and efforts are being made to broaden the fields of operation of the larger fund collectors. But little progress has been achieved in solving the fundamental problem, the setting of national goals proportioned to need. One university research director recently asserted that, while grants for research were doing great good, some large grants were endangering fundamental research. Said Dr. Starr[2]:

> Some agencies have more money than they know what to do with. Such groups, having raised their money by advertising their need, naturally feel it must be spent or next year's campaign would be conducted at a disadvantage. So they raise the ante and attract talent and personnel to their field without regard to the opportunities for advancing it. Good investigators leave promising problems to work in fallow fields simply because money can be so easily picked up. . . . Another temptation in a research investigator's path is to publish results prematurely or make exaggerated claims to insure next year's grant by producing what is desired this year.

Nevertheless, wisely apportioned gifts in the health field, particularly when devoted to research into ultimate causes, cures, and prevention of disease, have sometimes yielded spectacular dividends in the past, and may be expected to do so in the future. A newer trend is research into the causes and conditions of good health, rather than the problems of disease.

Agencies for Recreation and Character-Building

Another large group of voluntary agencies function in the fields of recreation and character-building. Some of these serve

[1] Gunn, Selskar M. and Philip S. Platt, *Voluntary Health Agencies*. Ronald Press Co., New York, 1945, p. 216.

[2] Dr. Isaac Starr, Hartzell Professor of Therapeutic Research, University of Pennsylvania School of Medicine, at the 1949 midyear meeting of the American Pharmaceutical Manufacturers Association.

boys and girls of elementary and high-school ages, as for example the Boy Scouts of America, Boys' Clubs of America, Camp Fire Girls, 4-H Clubs, Girl Scouts of the United States of America; others serve these and older groups, or only older groups, such as the YMCA, YWCA, the several Catholic and Jewish youth programs, National Federation of Settlements, American Youth Hostels. There are 22 national agencies in the Youth Division of the National Social Welfare Assembly, and 12 in the newly organized Young Adult Council.

Other agencies promote recreation activities, usually without age limitation. Recreation has been an important part of life since the cave man, and the founding fathers put it among the "unalienable Rights" in the Declaration of Independence in terms of the "pursuit of Happiness," but only in the past few decades has it become highly organized. Many of our recreational facilities are now provided out of tax funds—national, state, and local parks, playgrounds, public libraries, museums, swimming pools, civic centers, for example—and many others are commercially provided—professional baseball, football, boxing, racing, motion pictures, sponsored radio and television, the theater—but even in these fields voluntary agencies have been needed to perform advisory and other services. The National Recreation Association, for example, gives itself a broad mandate to "promote a program whose purpose is that every child in America may have a chance to play, and that all persons, young and old, may have an opportunity to find the best and most satisfactory manner of using leisure time." There is a National Conference on State Parks which promotes their development and informs the public concerning them. Twenty-seven organizations belong to the Education-Recreation Council of the National Social Welfare Assembly.

SOME AGENCY BUDGETS

Among so many and such diverse organizations, it is not possible to generalize on size of budget, how it is raised, or in what proportions it is spent. As illustrative examples, however, we present financial data for nine agencies. They were selected for diversity, relative importance in their fields, and willingness to cooperate. So far as available, figures are presented over an eleven-year span: for 1938, a fairly normal between-the-wars period; for 1943, a war year; and for 1948.

A standard reporting form was suggested, with the recognition that it would have to be adapted to the varying financial pictures of some of these agencies. The first report presented, that of the Child Welfare League of America, uses the reporting form as originally proposed. Reasons for departure from this form in some of the succeeding reports will usually be obvious in the nature of the data. Beyond a few explanatory footnotes, which were furnished by the named agencies and were checked by them, no attempt has been made to audit or to interpret these data.

It would be rash for the reader to draw detailed conclusions about an agency from these reports, which are merely samplings spread usually over eleven years, without much additional study of the agency, its program and policies, and special factors which may have affected one or more of the sample years. It would be even more rash to attempt general conclusions about financing voluntary welfare agencies on the basis of these highly diverse fragments. They are simply illustrative case studies, showing for certain agencies their chief sources of income and their major types of expenditure.

Even the "assets" item must be interpreted with much background knowledge. For example, the American Heart Association closes its fiscal year just after its annual fund-raising campaign; its reported assets therefore include almost all of its working funds for the year ahead. The National Foundation for Infantile Paralysis, on the other hand, now closes its fiscal year on December 31, at the low point of its financial picture, just a few weeks before the beginning of a new March of Dimes.

Child Welfare League of America

The Child Welfare League of America is a national organization intensively serving more than 200 local member agencies engaged in child care and protection, and offering information and other services to some 500 additional agencies. It develops standards, surveys individual agencies or groups of agencies, supplies information, and issues pertinent publications. It does not furnish direct child care. Its report follows exactly (except for a footnote) the suggested form, and may be compared with reports following to see changes which the reporting agencies have wished to make.

TABLE 22. FINANCIAL DATA SHEET, CHILD WELFARE LEAGUE OF AMERICA

Item	1938	1943	1948
Income			
Service fees[a]	$ 5,101	$ 1,809	$ 4,744
Endowment	..	..	..
Memberships	15,375	25,989	51,865
Contributions	13,734	25,047	36,237
Bequests	..	..	
Grants	17,043	13,881	14,605
Community chest	..	..	..
Sale of literature	3,575	3,635	5,871
Other	2,220	5,857	8,458
Total	$57,048	$76,218	$121,780
Expenditures			
General administration	$15,736	$18,783	$28,380
Fund-raising	2,577	3,508	5,629
Research	..	..	
Service[a]	37,653	50,069	85,238
Grants	..	..	..
Other	234	436	918
Total	$56,200	$72,796	$120,165
Assets			
Endowment	..	..	..
Unexpended balance	$ 217	$ 3,458	$ 2,870
Total	$ 217	$ 3,458	$ 2,870

[a] Includes surveys.

American Association of Social Workers

The American Association of Social Workers is the basic national association for professional social workers. It serves as a clearinghouse for professional activities in social work and carries on a program of interpretation, study, and promotion of legislation. It had in 1950 about 12,250 members.

TABLE 23. FINANCIAL DATA SHEET, AMERICAN ASSOCIATION OF SOCIAL WORKERS

Item	1938	1943	1948
Income			
Memberships	$63,820	$58,558	$92,003
Contributions	..	219	..
Grants	2,303	2,017	783
Sale of literature	1,205	..	2,806
Other	268	477	619
Total	$67,596	$61,271	$96,211
Expenditures			
General administration	$52,179	$43,960	$61,045
Committee service	9,578	6,043	13,754
Conferences and staff travel	5,425	2,555	6,397
Publications	4,956	4,224	11,206
Dues	..	..	500
Total	$72,138	$56,782	$92,902
Assets			
Unexpended balance	$ 2,024	$10,267	$ 2,807

TABLE 24. FINANCIAL DATA SHEET, AMERICAN HEART ASSOCIA-TION[a]

Item	1938	1943	1948
Income			
Memberships	$10,265	$11,940	$ 24,403
Contributions	1,312	8,139	1,610,879
Grants	..	..	51,499
Sale of educational materials	3,190	10,991	14,714
Other	22	149	12,274
Total	$14,789	$31,219	$1,713,769
Expenditures			
General administration	$10,598	$12,180	$ 151,272
Fund-raising	..	..	235,667[b]
Research	..	..	25,000
Service	858	..	10,705
Grants	..	..	59,495
Office furniture, equipment	..	..	23,322
Educational materials	3,291	9,364	19,353
Total	$14,747	$21,544	$ 524,814
Assets			
Research fund appropriated but not disbursed	..	..	$ 225,000
Unexpended balance, general	$ 2,723	$ 7,215	1,074,632
Total	$ 2,723	$ 7,215	$1,299,632

[a] This statement represents data on national headquarters only. It does not include financial information from affiliates.

[b] Of the 1948 fund-raising expenditure of $235,667, a total of $164,059 was for preparing and carrying on the larger 1949 campaign, on which no income is here shown.

American Heart Association

The American Heart Association and its affiliated heart associations and committees gather and disseminate information relating to the disorders of the circulatory system and diseases of the heart, and sponsor research training. Substantial efforts at national fund-raising were begun only in 1948; the national organization receives 30 per cent of the funds raised locally after the initial deduction of 10 per cent for expenses, or a net 27 per cent.

American National Red Cross

Little need exists to describe the American National Red Cross, since World War II the largest of the voluntary social agencies. The table on page 129 reflects finances of the national organization only; because of the unusual character of some of the Red Cross operations, it departs in many respects from the usual reporting form.

This statement does not include the records of some 3,700 Red Cross chapters. The national headquarters has supplied the following figures on "approximate income and expenditures of the chapters for the fiscal years under consideration." An estimate on assets of local chapters was not given.

Fiscal years	Income	Expenditures
1937–1938	$ 7,159,000	$ 6,805,000
1942–1943	41,000,000	35,000,000
1947–1948	42,000,000	47,400,000

Boy Scouts of America

The general activities of the Boy Scouts of America, with its more than two million members, need no description. The financial statement (page 130) is that of the national office only.

Community Service Society of New York

The Community Service Society of New York, a nonsectarian private family and health agency, is the only local social agency included among these samplings. It maintains research and other

TABLE 25. FINANCIAL DATA SHEET, AMERICAN NATIONAL RED CROSS

Item	1937–1938	1942–1943	1947–1948
Income			
Endowment and other invested funds	$ 857,868	$ 743,669	$ 1,219,574
Contributions:			
Campaign	2,871,155	85,719,536	38,976,017
Foreign war relief	..	3,365,554	..
Disaster relief	1,259,092	161,286	221,868
Junior Red Cross	4,251	187,467	724,956
Other[a]	98,823	467,904	2,151,389
Total	$ 5,091,189	$ 90,645,416	$ 43,293,804
Expenditures			
Service to armed forces and veterans	$ 596,248	$ 42,390,917	$ 20,976,482
Disaster relief	7,440,298	2,938,248	12,700,778
Health services	578,979	2,751,936	4,837,005
Junior Red Cross and college activities	144,953	447,218	1,787,496
Volunteer services	41,929	481,071	444,848
Service to chapters	657,752	2,048,084	2,903,313
Public relations and fund-raising	416,436	1,531,210	1,991,432
International activities	86,972	2,944,132	1,510,902
General administration	394,999	1,343,047	3,776,523
Total	$10,358,566	$ 56,875,863	$ 50,928,779
Assets			
Cash and securities	$15,225,987	$ 80,835,342	$ 94,066,653
Accounts receivable	321,582	591,033	5,980,375
Supplies	59,725	1,982,208	306,554
Working advances to employes	228,123	22,187,156	540,825
Advances to chapters	..	..	285,000
Land and buildings at $1	..	..	238
Miscellaneous	36	116,825	32,809
Subtotal	$15,835,453	$105,712,564	$101,212,454
Less: Liabilities	622,886	3,236,246	4,224,757
Net general fund assets	$15,212,567	$102,476,318	$ 96,987,697
Endowment and other invested funds[b]	14,371,104	15,864,738	22,308,749
Total	$29,583,671	$118,341,056	$119,296,446

[a] Includes receipts from salvage sales, adjustments in prior year commitments, and other miscellaneous income.

[b] Income only available for current expenditure.

functions, including the sponsoring of a school of social work, which give it national impact, and its budgets exceed those of the vast majority of national social agencies.

TABLE 26. FINANCIAL DATA SHEET, BOY SCOUTS OF AMERICA

Item	1938	1943	1948
Income			
Service fees	$ 165,119	$ 195,201	$ 218,515
Endowment	52,663	34,853	61,254
Memberships	594,155	750,241	1,008,540
Grants and contributions	75,509	108,156	129,353
Sale of literature, uniforms, camping equipment, etc.	230,581	696,861	789,714
Publications	147,591	165,796	344,697
Miscellaneous	10,817	14,841	12,839
Total	$1,276,435	$1,965,949	$2,564,912
Expenditures			
General administration	$ 205,973	$ 291,885	$ 511,027
Service	1,052,107	1,565,444	2,037,190
Miscellaneous	11,535	12,414	15,838
Total	$1,269,615	$1,869,743	$2,564,055
Assets			
Endowment	$1,707,245	$1,978,744	$2,179,748
Accumulated and unassigned income	42,573	145,919	168,038
Total	$1,749,818	$2,124,663	$2,347,786

TABLE 27. FINANCIAL DATA SHEET, COMMUNITY SERVICE SOCIETY OF NEW YORK

Item	1939–1940	1942–1943	1947–1948
Income			
Service fees[a]	$ 390,334	$ 463,725	$ 612,862
Endowment	1,143,169	1,114,667	1,302,987
Contributions	974,521	742,264	708,259
Greater New York Fund	151,427	156,023	142,575
Sale of literature	891	910	1,159
Workshop and Thrift Shop sales	27,398	30,613	30,599
Total	$ 2,687,740	$ 2,508,202	$ 2,798,441
Expenditures			
General administration	$ 276,549	$ 268,943	$ 436,454
Fund-raising, publicity, and public relations	127,783	96,153	129,324
Research	..	26,628	27,938
Service	1,980,244	1,893,001	2,169,946
New York School of Social Work	308,390	347,662	557,133
Bureau of Public Affairs, Committee on Housing	35,085	32,116	26,077
Total	$ 2,728,051	$ 2,664,503	$ 3,346,872
Assets			
Endowment (invested)	$26,319,245	$29,706,624	$30,285,257
Uninvested capital funds	802,773	226,041	430,343
Properties used in activities	864,115	817,135	618,859
Total	$27,986,133	$30,749,800	$31,334,459

[a] Includes dental clinic fees, School of Social Work tuition fees, institutional board and room rents, and the like.

Family Service Association of America

This Association promotes the development of family social work and wholesome family life through field work with governmental and voluntary family service agencies, assistance in developing qualified personnel in family casework, and various information services.

TABLE 28. FINANCIAL DATA SHEET, FAMILY SERVICE ASSOCIATION OF AMERICA

Item	1938	1943	1948
Income			
Service fees	$ 1,078	$ 1,032	$ 750
Endowment	..	..	188
Memberships	55,938	73,677	142,953
Contributions	9,217	5,343	3,787
Grants	32,227	27,092	17,500
Sale of literature	23,817	40,184	99,944
Other	..	..	1,466
Total	$122,277	$147,328	$266,588
Expenditures			
General administration	$ 35,286	$ 45,232	$ 76,177[a]
Research	1,200	1,800	6,590
Service	56,887	57,081	96,507
Publications	28,780	39,105	89,864
Other	..	..	2,406
Total	$122,153	$143,218	$271,544
Assets			
Endowment	..	..	$ 39,307
Unexpended balance	$ 2,386	$ 6,744	6,316
Total	$ 2,386	$ 6,744	$ 45,623

[a] Includes all administrative and office expense, plus considerable cost of maintaining liaison with other national agencies and relationships with government departments whose functions affect closely the field of family service.

National Foundation for Infantile Paralysis

The National Foundation for Infantile Paralysis has become the largest of the voluntary health agencies, unless one includes the American National Red Cross in that group. Its financial report is for the national office, and does not include funds available in the local chapters in most counties in the United States. The final year here reported, 1948, was a year of severe epidemic, as the figures reflect.

No complete report of the assets of local chapters, which number about 2,800, is available, but the national office has supplied a figure of approximately $7,441,000 for the close of 1948. In the epidemic year 1949 more than 1,000 chapters received advances from national headquarters, indicating that at least these chapters had used up their balances.

TABLE 29. FINANCIAL DATA SHEET, NATIONAL FOUNDATION FOR INFANTILE PARALYSIS

Item	1939[a]	1943[a]	1948[b]
Income			
Contributions[c]	$1,610,378	$2,686,923	$ 9,784,864
Donations, etc.	3,607	22,742	35,235
Interest	..	3,133	125,395
Total	$1,613,985	$2,712,798	$ 9,945,494
Expenditures			
General administration	$ 61,268	$ 87,750	$ 315,151
Pension plan	..	..	160,687
Service to chapters[d]	..	50,122	7,635,404
Virus research	130,219	428,969	1,936,181
Aftereffects care	293,269	293,367	361,776
Professional education	40,484	220,363	3,006,117
Medical care	..	255,592	752,023
Total	$ 525,240	$1,336,163	$14,167,339
Assets			
Prior unexpended balance	..	$1,755,427	$ 5,851,678
Balance for year	$1,088,745	1,376,635	4,221,845[e]
Total	$1,088,745	$3,132,062	$ 1,629,833

[a] Year ending September 30.   [b] Year ending December 31.

[c] Net to national headquarters; campaign costs and the 50 per cent retained by local chapters are not included in this item.

[d] Less repayments and epidemic aid deposits of $1,059,618 in 1948 by chapters.

[e] Deficit.

National Tuberculosis Association

The National Tuberculosis Association was the first important organization in the health field to organize a frontal assault on a single disease. Sale of Christmas seals is its characteristic fund-collecting method. Its financial report is for the national office, and does not include funds of the more than three thousand state and local tuberculosis associations. Because the seal sale takes place at Christmas and the national organization receives its share at the very end of its fiscal year, expenditures of a given fiscal year are based on receipts for the previous year, and bear no necessary relation to currently reported income.

TABLE 30. FINANCIAL DATA SHEET, NATIONAL TUBERCULOSIS ASSOCIATION

Item	1938[a]	1943[b]	1948[b]
Income			
Memberships	$ 8,157	$ 6,690	$ 8,410
Contributions	10,271	11,749	15,140
Sale of literature	..	..	986
Seal sale percentage	249,285	469,493	933,276
Interest and discount	8,467	193	218
Miscellaneous	1	3,571	5,954
Total	$276,181	$491,696	$ 963,984
Expenditures			
General administration	$ 43,885	$ 43,063	$ 95,400
Fund-raising[c]	27,805	23,076	41,929
Research and statistics	64,640	57,933	125,677
Service	122,412	135,756	447,176
Grants	7,003	6,874	29,176
Medical section (advisory)	..	5,553	21,719
Reserve, special publication	..	..	28,000
Magazine, net cost	3,766	..	80
Other[d]	9,253	46,255	40,828
Total	$278,764	$318,510	$ 829,985
Assets			
Reserve for next year	..	$469,493	$ 933,276
Emergency reserve	$314,237	457,401	907,680
General surplus	21,617	5,600	73,504
Total	$335,854	$932,494	$1,914,460

[a] Year ending December 31.   [b] Year ending March 31.

[c] Does not represent direct expense to raise funds, but an advisory service to affiliated associations.

[d] Such expenses as membership, library, archives, special activities not a regular part of program; and in 1943, $20,000 for a possible war emergency.

CHAPTER 8

Fund-Raising

IN MOST communities at the present time residents may expect one major charitable drive or another about once a month. In the winter and spring come the big health agencies and Red Cross, autumn is the usual season for the community chest, and any chinks left in the time schedule are filled in by drives for new hospital wings, churches, and university buildings, or supporting a wide variety of special agencies. In addition to the personal solicitors who call at one's home and place of business, the mailman brings all through the year a flood of appeals, reaching highest tide just before Christmas.

Fund-raising is necessary for nearly every voluntary welfare agency, though the chore may be delegated to a chest. Its costs vary from zero, where all the work is volunteered, to 100 per cent in the outright rackets. Its methods are as various as the combined inventions of all the many thousands of men—and women—who annually engage in this $3 billion activity. Many volumes have been written on its specialized techniques, and upon the programs of interpretation and public relations which are its usual adjuncts. Here, no more can be attempted than a description of various types of fund-raising efforts and organizations, with a view to helping the giver distinguish between the desirable and the dubious.

The Amateurs

Amateur fund-raisers carry a large share of the load, especially for local causes. The variety in method is tremendous. The

League of Women Voters may push doorbells and ask for cash contributions to supplement its membership dues. The Parent-Teacher Association organizes an opportunity sale, exchanging outgrown clothes or toys and taking a commission on the sales. Benefit bridges, barn dances, style shows, teas, and bazaars are popular in many parts of the country, and usually any prizes or objects sold are contributed, so that all the proceeds go to the benefiting organization. The American Institute of Graphic Arts sometimes auctions off rare books and typographic items. The Ladies' Aid bakes cakes, or serves a dinner, and repairs the church organ with the proceeds. Chances are taken on a new car, or a turkey, with the giver's conscience deciding whether he is making a contribution to the indicated charity, or gambling against heavy odds on making a cheap purchase.

Frequently volunteers are ticket-sellers for a benefit, a very common and often effective form of fund-raising for many local causes. The benefit may be a show staged by the organization itself, or arranged in cooperation with a local theater, or it may involve an outside attraction under commercial auspices. It may be a children's circus, a carnival, minstrel show, musicale, boxing match, or a percentage of the box-office receipts on a particular day at a regular show, or of the proceeds of a "sale day" at a store. Typically, the tickets are sold by the benefiting organization, with preferred seats at greatly inflated prices, and probably a program list of patrons from whom additional sums are received.

> We were visiting a wealthy friend who is on the lists of many charitable organizations. As we were about to leave, she reached into a large vase standing on her piano, and drew out a handful of tickets of various colors and sizes. Skimming them hastily, she laid aside two. "Could you use these for next Thursday? I can't be there." They were $50 apiece.

The benefit promoter deducts from receipts his costs and a profit. Difficulties arise when these two items together mount to a high percentage of the total. Many agencies in need of funds have listened to the smooth promises of a promoter and sold tickets to their friends, only to find that costs, unhappily, were so high there was little or nothing left. Cost percentages necessarily vary with the type of benefit, and the success of the agency in selling tickets. But if there is likelihood that the costs will exceed 40 per cent, the enterprise should be viewed with considerable doubt—by the agency, by the contributor, and by the amateur fund-raiser drafted to sell tickets. Many benefits, however, prove a successful and relatively painless way to raise funds at little or no cost to the soliciting agency.

Volunteers frequently work under experienced and probably professional direction. The campaigns of most community chests, and of such national agencies as the American National Red Cross and the National Tuberculosis Association, are carefully organized. The enlistment of many unpaid local workers in such drives not only saves expense, but ensures a friendly—and contributing—local group. The Red Cross has been outstandingly successful in enlisting volunteers all over the country in its programs, not merely in fund-raising, but in blood banks, bandage rolling, and similar activities. There is reason to believe the sweater- and sock-knitting craze during both world wars was more useful in its effects on the knitters than as a means of producing wearing apparel for the armed forces, which machines could have turned out more efficiently. But the participation of local volunteer workers, in fund-raising or other activities, is an asset to philanthropy of both monetary and other values, which does not appear on balance sheets.

Professional Fund-Raising

Campaigns that run into the millions, as do those for many educational institutions and national agencies, are usually conducted by special fund-collecting firms whose sole business is organizing solicitations.

The smaller, weaker firms sometimes work for a percentage of the funds raised, and in their efforts to increase their own income have been known grossly to misrepresent the agency and to engage in other objectionable practices. The larger firms do not work on a percentage basis. They insist on a preliminary investigation fee, and may refuse a campaign where the services of the agency seem to them in some respects faulty, and the chances of success meager. If they accept a campaign, they charge a flat fee based upon the size and nature of the task, without consideration of final result. They claim that these fees usually work out to between 6 and 9 per cent of the money eventually raised.

Such fund-raising campaigns are highly organized. Operatives are often in the offices of the agency or university six months before the solicitation begins, getting into the spirit of the organization, working on local lists, preparing the elaborate printed pieces which both precede and accompany a major campaign. The fund-raising company takes no part in the actual solicitation of givers, its name appears on none of the literature, and the giver is usually unaware of its existence. But it prepares every detail of a campaign that, at least on paper, should work with clocklike precision.

All potential contributors are listed, with an estimate of their incomes and how much should be expected from them. A special-gifts committee secures in advance a few large contributions, which can be mentioned at appropriate moments. Trained operatives of the fund-collecting agency visit team captains in the larger cities, and instruct them in the organization of lieutenants and actual solicitors. The advance literature goes out. The team captains hold organization dinners—"The menu should be simple to eliminate the mental reaction following heavy eating," one such organization says in its 12-volume guide to standard practice. There follow kick-off dinners, report luncheons, and perchance a victory dinner. "Spread the work" is the principle, perhaps because a solicitor, even if he calls on as few as three people, can then scarcely avoid being also a contributor.

If we are distressed at this degree of organizing generosity, the professional firms can point to their excellent record. It does work. The poor showing in the United States of the 1948 United Nations Appeal for Children was attributed to "amateurish organization," and an editor hoped that the 1949 Appeal would get off to a good start "with full and bold support undertaken by professional fund-raisers."[1]

[1] *New York Times* editorial, April 5, 1949.

The eleven leading fund-raisers of this type, who are organized into the American Association of Fund-Raising Counsel with a definite code of approved practice, are—CHICAGO: the American City Bureau; Beaver Associates; NEW YORK: Reuel Estill and Company, Inc.; John Price Jones Company; Kersting, Brown and Company, Inc.; Marts and Lundy; Pierce, Hedrick and Sherwood, Inc.; Tamblyn and Brown; Ward, Wells and Dresham; Will, Folsom and Smith; PITTSBURGH: Ketchum, Inc.

THE FEDERATION IDEA

An important development in the field of fund-raising was the formation of federations, of which community chests are the outstanding though not the only examples. Such federations of social agencies often have functions of planning and community organization of great significance, but it is their fund-raising and distributing functions which are the necessary focus of this chapter.

It was pointed out in Chapter 2 that growing complications in the social field resulted in attempts to "organize charity" about the turn of the century. These attempts to plan and coordinate services did not extend to financing until World War I, except in isolated instances. In 1887 a group of relief agencies in Denver formed a federated plan, and the following year a number of them began uniting their appeals for contributions. But the first real community chest is considered to be the Federation of Charities and Philanthropy organized in Cleveland in 1913.

During World War I the multiplication of appeals of all sorts, including those for relief of sufferers in Europe, induced some 400 communities to organize war chests for joint solicitation of funds. Many of these were disbanded after the end of the war emergency, but the idea had been firmly planted; permanent chests began to increase in number in the early 1920's.

In 1918 the chests formed a national association known first as the American Association for Community Organization, now Community Chests and Councils of America, Inc. Under guidance of this agency, experience has been exchanged and fairly uniform policies adopted; since 1945 most chests and their participating agencies which are affiliated with the national organization have been using the Red Feather as a common symbol. There are now some 14,000 participating agencies of local chests.

In essence, the community chest ("fund" and "federation" are alternative names) is a citizen-and-agency-controlled organization which has the principal duties of acquiring and spreading information on welfare needs; coordinating the work and reviewing budgets for the participating agencies; campaigning for voluntary contributions to meet the chest's accepted share of these budgets, and disbursing these funds to the agencies.

Chest executives believe that this plan results in wider public participation in both the planning and the support of social agencies. Usually all contributors are "members" of the chest, entitled to vote at the annual meeting, and sooner or later in smaller communities a number of these persons become members of the board of directors and gain intimate knowledge of the activities of local agencies and their budgeting problems. The fall campaign is highly organized, and draws in a veritable army of solicitors (Boston used more than 35,000 in its 1949 campaign), who attend district and general meetings, receive special publicity, and by their voluntary activities are given a sense of participation. Finally, in a well-conducted campaign every resident is invited to contribute.

The chest form of money-raising, it is contended, has substantially increased both the number of givers and the total amounts contributed to social welfare. In support of this contention the chests present figures for many communities showing increases for the first chest year, often more than 50 per cent above collections by the agencies themselves the previous year. Since, obviously, a chest would put forward a major effort in its first year, these figures are not entirely conclusive, and certain other evidence will be examined later.

Chests believe that programs of the participating agencies are favorably affected by their requirement of annual review and by budgetary control. Duplications with other agencies are often eliminated, economies in operation effected, and sometimes needed extensions of service suggested. In addition, the service agencies do not themselves need to devote staff time and money to fund-raising; they can concentrate their attention upon program.

Community contributions for welfare are apportioned by an informed budget committee (after budget hearings for the agencies and the right of review by the board of directors) in proportion to need as judged by this committee rather than on the basis of skill in fund-raising or the "heart appeal" of the particular cause.

Typically, community chests are manned chiefly by volunteers. In small communities there may be no paid personnel, except possibly for secretarial services during the period of the active campaign. In larger communities the chest has usually a paid all-year executive and sometimes a small staff. If the chest is combined with the council of social agencies, a larger staff is probable.

Most chests endeavor to include all local fund-collecting agencies of approved status, and local chapters of national agencies which conduct local programs—as for example, the Boy Scouts and the YMCA. Many of them invite state and national agencies, and some of them regard so seriously the competition of outside "drives" by national and other agencies that strong pressures are exerted to bring them in.

It is a fundamental principle of chest operation that agencies which participate must agree not to conduct within the given year other fund-raising drives in the community, with exceptions sometimes permitted in behalf of drives for capital expenditure, such as a new building, and solicitation of their own membership. The contributor is therefore promised "immunity" from further solicitation by these agencies. In recent years the mounting number of drives by agencies outside community chests has severely reduced the value of this immunity.

The types of agencies to which chests contribute and the proportion of chest income given to each type of agency differ from city to city, but for a chest disbursing $1,000,000 the distribution might approach the generalized figures of Table 31, which can be translated into percentage by pointing off four places.

TABLE 31. DISTRIBUTION PATTERN FOR A COMMUNITY CHEST

Type of service	Amount
YOUTH SERVICES: Boys' Clubs, Boy Scouts, Camp Fire Girls, Girl Scouts, neighborhood houses, summer camps, YMCA, YWCA, etc.	$ 307,000
CARE OF CHILDREN: Protection, foster home care, children's institutions, day nurseries, maternity homes, vocational training for children	170,000
FAMILY SERVICE: Assistance to the handicapped, legal aid, transients, adult vocational and employment aid	178,000
HOSPITAL CARE	70,000
OTHER HEALTH SERVICES: Visiting nurses, clinics, medical, social service, mental hygiene, child guidance, fresh air and health camps	83,000
CARE OF THE AGED	13,000
COMMUNITY WELFARE PLANNING: Information centers, social service exchange, and other common services	47,000
MISCELLANEOUS SERVICES: Safety leagues, Americanization activities, interracial committees, national and state appeals, etc.	25,000
YEAR-ROUND ADMINISTRATION: Budgeting, collections	27,000
CAMPAIGN	43,000
RESERVE FOR COLLECTION LOSSES	37,000
Total	$1,000,000

SOURCE: Adapted from Community Chests and Councils' analysis of 1949 chest budgets.

Growth of the Movement

The growth of community chests in numbers has been relatively steady and is impressive. In 1920, after the war-chest flurry had subsided, there were only 39 chests, which raised about $20 million. By 1925 there were 240 chests; subsequent growth to the present total of 1,318 is indicated by chest years in Table 32. For reasons later discussed, New York does not have a community chest of the usual pattern. Aside from this largest city, all cities in the United States with a population of 50,000 or more are served by community chests except Hoboken and Union City, New Jersey; many small communities also have chests, or are served by a neighboring chest. It is estimated that the areas with community chests have a total population of 84,000,000, so that some 57 per cent of United States citizens are exposed to the chest-type of federated giving.

Growth in funds collected is less impressive when the dollar amounts are analyzed. In 1924 (chest year 1925), chests in only 240 communities collected $58 million, or 8 cents out of each $100 of the total national income of $69 billion. Collections for chest

TABLE 32. TOTALS RAISED BY ALL RECORDED COMMUNITY CHESTS, 1925–1950

Chest year[a]	Number of campaigns	Amount	Per cent of goal
1925	240	$ 58,003,965	94.0
1926	285	63,677,235	94.7
1927	308	66,432,072	94.4
1928	314	68,664,042	96.2
1929	331	73,276,688	95.9
1930	353	75,972,555	95.5
1931	386	84,796,505	98.7
1932	397	101,377,537	96.8
1933	401	77,752,954	83.7
1934	399	70,609,078	83.2
1935	406	69,781,478	87.2
1936	429	77,367,634	91.8
1937	452	81,707,787	93.8
1938	475	83,898,234	93.3
1939	523	82,771,362	91.2
1940	561	86,297,068	95.3
1941	598	90,379,099	98.0
1942	632	104,575,890	99.6
1943	649	162,334,486	107.0
1944	703	210,415,187	100.9
1945	772	221,272,950	101.9
1946	798	197,048,839	89.8
1947	841	168,521,984	96.6
1948	1,010	177,082,356	95.3
1949	1,152	188,061,328	91.9
1950	1,318	192,933,988	93.1

[a] Year in which funds are to be expended. In most instances the campaign was conducted the previous fall, but collections continue through the chest year.

SOURCE: *Trends in Community Chest Giving, 1950.* Community Chests and Councils of America, Inc., New York, 1950, p. 9.

year 1949 were $188 million, but were made by more than four times as many chests covering about 57 per cent of the population, and the relation to the national income of $226 billion was still 8 cents to $100.

Chart 4 compares rates of growth of national income and contributions of 180 community chests continuously reporting from 1929 through 1949.

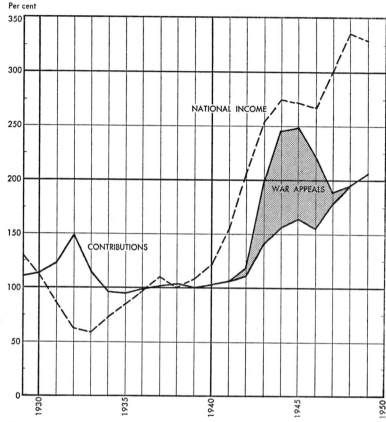

CHART 4. CHANGES IN NATIONAL INCOME AND IN CONTRIBUTIONS TO 180 COMMUNITY CHESTS, 1929-1949

1935-1939=100

SOURCES: National income figures are from *Survey of Current Business*, Department of Commerce, for calendar years indicated. Chest figures are from Community Chests and Councils of America, and represent chest campaign years (e.g. 1929 = September 1, 1928 through August 31, 1929).

As the chart shows, when national income dropped sharply at the beginning of the depression, chest contributions at first rose to meet the severe needs of the emergency. But this increase could not be sustained, and by 1934 contributions had fallen well below the 1929 records, and remained almost stationary for eight years. During most of this period national income was climbing, and by 1941 was in steep ascent, owing to war-induced employment. Chest contributions, aided by war chests and special drives, rose almost as sharply, reaching a peak of 249—almost two and a half times their 1935–1939 average—in 1945, but then dropped. With elimination of the special war funds (the shaded portion of the chart) a fairly consistent increase is indicated, beginning in 1940, but at a much slower rate than national income, which continued to climb, standing recently at well above 300. The chest index has leveled off for the past several years at around 200. A significant gap has opened between national income and the contribution rate for this group of chests.

Some Recent Developments

In addition to the older procedures of door-to-door canvass and special-gifts committees who approach the larger givers individually, many chests now conduct carefully organized industry drives, soliciting both workers and management for a proportion of wage or salary, often to be paid in installments. In 1949 Detroit asked for five hours' pay from hourly rated employes, and from executives one-half of 1 per cent of annual salary beginning at the $3,600 level to 2 per cent for those receiving $20,000 or more.

In addition, contributions are sought from the corporations themselves, as a matter of good citizenship, good public relations, and on the basis that the chest agencies contribute directly to the health and welfare of employes of the corporation. As is elsewhere noted,[1] corporation contributions to philanthropy have tremendously increased, particularly during the war period of excess-profits taxes. Corporation gifts had been 26.7 per cent for a small group of reporting chests in 1941. They were 40.2 per cent of the aggregate amount raised by 64 community chests which reported on this subject for 1950. Nearly half of corporation gifts

[1] See p. 64.

in a recent year came from manufacturing industry; about one-sixth from banks, insurance companies, and utilities; another sixth from retail stores; the remaining sixth were miscellaneous.

While community chests are primarily concerned with collecting current funds for disbursement within the year, their directors sometimes endeavor to build up "rainy day" reserves, and in recent years some chests have received bequests or other restricted funds which represent permanent endowment. When this occurs, the chest assumes some of the additional functions of a community trust.[1]

Chest experience with capital funds has been too recent for much uniformity. In 1949 the Cleveland Community Fund reported slightly under $300,000, but is also the beneficiary of a number of funds set up within the Cleveland Foundation, the first and one of the largest of the community trusts. The Cleveland chest "does not actively solicit legacies or capital gifts, reasoning that its function is annually to obtain current gifts from living sources, whereas its member agencies cultivate capital giving for endowment or building purposes and the [Cleveland] Foundation is especially designed to obtain capital sums."

Another Ohio chest has $714,000 "in trust and escrow." Much of this sum was built up by corporations in fat years (when they had the ability to give and could take maximum tax advantage from such gifts) with a gentlemen's agreement that it would be held for a lean year when the chest would be in need and the corporation less able, or unable, to contribute. In this case the chest is serving, informally, most of the functions for which business firms in recent years have sometimes set up their own charitable foundations.

Rochester, New York, which led in this movement of setting up capital funds within a chest, now has 60 different gifts and bequests, worth $1,022,000. Detroit reports minor funds of a similar nature. Newark has 75 separate funds amounting to $520,000. San Francisco has miscellaneous bequests totaling $341,000. The Springfield (Massachusetts) Chest is trustee for the single Eugene A. Dexter Charitable Fund, amounting to

[1] See pp. 105 ff.

$1,750,000. The Madison (Wisconsin) Community Chest has developed a special trust agreement growing out of war-chest funds contributed for "postwar needs"; it amounts to $581,000.

In communities where both a chest and a community trust exist, the Cleveland position seems the logical one—that the chest should not solicit capital gifts, leaving these to its agencies and to the community trust, which has been especially organized for the purpose. The National Committee on Foundations and Trusts for Community Welfare, organized jointly by Community Chests and Councils, National Social Welfare Assembly, and a group of the larger community trusts, takes the further position that restricted bequests which come to the chest should be placed with the trust for administration, and if no community trust exists, the chest should aid in organizing one.

Federation in Large Cities

In our greatest cities federation in the usual community chest pattern is difficult. The amounts needed, the tasks of organization, and the vast numbers and varieties of agencies which have to be considered are staggering problems. The giver who is asked to contribute to more than one hundred different agencies at once finds it hard to individualize their work, and sees his own contribution divided into insignificance as respects any particular agency. Chicago and New York have partially solved these problems in diverse ways.

In Chicago joint financing did not begin until the depression of the 1930's forced the organization of joint emergency relief funds, which in 1933 grew into the Community Fund of Allied Chicago Charities, and is now the Community Fund of Chicago.

The Community Fund of Chicago included 192 agencies in 1949. The expenditure budgets of these agencies aggregated $23.8 million, with expected earnings and endowment income of $8.4 million, leaving a "need" total of $15.4 million to be collected from Chicago givers. The Community Fund appropriated $7.5 million for 1949 for these agencies, leaving approximately half of the "need" to be collected by the agencies themselves.

The Chicago Fund therefore differs from the usual community chest pattern in urging its agencies to seek contributions from individuals. The Fund completely covers corporations and employe groups, offering them the usual immunity; it solicits from individuals, but does not guarantee them against separate solicitation by the individual agencies.

Although it does not undertake to meet the whole financial problem of its participating agencies, the Chicago Community Fund, raising $7.9 million in its 1949 campaign, is one of the largest of the Red Feather funds. Only five others raised over $5 million in that year; the Cleveland Community Fund, $5.2 million; the Community Chest of Metropolitan Detroit, $5.8 million; United Community Services of Metropolitan Boston, $6.1 million; Welfare Federation of Los Angeles Area, $6.4 million; and the Community Chest of Philadelphia and Vicinity, $8.3 million. Chicago is a "chest" city, though in a modified sense, and statistics of the Community Fund of Chicago are included in chest summations.

New York is not a chest city. It does have a Greater New York Fund, organized in 1938, which helps support most of the city's voluntary hospitals, health and social agencies. The agencies for its 1949 campaign numbered 423. In 1949 these agencies spent $164 million, of which $123 million was earned by services or received from endowment income and similar sources. Of the remaining $41 million "need," the Greater New York Fund hoped to raise from business firms and employe groups $8 million —some 20 per cent as compared with Chicago's 50 per cent. (It raised $5.2 million, mostly from corporations.)

Unlike the Chicago Fund, the Greater New York Fund does not solicit from individuals except as members of employe groups. It does not accept individual contributions of more than $100 to employe group gifts, so as to leave the field of solicitation for large individual gifts entirely open to its agencies. Because of its many divergences from the chest pattern, therefore, New York is not regarded as a chest city, and the Greater New York Fund is not included in chest statistics.

Other Forms of Federation

While the community chest, serving a single town or one town and its immediate neighborhood, is the best-known form of fund-collecting federation, many other types exist.

In larger cities hospitals sometimes unite for fund-raising purposes in a United Hospital Fund. Solicitations may be for deficits in ordinary running expenses and for building additions, or only for the latter. Community chests often include current needs for hospitals in their campaigns, but ordinarily they do not cover building programs or other capital expenditures for any of their agencies.

The United Negro College Fund is an example of federation among colleges, but most colleges and universities go it alone; their chief contributors are their own alumni and their local communities.

Many religious agencies are federated on a sectarian basis. Among examples are the Federation of Protestant Welfare Agencies in New York City; Catholic Charities, organized in more than a hundred separate dioceses of this Church; and the tremendous operations of the United Jewish Appeal, the central fund-raising agency for the United Palestine Appeal, the Joint Distribution Committee, and the United Service for New Americans. Chapter 10 discusses giving through religious agencies.

Certain national agencies, including several which vigorously oppose federated fund-raising, are themselves examples of successful federation. The American National Red Cross is structurally a vast federation of local chapters, some 3,700 in number, and functionally it raises funds for such diverse purposes as services to members of the armed forces and their dependents, including guidance on personal and family problems; recreational activities in military hospitals; disaster relief, including provision of food, clothing, shelter, and supplementary medical care; a national blood-donor program; instruction courses in first aid, accident prevention, water safety, and home nursing; and still other functions.

The National War Fund

Group fund-raising reached its highest concentration in the National War Fund. Organized in January, 1943 at the specific request of the President's War Relief Control Board, this super-chest operated about four years. To it fell the tremendous task of considering the appeals of the hundreds of special war relief agencies, of establishing budgets for these agencies, and of devising a quota system for the various states. It did not itself directly raise funds, but worked through local war chests usually affiliated with community chests where these were available. Its member agencies included the United Service Organizations (USO), United Seamen's Service, War Prisoners' Aid, and, for varying periods, 27 other major foreign and domestic war-relief agencies. Among its by-products its historian claimed:

> . . . the organization of some 43,000 American communities in the interest of war-time unity; an increase in the number of contributors to local chests from some 16,000,000 to 20,000,000; an extension of health and welfare programs to small towns and rural communities; a sharp rise in the total number of community chests; and a war-time dividend to local home-front agencies, admittedly as a result of the deep and broad strength of the war appeal, in the form of an average budget increase of 34 per cent.[1]

Collections for the three campaigns of the National War Fund were $121 million in 1943, $113 million in 1944, and $87 million in the fall of 1945, this final campaign being conducted after Japan's surrender.

State Federations

The National War Fund operated through state organizations, which were assigned quotas and given the task of dividing these quotas among the cities and counties of the state, and supervising local efforts. These state organizations were nearly all dissolved at the end of the war, and federation went back almost entirely to a local community basis.

[1] Seymour, Harold J., *Design for Giving:* The Story of the National War Fund. Harper and Bros., New York, 1947, p. 1.

But the state rather than the locality is the important unit in many welfare activities, particularly when the federal government participates in supplying funds, where state planning and state legislation may be involved, and in assigning local quotas for nonlocal appeals.

A start has been made in the organization of peacetime state chests. The United Health and Welfare Fund of Michigan is the most prominent of these; it conducted a statewide campaign in 1949, and in the process raised explosive issues. Oregon has a state chest which confines itself to organizations within the state. The Massachusetts Community Organization Service is chiefly advisory.

The National Budget Committee

Proponents of federation set up as their goal a joint appeal to the public, seeking gifts in proportion to ability to give, to be distributed as nearly as possible in relation to need. But, obviously, the budget committee of Middletown's community chest is in no position to determine what is the national need for cancer research and treatment, or how that need is related to requirements for heart disease, and what proportion of either is the equitable share of Middletown's citizens. These are questions which should be answered—if the Middletown chest is going to contribute to either of these causes.

In an effort to handle such problems, Community Chests and Councils of America set up a National Budget Committee, after the dissolution of a similar committee it had formed in 1942 to consider war appeals, which later functioned for the National War Fund. It began its new operations in 1946; from 1947 it has been sponsored jointly by Community Chests and Councils and the National Social Welfare Assembly. Neither sponsoring organization has any right of review over the decisions. National organizations seeking funds from the public and reviewed for accrediting and approved by the National Information Bureau are invited to submit their proposed budgets, but cannot be compelled to do so. The 24 organizations submitting their 1951 budgets for review to the National Budget Committee are the following:

American Federation of International Institutes
American Hearing Society
American Heart Association
American Social Hygiene Association
Associated Services for the Armed Forces, Inc.
Big Brothers of America, Inc.
Boys' Clubs of America, Inc.
Camp Fire Girls, Inc.
Child Welfare League of America, Inc.
Community Chests and Councils of America, Inc.
Family Service Association of America
Girls Clubs of America, Inc.
International Social Service

National Child Labor Committee
National Committee on Alcoholism
National Conference of Catholic Charities
National Federation of Settlements
National Legal Aid Association
National Organization for Public Health Nursing, Inc.
National Probation and Parole Association
National Social Welfare Assembly
National Travelers Aid Association
National Urban League
United Cerebral Palsy Association

Several of the largest fund-collecting agencies are conspicuously absent.

As a necessary adjunct to the National Budget Committee, a National Quota Committee is charged with determining the proportions of these budgets which should be raised in each of the states. These state ratios are based on 13 factors, ranging from number of households to number and amount of individual income taxes, passenger automobile registration, telephones, effective buying income, and admission taxes. Proposed quotas for the various states for national campaigns are listed in Table 9, page 61. The National Quota Committee also recommends quotas for campaigns restricted to areas covered by community chests, and works with local and state organizations with respect to the county and local quotas.

Opposition to Federation

Giving through community chests or other types of federation has been sharply challenged. Some of this opposition is individualistic, on the part of agencies that believe they can raise larger sums independently than they would receive as their portion of chest campaigns. Nearly all chests have experienced withdrawals of dissatisfied agencies. Some of them later came back, but others have remained outside.

The American National Red Cross formerly was included in many chest campaigns, but the national organization now forbids its locals to join other organizations for federated fund-raising. Other national organizations that conduct large campaigns usually independent of chests are the American Cancer Society, National Foundation for Infantile Paralysis, National Society for Crippled Children and Adults, and National Tuberculosis Association.

It is probable that any one organization with an appealing cause, be it local or national, can raise more money than it is likely to be assigned from a federated drive for all agencies. But can it continue to do so if great numbers of other agencies also conduct independent drives? And is ability to collect a satisfactory basis for apportioning contributors' dollars?

Federated fund-raising is more fundamentally challenged with the contention that it does not and cannot raise enough money to meet the reasonable needs of all philanthropic agencies. Typically, chests conduct a single campaign, usually in the autumn. Most people, probably, will contribute a greater total amount if they are asked for money perhaps eight or ten times in the year, instead of just once. Chests try to meet this difficulty by arranging for installment payments. But in the house-to-house canvass, the installment plan has not been notably successful; most contributors make a single contribution, and many of them regard the community chest drive as simply another "appeal," similar to other drives for single agencies; their contribution to the whole group of chest agencies may be even less than to the single agency if that agency happens especially to interest them. In industry the chests have had better success with installment payments. Where both labor and management have strongly favored a federated drive in place of numerous plant solicitations, it has usually been possible to arrange pledges covered by payroll deductions once a month, or even weekly.

To the contention that giving should be proportioned to the varying abilities of the givers, and not on the basis of a march of dimes—or of dollars—from everybody, the independents which have used the mass appeal point out that it works. Christmas seals for tuberculosis, March of Dimes for polio, individual memberships for the Red Cross, these and similar campaigns have raised outstanding sums. These three causes collected a total of $113 million for 1949, as compared with the 1949 chest total of $188 million for 1,152 chests.

To the arguments that federation is necessary because multiple drives have become an intolerable nuisance to givers, are a heavy drain on volunteer workers, and are costly, the opponents of federation make these replies. Givers need to be prodded hard and often, for giving is at a shamefully low level. Volunteer workers can still be obtained—one sampling revealed that only one-quarter of all people have been volunteer workers in fund-raising, and 30 per cent of the remaining said they were willing to serve—and recruiting and training such workers introduces the agency to an important additional public. Finally, while the costs of raising these separate funds are considerable, some of these expenditures might properly be charged off to education of the public concerning the particular disease or social condition involved.

The National Foundation for Infantile Paralysis points out that it has a "spreading the risk" function. When a disease becomes epidemic in a particular locality, that locality may be unable to bear all of the heavy costs from its 50 per cent of March of Dimes funds. The national organization sends in money from its 50 per cent share, part of which is allocated to epidemic relief, and in emergencies may augment this by contributions from localities which have had few cases. The national also combines funds received from all localities for research and professional education needed by all.

Chests point out that they also are usually open to inclusion of national agencies, and already do include many. The new state chest idea would prove useful in spreading the load.

"Distribution in proportion to proved need" is another strong plank in federation's platform. The independent fund-raisers have refused to submit to the procedures of the National Budget and the National Quota Committees. They take the position that no cause has yet received all the financial support it could usefully employ; that they are entitled to put their cause before the public as effectively as they can, and to receive what the public, rather than an "authoritarian body of officials," decides they should have.

Preservation of the giver's choice in the destination of his gift is one of the chief stumbling blocks in federation's path. The giver favorably disposed toward a particular cause, either because of some experience of his own or because of the agency's superior publicity, may reasonably desire the whole of his gift to go to that special purpose. He may refuse to contribute to the chest if this agency is not included. Even if it is, the budgeted amount may seem to him too small. Probably the chest permits him to designate the whole of his gift for this agency, but this is an illusory privilege; unless the contributions designated for this particular agency exceed its budgeted total, it will get no more than if no designations were made.

The more ardent attackers of federation have lately engaged in broad charges. "We are reaching the point," said Basil O'Connor,[1] "where there is going to break out an open warfare between the school of federated financing and the school of independent financing. . . . Frankly, I cannot personally go along with what I refer to intentionally as the communization of either health or welfare activities or in fund raising in connection with them."

Michigan Skirmish

The two groups met head-on in Michigan in 1949. The recently organized state chest, the United Health and Welfare Fund of Michigan, conducted its first general campaign in the spring of that year, endorsed by labor, farm groups, and industry. The UHWF campaigned through local units for 18 national member agencies and, under varying arrangements in different localities, for certain additional agencies and sometimes in the name of a

---

[1] Address before National Social Welfare Assembly, May 6, 1947. Mr. O'Connor is president of the National Foundation for Infantile Paralysis.

cause or disease. The "big five," cancer, crippled children, polio, Red Cross, and tuberculosis, did not join.

Detroit became a storm center. Industry, led by Henry Ford II and other industrialists, with the support of the labor unions, had decided that the losses in time and the heavy costs of numerous individual solicitations in plants were no longer to be endured. They helped organize in Detroit a drive limited to plant and industrial solicitation under the name of United Foundation of Detroit, which "invited" all national fund-collecting agencies to join, with notice that no other plant solicitations would be permitted, and campaigned for $893,500 in February and March, 1949. Its campaign literature headlined "Unite to fight disease. Give to your United Foundation, one campaign to unite national health and welfare fund-raising appeals. Saves time, saves money, saves lives." And it listed various diseases, including cancer and polio. The American Cancer Society had refused to come in, but $140,969 was paid to the Michigan Cancer Foundation. The National Foundation for Infantile Paralysis had announced in advance that it would accept no money from this drive; a payment of $30,294 was made to the Sister Kenny Foundation. Various arrangements were improvised in different plants to meet the National Red Cross insistence upon joining in no federated drives; in the Ford plant, the subscription card for the drive as a whole included a separate line, printed in red, permitting separate subscription for the Red Cross. The hastily organized campaign did not reach its full goal in Detroit, but it raised $750,000.

In the fall of 1949 the United Foundation took the next step by including the local agencies of the Detroit community chest ("143 campaigns in one!") in its Torch Drive for $8.55 million. It went over the top, raising $9.2 million. The Detroit Red Cross chapter had been threatened with suspension if it joined in the drive, but a face-saving formula was finally found whereby, during the single solicitation, a separate Red Cross pledge could be made, with the usual membership card to be issued and the payroll deduction taken at the time of the normal Red Cross drive in the spring of 1950, and paid directly to the Red Cross.

A similar arrangement was made for the National Foundation for Infantile Paralysis. Both organizations limited the pledge arrangement to plant solicitations among 650 firms and government employes, retaining the right to campaign separately elsewhere. The United Foundation dealt with the local chapters; both of these national organizations felt that even this degree of "cooperation" was forced upon them and was against their national interest.

Limited Federation?

Givers have not, in general, been much concerned over this warfare between the embattled camps of federation and antifederation in fund-raising. Many have not been aware of its existence. But the decision will be made by givers, through the tightening or loosening of their purse strings. It is quite likely that this decision will vary with the size and degree of industrialization of communities, and with their habits of thought and action.

Welfare needs that affect a large majority of the population and are capable of mass handling will probably remain under, or drift toward, governmental auspices. These include care of dependent children, education for all children, unemployment insurance, health and dental care, assistance to the needy blind and other large groups of the handicapped, relief up to a subsistence level, and pension plans or outright aid for the aged.

To these causes we "give" through taxation or, in the insurance-type plans, through enforced and often matched contributions. Our control is the very remote one of influencing legislation by the ballot and by pressures. In most of these fields some private agencies will still be needed to supplement program and to serve as pilot plants for new experiments and measuring rods of governmental performance—much as private schools continue to serve useful functions.

Beyond the present or probable orbit of government a vast variety of needs remain, many of them appealing and important, some of them important but with little pull on the heart strings, and some of them, alas, merely appealing. For the needs which are important, support must be found. In spite of efforts at mergers and combinations, the number of agencies in all but the smallest communities will remain large. No giver will have either the knowledge or the time to consider all of them on their merits. Besides, individual campaigns would be prohibitively expensive and burdensome. In this situation federated fund-raising has been a useful device in the recent past and is likely to remain so.

Such fund-raising is not wholly satisfactory to givers. Said one contributor:

> When Christ says to "help your neighbor" one doesn't visualize giving to an impersonal organization such as the Community Chest. It's probably more efficient, but something is missing. Probably what psychologists call the selfish satisfaction of having helped another individual.

Several recent surveys attempted to find out how people feel about federated versus independent fund-raising. One undertaken by the Greater St. Louis Community Chest concludes for St. Louisans:

> Despite their generally favorable attitude toward the Chest, more than half of the respondents in this survey think that it is more important to give to needy people they know, than to give to the Chest. Fifty-six per cent of the population think that there is too much red tape in welfare agencies, but only 14 per cent think that private welfare agencies should be abolished. About one-fourth of the people would prefer supporting welfare work through taxation, rather than through contributions. The majority (62 per cent) would like to see all appeals included in the one Community Chest drive.[1]

Community chests will lose ground if they permit themselves to become professionally controlled, agency-minded machines for presumed efficient giving, taking the public into their confidence only once a year, when the annual drive is due. They were invented as an aid to givers, to bring order and understanding into the chaos of multiple appeals. To the extent that they remain responsive to the giver, speaking his language, and inviting his participation, to that extent the chests are useful to the giver, and may expect his larger support.

Most chests were started by the people on the wealthier side of the railroad tracks. Many of them have taken pains, especially

[1] *St. Louis Looks at Its Community Chest*, 1947, p. 7.

recently, to represent the whole community by including labor and other groups on their boards. They have been less successful in interpreting to the contributor the wide variety of agencies they represent, and in making him feel that his own dollars are going to causes that are important to him.

Possibly the chests will find a formula by which the individual contributor may select two or three agencies within the chest (instead of the 15 to 400 the chest may include), be kept in close touch throughout the year with the work and the needs of these particular agencies, and designate half his chest contributions to that work, with the remaining half left to the discretion of the budget committee. Such a formula might restore the keen interest and sympathy of individuals who now give perfunctorily or not at all, lost in the maze of agencies the average chest tries to represent equally; it might stir the chosen agencies to a better job of interpreting their work, and still give the chest enough flexibility—with the aid of undesignated corporate gifts—to perform its important function of distributing funds in accordance with community needs.

Chests are troubled by the number of independent drives, usually by national agencies, that compete with their own campaign. In theory, chests would like to see all welfare agencies brought into the common fund-raising effort, and subject to the budget controls that seem to them reasonable and desirable. In practice, chests sometimes do not open their doors soon enough to new causes that capture the interest of givers. Even if they do so, a strong independent may regard its own case as unique, requiring special consideration not likely to be received from a general budgeting committee, or act on the still simpler premise that it can collect more money, even if at a high collection cost, by going it alone.

Since communities differ widely in their organization and in their traditional attitudes, it seems unlikely that the "open warfare" predicted by Mr. O'Connor between the forces for and against federated giving will become general, or will at any near date reach a decisive conclusion, nationally. Highly industrialized communities, like Detroit and Pittsburgh, are likely to find single plant solicitations, with periodic wage deductions, so efficient and convenient a device that even the most resistant independents will find it necessary to federate to this extent. Small residential towns with a leisure class for volunteer workers may support a chest covering many local and a few state and national agencies, tolerate a number of independent drives, and still have ample resources for solicitations by universities, hospital building funds, and many special causes. The village and the farm may continue to do much of their giving through the local church and by simple neighborly action.

In view of the difficulties of collecting sufficient funds from householders in one solicitation, federation itself may find division desirable. For example, family service and recreation (character-building) agencies might join in the regular fall chest drive. Health agencies, national and local, might conduct a federated spring drive. At another convenient season the hospitals might join in a United Hospital Fund solicitation.

The giving we do through government by way of taxes is a duty, with our portion decided by law. The giving we do through voluntary agencies is a privilege, with the amount and channel of the gift determined by our understanding of the need. Since givers differ, no one "right" channel exists. Ample opportunity should remain for the individualist who sees one particular need as more important than all others. Givers should have full information on the advantages and disadvantages of the various methods so that, community by community, the ends of giving in terms of human welfare may be well and willingly served.

CHAPTER 9

Avoiding Charity Rackets

THE GULLIBILITY of some givers had its classic illustration when Robert E. Hurst, just for a gag, began circulating in Memphis, Tennessee, a paper asking contributions to the "Fund for the Widow of the Unknown Soldier." In a few minutes Mr. Hurst collected $11, which he later returned, explaining to the red-faced givers that it might be difficult to locate the *Unknown* Soldier's widow.

In a New York City bank a mother, her hands full of shopping parcels, forgot to pick up her child's coin bank after depositing its contents. An hour later she returned to find it still standing on the table in the bank, but already half full of small coins contributed by "givers" who felt the urge to give, though there was not the slightest indication of a cause.

The careful giver does not tumble into such obvious pitfalls, but even for him there are dangers and difficult choices. Organizations soliciting funds for philanthropic causes may be divided into three groups. First are organizations of sincere purpose, run efficiently, and attempting to raise a budget well proportioned to a real need. Second are the many organizations which may be equally sincere in purpose, but are badly run; or are directed toward a need outmoded, not important, or now being otherwise met; or have become involved in wasteful collection procedures. Finally, come the outright charity rackets, where the profit of the promoter is paramount and the cash receipts of the high-sounding cause are negligible or nothing.

CHARITY RACKETS[1]

Although the money lost to useful work through charity rackets is not large in proportion to total philanthropy, it is important to expose, suppress, and starve out of existence all such endeavors. Charity rackets diminish regular giving by planting doubts in the minds of contributors.

Some Examples

Panhandling is still the most common individual racket, though the "need" it pretends is usually sham and could be better met by other means. No one need starve in these United States. In every town and city agencies exist which will take care of dire immediate want. It has been demonstrated countless times that the "dime for a cup of coffee" is usually spent for something more potent; even if not misspent, it is likely to contribute toward making an incorrigible beggar.

William Beck,* 69, white-haired, clad in rags, was picked up on Broadway for begging. On him were bank books showing deposits of $26,832.63 which soft-hearted folk had given him, and in his pockets were $127.53 in bills and coin. After he was fined and dismissed with a warning, it was learned that he had just collected an additional 25 cents from a fellow prisoner in the detention pen.

One step above the outright panhandler is the licensed peddler, usually a cripple, who "sells" pencils or shoelaces on the streets of many of the larger cities. His handicap may be real—or it may be cleverly simulated; in either case his "take" may be out of all proportion to his need. Government-financed programs of vocational rehabilitation are now widely available; 53,131 disabled men and women were rehabilitated into gainful employment by such services in 1948. Also, sheltered workshops and services for special disabilities are maintained in many communities by private agencies.

[1] Incidents in this chapter are factual, taken usually from newspaper accounts or the files of welfare agencies, but starred names are fictitious.

* Name fictitious.

Street solicitors, however garbed or equipped, are not always what they seem to be:

> Edwin R. Ramsay* was fined $50 in Municipal Court (Chicago) for obtaining money under false pretenses as collector for Samaritan Army, Inc. He said he received 50 per cent of his take, but admitted under questioning that he hadn't been turning in anything.
>
> According to the Better Business Bureau in New York, women in nuns' garb, who had "little if any genuine religious affiliation," were reaping golden profits for themselves by soliciting alms in bars, subways, restaurants, and railway stations. They paid $2.50 a day, in advance, to [organization not revealed] for their credentials, and kept all they collected.

Many rackets are highly organized. A favorite device is the "boiler room" for telephone solicitation. In a room crowded with desks and telephones a group of men, representing themselves as "Father Callahan" or "Judge Brown," call long lists of "suckers" and in trained, persuasive tones plead an appealing cause; the need is so urgent that a messenger will come to pick up the contribution. Some of the money may even go to a charitable purpose in order to maintain some appearance of legality. One professional boiler-room man testified that a usual distribution of a $10 contribution would be:

Commission to telephone salesman	$3.00
Cost of this and nonproductive phone calls	1.00
To the pick-up man	.30
To rent and general overhead	1.50
Total	$5.80

Of the remaining $4.20, the manager of the racket took anywhere from 50 cents to $2.00, leaving for the charity as little as $2.20 of a $10 contribution.

Sometimes there is no charity at all:

> The chief of police, the police lieutenant, and three civilians were found guilty in the Court of Special Sessions on charges of conspiracy to defraud in the operation of a charity scheme in which several thousand persons were said to have been victimized, with a take of $30,000. In the chief's home were 5 telephones, desks, and a sucker

* Name fictitious.

list. Persons were invited to contribute to the Police Relief Fund for orphans and widows of Terryville* policemen killed in the line of duty. Donors would receive a "courtesy card" which would give immunity from prosecution for traffic violations. Testimony indicated that the police force consisted of only 5 men, and no Terryville* policeman ever had been killed in the line of duty.

The joker may be more insidious. Here is an excerpt from the by-laws (now changed!) of a certain organization for the crippled and disabled:

> In the event that any one or all of the founders of this organization, [names here], decide to retire after 10 years of service or because of inability to continue, they shall be paid for the remainder of their lives the compensation received at the date of retirement.

The "Take" of Charity Rackets

No authoritative figure can be given, obviously, for the annual "take" of charity rackets. They flourish in the dark, never boast of their successes, keep few records, and publish balance sheets only under legal compulsion. Variations must be great from year to year, as people have more or less money with which to be careless, as operators invent bright new ideas, or as efforts to clean up rackets drive them temporarily under cover. Only informed guesses, therefore, are possible.

For New York City, figures between $25 million and $30 million a year have been cited by authorities close to the situation. Nationally, the round figure of $100 million is often used, but with little statistical evidence to support it.

If, for the sake of concreteness, we accept for the moment this guess of $100 million as philanthropy's annual loss to rackets, we see that this loss is not tremendous in relation to the whole—it is less than 3 per cent of the philanthropic dollar. It represents, however, nearly as many dollars as all the endowed foundations together are able to spend. Quite aside from the ill effects on regular giving of publicity about such rackets, any business losing 3 per cent to "bad accounts" would take vigorous measures to

---

* Name fictitious.

diminish these losses. Philanthropy can do that only with the informed cooperation of many givers.

Information Agencies

The first line of defense against rackets, and toward more effective choices, is the information agency. Several cities maintain separate agencies of this sort. In New York it is the Contributors Information Bureau maintained by the Welfare Council, established in 1882 as the Bureau of Advice and Information by the Charity Organization Society. The Chicago Association of Commerce and Industry publishes an excellent directory of approved local civic, health, and welfare organizations annually, issues a weekly bulletin, and maintains a Contributors Information Bureau. In Cleveland the Chamber of Commerce maintains an information service. In Los Angeles it is the California Intelligence Bureau. In Seattle a special citizens' committee called the Public Appeals Board performs this function.

These bureaus offer free information to anyone who has been solicited on any cause represented in their files. They will also "clear" an annual list of proposed charitable contributions. The New York "CIB" received 3,923 inquiries in 1949, and reported on 714 organizations. They supply name, principal officers, purpose, recent program, budget, and usually report if other organizations are performing a similar task. They investigate new organizations where possible, and relay requests for information on national agencies and others outside their field to the appropriate sources of information. If they can supply no information, the contributor had better beware.

In cities where such separate agencies do not exist, a similar function is often performed by the community chest, the council of social agencies, and sometimes the chamber of commerce or the better business bureau. A call to the council of social agencies or the community chest will determine which agency is the best source of information in a particular city.

For national rather than local agencies, the most important source is the National Information Bureau, established in 1918, when the multiplicity of the appeals growing out of World War I created a serious problem. This Bureau has investigated and reported on more than 4,000 national, international, and interstate agencies. For legal reasons it cannot publish its reports, but they are available to members.[1]

A person lacking such membership can nevertheless discover whether a given organization is on the Bureau's approved list by making inquiries of the community chest or local council of social agencies, which has membership through its national association.

The *Basic Standards in Philanthropy*, which the Bureau has set up for judging national agencies, are in so many respects standards which the individual giver might well apply in nearly all his giving that they are presented on page 166, with slight abbreviation.[2]

Information in certain fields should be sought from the special accrediting agencies which have been set up for those fields. National Jewish agencies are reported on by the Council of Jewish Federations and Welfare Funds, Inc.[3] The National Catholic Welfare Conference[4] performs a somewhat similar service in its field. The Advisory Committee on Voluntary Foreign Aid of the United States Government[5] furnishes some information on voluntary agencies engaged in relief abroad. The Child Welfare League of America[6] will supply information on many children's agencies; and so on.

Informational and accrediting agencies serve a double purpose. In addition to warning the contributor away from doubtful causes, their refusal of approval has often brought back into line an inefficient agency, or one using some objectionable practice. Agencies unwilling or unable to bring their practices up to the standards which have been set sometimes make violent accusations of bias or favoritism against the accrediting and information bureaus.

---

[1] The cost of membership in 1950 was $10 for an individual, $25 minimum for a corporation. The address is 205 East 42d Street, New York 17, N. Y.

[2] *Giver's Guide to National Philanthropies, 1949–50*. National Information Bureau, New York, 1949, pp. 3–4.

[3] 165 West 46th Street, New York 19, N. Y.

[4] 1312 Massachusetts Avenue, N.W., Washington 5, D. C.

[5] Care of Department of State, Washington 25, D. C.

[6] 24 West 40th Street, New York 18, N. Y.

BASIC STANDARDS IN PHILANTHROPY

1. An active and responsible governing body serving without compensation, holding regular meetings, and with satisfactory forms of administrative control.

2. A legitimate purpose with no avoidable duplication of the work of another efficiently managed organization.

3. Reasonable efficiency in conduct of work, management of institutions, etc., and reasonable adequacy of equipment for such work, both material and personnel.

4. No solicitors on commission or other commission methods of raising money.

5. Non-use of the "remit or return" method of raising money by the sale of merchandise or tickets.

6. No organization shall make a practice of giving entertainments for money-raising purposes, the estimated costs of which, including compensation under the terms of the agreement, exceed 40 per cent of the gross proceeds.

7. Ethical methods of publicity, promotion, and solicitation of funds.

8. Evidence of consultation and cooperation with the proper welfare agencies in local communities with reference to local programs and budgets.

9. Complete annual audited accounts prepared by an independent certified public accountant or a trust company showing receipts and disbursements classified, and itemized in detail.

10. Itemized and classified annual budget estimate indicating an attainable program.

11. No telephone solicitation to the general public for money or donations or for the purchase of tickets for benefits.

Adapted from standards formulated by National Information Bureau

Legal Protection

Some protection against the worst abuses is afforded by law—local, state, and federal—and more legislation is pending. In many cities organizations intending to raise funds must get a license, which permits at least some examination of their purpose, auspices, and officers.

In New York City, for example, such licenses must be obtained from the Bureau of Public Solicitations of the Department of Welfare except for "religious corporations," which are exempt. No agency is licensed to use outdoor solicitors for more than three days in any six months' period, and the name of the agency, dates of permitted solicitation, and seal of the Department of Welfare must be on the person of every solicitor, or on the canister or other receptacle used in the solicitation.

Appeals by mail are not covered by such licensing, nor those in newspapers or by telephone, unless a messenger is used to pick up the contribution. Exemption of religious corporations has proved a dangerous loophole, since in New York State any seven persons may band together, declare themselves a religious corporation, and avoid the licensing provision.

> Certain so-called "religious corporations" have from time to time secured charters under the Religious Corporations Act. During the past four years the Department of Welfare, in cooperation with the Police Department and the district attorney's office, has secured convictions and appropriate sentences of some twenty persons for fraudulent solicitation. These persons represented the following organizations: The Gates of Mercy, The Charity Church of Christ, and The United Relief Association.[1]

In other cities the licensing of charitable drives may be entrusted to the police department or to an independent board. In Cincinnati a Public Solicitations Commission—the city treasurer and two appointees of the city manager—supervises all public solicitations, has set up a licensing procedure, and reviews financial statements which must be submitted within ninety days of the conclusion of any drive. St. Louis has a Charities Solicitations

[1] Letter from William Hodson, Commissioner of Welfare, to Mayor F. H. LaGuardia of New York, September, 1940.

Commission of nine persons who meet twice each month to pass on appeals. The mayor of Detroit issues permits on the basis of recommendations made by a Solicitation Authority Committee. In Chicago, charitable solicitations are not subject to licensing, but for the "tag day" type of solicitation an order of the City Council is required.

These licensing procedures are no better than the laws on which they are based and the sometimes perfunctory personnel who are charged with enforcement. The three-day limitation in New York City is widely violated, and convictions are difficult to secure since violators are represented as merely earnest persons who, in their zeal for the cause, went out ahead of, or after, the prescribed dates.

It is reported that in some of the "tag day" type of drives, the high-pressure street solicitor buys the tokens at so much apiece, and keeps whatever larger amount he can wheedle from contributors.

Street beggars who "sell" pencils and shoelaces are salesmen, not solicitors, and operate under a commercial license, if they are licensed.

Legislation controlling solicitations is being attempted at the state level.[1] Pennsylvania passed a Solicitation Act in 1925 which, as amended, makes unlawful any appeals for funds (certain religious, educational, and similar organizations excepted) for agencies or individuals not holding certificates of registration issued by the Pennsylvania Department of Welfare.

In 1947 North Carolina amended its 1939 statute, limiting solicitations within the state (except for purely local agencies or those soliciting only from their own memberships) to organizations "holding a valid license for such purpose from the state board of public welfare," issued for only one year and after due study of "proof of the worthiness of the cause, chartered responsibility, the existence of an adequate and responsible governing board to administer receipts and disbursements of funds, goods, or other property sought, the need of public solicitation, proposed

---

[1] On the constitutionality of such legislation, see *Yale Law Journal*, vol. 39, March, 1930, p. 745.

use of funds sought, and a verified report . . . to show reserve funds and endowment funds as well as receipts and disbursements."[1] An individual "soliciting alms or begging charity for his or her own livelihood or for the livelihood of another individual" must obtain a license and furnish reasons for soliciting help publicly instead of pursuing a legitimate trade or accepting benefits available under various programs; offering merchandise for sale does not exempt him from this provision.

Federal legislation has largely been confined to agencies operating in the international field. During World War II such a multitude of foreign-relief agencies sprang up that the President's War Relief Control Board was established, in which such agencies were required to register. With the end of the war the close supervision of the Board was abandoned but some measure of control survives in the Advisory Committee on Voluntary Foreign Aid of the United States Government.[2]

Charity rackets which attempt to use the mails come under the provisions of the postal laws relating to frauds and swindles.

> Whoever, having devised or intending to devise any scheme or artifice to defraud, or for obtaining money or property by means of false or fraudulent pretenses, representations, or promises . . . knowingly causes to be delivered by mail . . . any such matter or thing, shall be fined not more than $1,000, or imprisoned not more than five years, or both.[3]

In spite of the laws, many dubious schemes still come through the mails. New York papers carried this story in April, 1949:

> Although the 32 winners in the metropolitan area—including Sid Krakower* holding the grand prize ticket for $100,000—have not been paid off for the Mexican Sweepstakes run last December, new tickets worth at least $450,000 are flooding the city. Although the incoming tickets state that they are "authorized by the Department of the Interior of the Mexican government" and are "for schools and public welfare," Rafael de la Colina, Mexican ambassador in Washington, stated that his government neither backed nor authorized the sweepstakes.

[1] Text of the complete statute appears in Appendix C.
[2] Operations under these controls have been described in Chapter 5.
[3] 18 U.S.C. 1341 (Cum. Supp. 1949).
* Name fictitious.

Marginal Causes

More serious than actual rackets, in terms of money wasted, are the vastly greater sums which go every year to honest, well-intentioned organizations which can pass any financial audit, but achieve little social benefit with the funds they spend.

The very purpose of the organization may be outmoded. For instance, a private industrial school may have filled an important community need for many years. The character of the neighborhood changes, or adequate public facilities become available. But the trustees and staff, bound by tradition or desirous of keeping their jobs, seek contributions to maintain a school for which there is little use.

There may be unnecessary duplication. During World War II, 596 different agencies for foreign relief were registered! Of course, some duplication may be desirable and useful. Two competing colleges are probably each better for the presence of the other. Many separate attacks on a research problem are sometimes required before a solution is reached. And elimination of duplication is not always possible. "Not all the powers of the President's Board," said the National War Fund's general manager,[1] "nor all the king's horses and all the king's men, were ever able to resolve the fundamental cleavage between the political sympathies of the two main groups of Americans of Yugoslav sympathies or descent."

Management may be wasteful, though the purpose of the agency is wholly desirable. Business enterprises, even under the watchful eyes of boards and stockholders intent on profits, often fall into management ruts and require drastic overhauling. Board members and contributors to philanthropic organizations should take a keen interest in their operations and see that they remain effective.

Costs of solicitation may be too heavy, or some of the methods objectionable.

A "man in uniform" association in California received $24,200 from the contributing public during a nine months' period to provide

[1] Seymour, Harold J., *Design for Giving*. Harper and Bros., New York, 1947, p. 9.

temporary relief for members in financially distressed circumstances. Files of the California Intelligence Bureau revealed that only $4,672 finally reached those in whose behalf the appeal had been made— 19 per cent of the amount raised.

Three organizations conducting cancer drives (not including the American Cancer Society) recently mailed crisp dollar bills to their prospect lists, inviting the startled recipient to mail back the dollar bill with his own contribution to the cause. Full results are not known, but in one such mailing 70,000 of the dollar bills were not returned. Contributors who wanted to help cancer work by giving to this organization had to make up the missing $70,000 plus the costs of the complete mailing before any part of their dollar could go to the cause of cancer.

The size of the budget with relation to other needs in the community is a subject on which the leaders of a particular cause can seldom be expected to have objective judgment. The problems of national and local budgeting among the various agencies have been discussed in the two preceding chapters.

The contributor who examines his charitable list with care, seeks information on any doubtful items, and takes an intelligent and continuing interest in the organizations he does assist is giving more than money. He is helping raise standards in the field.

Giving Through Religious Agencies

R ELIGION," says Edward C. Jenkins,[1] "has been the seed plot in which grew nearly all the organizations included in philanthropy." In certain periods, we have noted, the church was almoner for many causes now supported by secular agencies or by government. About 50 per cent of present voluntary giving still goes to religious agencies, though not all of it for direct church purposes.

Characteristics of Religious Bodies

Church membership has been increasing in the United States, both absolutely and relative to total population. Membership, however, is a somewhat variable term, its definition depending upon the body reporting. Some churches report only communicants, usually those thirteen years of age or older; others report all baptized persons; still others list as members known persons in the cultural or nationality groups represented by the churches. Duplications and errors exist through the failure of some churches to clear their records of persons long inactive. The Church of Christ, Scientist, furnishes no figures, its manual forbidding "the numbering of people and the reporting of such statistics for publication." With these qualifications, reported church member-

[1] *Philanthropy in America.* Association Press, New York, 1950, p. 8.

ship in the United States totaled nearly 80 million, divided as indicated in Table 33.

This membership represented about 54 per cent of the estimated 1948 population—an all-time high. In 1880 officially counted members were less than 20 per cent of the population; in 1900, 34.7 per cent; in 1920, 39.8 per cent.[1]

These nearly 80 million persons contribute through their churches and nonsectarian religious agencies an amount which cannot be exactly determined, but may be in the neighborhood of $1.9 billion. A varying but substantial part of the contribution in any congregation goes directly toward the maintenance of local religious services, including salaries of the minister, priest, or rabbi, the janitor, organist, and possibly a paid choir; fuel, light, and building maintenance; and supplies.

TABLE 33. REPORTED CHURCH MEMBERSHIP IN THE UNITED STATES AT THE CLOSE OF 1948

Protestant religious bodies	47,557,203
Roman Catholic Church	26,075,697
Jewish congregations	4,641,000
Other	1,302,452
Total	79,576,352

SOURCE: *Christian Herald*, September, 1949. In a few instances where 1948 figures were not available, earlier totals have been used.

Members also contribute toward "benevolences," a word widely interpreted. The term may include only care of the parish poor, or may cover a program worldwide in extent and varied in character. Table 34 presents a typical budget for a small Protestant church and the actual 1950 budget of The Riverside Church in New York City.

Radical differences arise not only from variations in size and resources, but from religious tradition. Jewish, Catholic, and Protestant churches exhibit marked differences in their attitudes toward philanthropy, and therefore in the programs beyond mere church support which channel through them.

[1] *Christian Herald*, September, 1949.

The Jewish religion has the oldest tradition. The Talmud exhorts Jews to many quite specific forms of charity, which assume the character of duties. As a result, Philip Bernstein says of Jewish social work that although it is "supported by voluntary contributions, these gifts have much the character of self-taxation, with a deep consciousness that each member is expected to bear his fair share of group responsibilities."[1] This "self-taxation" and the pressures that a closely knit minority group is

TABLE 34. BUDGETS OF A TYPICAL SMALL CHURCH AND OF THE RIVERSIDE CHURCH

Typical small church		The Riverside Church	
Receipts		Receipts	
Contributions	$2,400	Loose plate collections	$ 24,000
Special offerings	350	Members' contributions	196,250
Women's society	150	Endowment income	160,197
Special events	100	Other income	118,059
Total	$3,000	Total	$498,506
Expenditures		Expenditures	
Minister's salary	$1,800	Public worship	$108,952
Organist's salary	150	Religious education	90,750
Janitor's salary	125	Church fellowship	4,245
Fuel and light	125	Organized activities	1,200
Repairs	65	Benevolences	79,589
Supplies	135	Support and interpreta-	
Foreign missions	300	tion	12,427
Home missions	200	Church office	43,865
Other benevolences	100	Building operation	146,537
		Contingencies	10,941
Total	$3,000	Total	$498,506

SOURCES: For the small church, *America's Needs and Resources* by J. Frederic Dewhurst and Associates, Twentieth Century Fund, New York, 1947, p. 327. For The Riverside Church, *A Guide for Giving*, The Riverside Church, New York, 1949.

able to bring upon its members are perhaps part of the explanation of the extraordinary recent record of Jewish philanthropy. Most of these contributions, however, do not channel through the synagogues and temples, and the welfare agencies are usually secular. It has always been difficult to draw a clear line between the religious and secular giving of the Jewish people, and it has become more so since many large contributions are being made to welfare agencies of the new state, Israel.

[1] Bernstein, Philip, "Jewish Social Work," *Social Work Year Book, 1949*, p. 260.

Reinhold Niebuhr says of the Christian faiths:

> Various religious motives helped to emphasize the love spirit in the early church—the inspiring example of Jesus, the sense of kinship under a common father, the Christ-mysticism of Paul by which members of the church felt themselves united in "the body of Christ," and the sense of abandon which was derived from the millenial hopes of the early Christian community.[1]

For the Roman Catholic, almsgiving is closely associated with the Church and its doctrine. Its importance toward individual salvation was stated by St. Thomas Aquinas: "Almsgiving may be made meritorious of eternal rewards and expiatory of the temporal punishment due to sin."[2] A wide variety of welfare services have sprung up directly under the control of the Church and its special orders.

The Protestant feels a deep responsibility for the welfare of his fellow man, but is content, and may prefer, to have that responsibility discharged through a secular agency which he supports, or even by the government.

These quite diverse attitudes make it necessary to examine giving through religious agencies under separate categories.

Jewish Giving

The Jewish population of the United States—no accurate census exists; in round numbers 5,000,000 may be a reasonable estimate—is relatively small, but the group is so closely knit by common tradition, religious practice including special dietary laws, and the problems of a minority that it exerts an influence beyond its numbers.

Religiously, the Jews are divided into three principal groups, Reform, Conservative, and Orthodox. No central tabulation of giving for congregational purposes exists in these three bodies, but data from the 1936 *Census of Religious Bodies* adjusted for recent changes in membership and rates of giving suggest that the current contribution for support of synagogues and temples

---

[1] *The Contribution of Religion to Social Work.* Columbia University Press, New York, 1932, pp. 4–5.
[2] *Catholic Encyclopedia*, vol. 3, p. 599.

and directly religious purposes may be in the neighborhood of $35 million.

For the remainder of Jewish philanthropic giving, better records exist through the reports compiled by the Council of Jewish Federations and Welfare Funds. Most of the organizations reporting to this agency are secular in the sense that they are not under control of synagogue or temple; but they are maintained by a people whose religious traditions pervade so much of their living that dividing lines can scarcely be drawn. For convenience, therefore, the whole of Jewish giving for philanthropic purposes is here presented, so far as facts are available.

TABLE 35. RECEIPTS OF JEWISH OVERSEAS AND NATIONAL BENEVOLENT AGENCIES, 1948

In thousands

	From federations and welfare funds	Other contributions	Other income	Total
Overseas				
United Jewish Appeal	$150,000[a]	..	..	$150,000[a]
Other Israel agencies	1,414	$13,255	$2,844	17,513
Other overseas agencies	1,222	2,962	844	5,028
Total	$152,636	$16,217	$3,688	$172,541
National				
Civic protective agencies	$ 6,056	$ 846	$1,643	$ 8,545
Health and welfare agencies	339	2,612	281	3,232
Religious agencies	430	3,687	1,030	5,147
Cultural agencies	649	1,081	589	2,319
National service agencies	1,241	204	287	1,732
Total	$ 8,715	$ 8,430	$3,830	$ 20,975
Grand total	$161,351	$24,647	$7,518	$193,516

[a] Estimated pledges.
SOURCE: Council of Jewish Federations and Welfare Funds, Inc.

Table 35 records receipts of overseas and national agencies for 1948. The item "Religious agencies" probably includes some sums already reported in the congregational figures. Jewish health and welfare agencies in community chest cities usually receive some or all of their support through the chest; this figure therefore is not a direct reflection of Jewish giving. Non-Jewish persons also give as individuals to Jewish causes.

On the other hand, many Jews contribute liberally to non-sectarian philanthropies, and some of the Jewish agencies extend their services to non-Jews. This is particularly true of Jewish hospitals, over half of whose patients are not Jewish. Their generous establishment seems also to have been motivated to aid observance of dietary laws, and to give professional opportunities to Jewish physicians, who have sometimes faced discrimination in other hospitals.

In addition to items shown in Table 35, Jewish federations and welfare funds budgeted $44.3 million in 1948 for local services and administrative costs, including $8.7 million from non-sectarian community chests. Other sources of income, for which figures are not available, include (1) as already noted, the congregational offerings; (2) sums contributed to local organizations or institutions through sources other than federations; (3) results of campaigns for capital expenditures, such as buildings, which usually are conducted independently.

The recent record of the United Jewish Appeal is one of the most remarkable in modern philanthropy. Beginning with collections of $15 million in 1939, it rose gradually to $34 million by 1945, and then in each of the years 1946 through 1949 exceeded $100 million, approaching $150 million in the peak year 1948. The 1949 pledges are estimated at $112 million. Funds of the United Jewish Appeal are divided among three organizations. The American Jewish Joint Distribution Committee, which received about 51 per cent in the period 1939 through 1948, takes care of emigration, displaced persons camps, and in general the problem of the dispossessed Jew. The United Palestine Appeal (41 per cent) finances a broad program of settlement and reconstruction in Palestine. United Service for New Americans (8 per cent) looks after Jewish immigrants in the United States. The United Jewish Appeal, obtaining funds almost exclusively from a Jewish population of only about five million, including children, secured for its three agencies in its peak year almost as much money as all the community chests in that year, seeking funds in 1,000 communities from the whole population for a wide variety of local agencies.

Total Jewish giving for philanthropic purposes in 1948 may have exceeded $250 million, or perhaps $50 per capita. This is substantially above estimates for the whole population.

Roman Catholic Giving

There are now more than 27 million Roman Catholics in the United States. These persons support not only the local churches and international ecclesiastical activities of this Church with its center in Rome, but a wide variety of philanthropies. The Church takes direct charge of these philanthropies, and alms-giving is itself a religious exercise.

Members should give "not merely tithes," said the Reverend Michael J. Deacy in a recent sermon, but "all surplus goods." He defined surplus goods in the words of St. Basil: "The bread in your box belongs to the hungry; the cloak in your closet belongs to the naked; the shoes you do not wear belong to the barefoot; the money in your vault belongs to the destitute." Moreover, this giving is not giving up anything, said Monsignor Fulton J. Sheen, but exchanging temporal wealth for spiritual wealth. Appealing for the New York Catholic Charities fund, he added, "The Catholics of New York are not asked to 'give up' $2,500,000. Catholic Charities has no 'drive.' It is conducting an exchange."[1]

In education, where the Jews and Protestants support Sunday schools, theological seminaries, a few institutions of higher education,[2] and some extracurricular religious training, the Roman Catholics support a complete educational system with 11,497 educational institutions in the United States, Alaska, and Hawaii in 1950. These include 225 colleges and universities for men and women, 388 seminaries, 1,576 diocesan and parochial high schools, 806 private high schools, 7,914 elementary parochial schools, and 588 private elementary schools.

There are 739 general and 110 special Catholic hospitals, with a combined bed capacity of more than 100,000. These hospitals

---

[1] *The New York Times*, March 28, 1949.

[2] The Jews have the beginnings of an elementary school system in 125 all-day schools serving 18,000 pupils. A few private elementary schools function under Protestant auspices.

are partially maintained by the fees of patients, not all of whom are Catholics, but about 15 per cent of their budgets must come from other sources. In addition, these hospitals are largely directed and served by members of religious orders—22,000 Sisters and Brothers by recent count—who receive maintenance but no salaries. These members of religious orders, in hospitals and elsewhere, are making a contribution not in cash but of their lives. It was recently estimated that such "free" service in the hospitals was worth $30 million a year.

Total figures on Catholic giving are not available. Each of the more than a hundred dioceses in the United States is a separate financial unit, apparently reporting only to Rome. The picture is further complicated by the tremendous number of orders, funds, and causes for which separate collections are made.

Individual items are frequently available. Catholic Charities in all the larger cities support a wide range of social services, including care of children, family casework, recreation, care of the chronically ill and the aged; they are designed primarily to serve Catholic communicants, but do not exclude people of other faiths if they may be served without slighting the primary beneficiaries and "without offense to religion." Some of their funds are derived from community chest (and therefore non-denominational) allocations, but the larger part from direct Catholic giving. Receipts for Catholic Charities in all the dioceses are not available, but the New York Diocese alone received $2.7 million from individual givers in 1949. Some of the volunteer organizations operate under substantial budgets. The Society of St. Vincent de Paul received contributions amounting to more than $3 million in 1947 for assisting the poor and the sick and giving spiritual counsel under direction of parish clergy.

The accumulated holdings of the Roman Catholic Church—not only in ecclesiastical buildings, many of which are magnificent—but in grounds and buildings for schools, hospitals, monasteries, convents, children's and other institutions, and in invested funds, represent a very substantial base for present and continuing activities. In the absence of data, the present value of the real-estate holdings of this Church can be little more than a guess, but is probably not less than $2.5 billion. No estimates can be made of the value of invested funds.

Current giving is additional to these resources. Reliable data are not available, but a few samplings suggest that giving is relatively generous in proportion to income. For direct church support it may be in the neighborhood of $500 million. In addition, contributions are made to the special orders, to Catholic Charities, and for support of the many separate institutions, including capital outlay for buildings.

Protestant Giving

In dealing with Protestant giving the problem is not absence of data—though gaps do exist—but multiplicity of sources and wide differences in program and methods of reporting. Some 222 Protestant denominations are in existence in the United States, of which 52 have memberships exceeding 50,000. These 52 larger groups contain nearly 97 per cent of the total Protestant membership of 47.6 million persons.

Before 1920, data on Protestant giving are fragmentary. Charles H. Fahs[1] reports total giving for current congregational expenses, but for only 11 Protestant bodies, for the fifteen years ending in 1927. During this period these contributions "steadily and greatly advanced" (from $123 million to $305 million) but from 1915 through 1922 the rate of advance was not enough to compensate for decrease in value of the dollar.

Another series, beginning in 1920 and running to the present, has been compiled by the United Stewardship Council under the direction of Harry S. Myers, covering 15 religious bodies throughout this period. The sample is large enough to permit generalization and annual comparisons.

According to this table, membership has increased rather steadily, except for a leveling off in the depression. The record on per capita gifts is more disturbing. By 1934 the per capita rate had dropped to $11.76, scarcely more than half the previous high of just a decade earlier, $23.03 in 1924. A slow recovery followed,

---

[1] *Trends in Protestant Giving.* Institute of Social and Religious Research, New York, 1929, p. 65.

bringing the numerical rate to a new high of $28.29 in 1949. But meanwhile the purchasing value of the dollar had severely declined. The per capita contribution of $28.29 in 1949 was worth only $20.43 in 1924 dollars.[1]

TABLE 36. CONTRIBUTIONS TO AND MEMBERS OF 15 PROTESTANT RELIGIOUS BODIES, 1920–1949

Year	Contributions (thousands)	Members (thousands)	Contributions per member
1920	$214,920	12,260	$17.53
1921	281,173	17,460	16.10
1922	345,996	18,257	18.95
1923	415,557	18,867	22.03
1924	443,188	19,245	23.03
1925	412,658	19,475	21.19
1926	368,529	17,054	21.61
1927	459,528	20,267	22.67
1928	429,948	20,911	20.56
1929	404,002	20,595	19.62
1930	441,452	20,050	22.02
1931	418,075	20,837	20.06
1932	362,494	21,450	16.90
1933	320,365	21,839	14.67
1934	256,803	21,840	11.76
1935	270,713	22,137	12.23
1936	260,528	22,215	11.73
1937	282,185	21,760	12.97
1938	292,554	20,910	13.99
1939	307,870	22,344	13.78
1940	300,729	23,108	13.01
1941	351,391	23,672	14.84
1942	350,807	23,121	15.17
1943	356,468	23,556	15.13
1944	398,773	24,680	16.15
1945	459,707	25,217	18.23
1946	549,884	25,899	21.23
1947	606,619	26,179	23.17
1948	655,641	27,104	24.18
1949	765,386	27,059	28.29

SOURCE: United Stewardship Council.

In addition to the continuous series for 15 religious bodies, the United Stewardship Council has current figures for 47 religious bodies in the United States, comprising 35.4 million members. In 1949, contributions for this larger sampling totaled $971.9

[1] The Bureau of Labor Statistics Consumers' Price Index was 122.2 in 1924; 169.2 in 1949.

million, of which $756.7 million was for congregational purposes, the remainder for benevolences. This represented a per capita contribution of $27.43. Applied to the total Protestant membership of 47.6 million, this rate suggests a total Protestant contribution made directly to the churches of about $1.3 billion.

Protestant churches also maintain welfare agencies of various types, but these are not so numerous in proportion to church membership as Roman Catholic institutions, nor so closely integrated with the churches. Many colleges, for example, are affiliated with particular denominations, but they usually accept students of all faiths[1] including non-Christians, and function largely as community colleges. Protestants pioneered in the establishment of many types of social agencies in their communities, particularly those for child care, homes for the aged, and hospitals. But the disunity among Protestant bodies in the same community made the secularization of many of these agencies inevitable.

Others, particularly children's agencies, hospitals, and homes for the aged, are maintained by individual denominations, often in substantial numbers. Totals are not available, but three large denominations recently reported 649 institutions:

	Methodist Church	Protestant Episcopal Church	National Lutheran Council
Hospitals, convalescent homes	71	70	87
Homes for the aged	55	56	108
Children's institutions	55	62	85
Total	181	188	280

Such services are maintained by the churches in the belief that the religious ministry is itself a part of the service which should be offered, and with a desire that children shall be brought up, and the sick and the aged cared for, in "the faith of their fathers." For children there are additional legal reasons. In most states the law specifically requires that dependent children who become wards of the state shall be assigned to homes and institutions, or

[1] As do Catholic colleges, but the proportion is usually much smaller.

in charge of persons, of the same religious faith as the children.[1]

In some cities most of the denominational agencies have joined in federations of Protestant welfare agencies. To the many administrative advantages of cooperation has usually been added the feeling that the independent Protestant agencies were at a disadvantage in seeking funds from local community chests as compared with the strong cases possible for the Catholic and Jewish federated groups. But within the Protestant churches themselves have been strong voices against attempts to put social welfare in general under denominational auspices.

> I look with concern upon the agitation for Protestant councils of social welfare, called by whatever name. The aim seems to be to segregate a Protestant social work clientele for care under Protestant auspices. . . . If the idea is that the church must do its welfare work for its own people, or that Protestant funds must be expended among a Protestant constituency, the move is reactionary.[2]

Most of the welfare program of the Protestant churches is supported by the "benevolences" portion of regular contributions, and is included in the figures already presented. Certain additions need to be made, however. Contributions for special institutions and for overseas—in cash, or in food and clothing—are reported among benevolences by some church groups, but omitted by others. Church colleges receive substantial gifts as a result of special drives, and from sources outside their church affiliation. Where a federation of Protestant agencies exists, it often runs a separate campaign or receives funds from the local community chest.

The value of Protestant church property can be estimated only roughly. It consists of some 160,000 church buildings, usually with parsonages, some 320 church colleges and theological seminaries under varying degrees of denominational control, and a variety of special institutions such as children's and old people's homes, hospitals, and recreation centers. Total value is probably not less than $7 billion.

[1] See "Legal Basis of Sectarian Social Work" in *Sectarian Welfare Federation* by Leonard A. Stidley. Association Press, New York, 1944, pp. 145 ff.

[2] Johnson, Frederick Ernest, *The Church and Society*. Abingdon Press, New York, 1935, pp. 152–153.

A Total Picture

The difficulties in presenting any complete and accurate picture of total giving through religious agencies have been indicated. The most recent governmental religious census[1] is for the year 1936. It was admittedly incomplete when taken, is now seriously out of date, and happened to coincide with the year which, our other figures indicate, marked the low point in the recent history of religious giving. Moreover, the value of the dollar has so radically altered that a 1936 dollar was the equivalent of about $1.70 in 1949.

Table 37, summarizing data from the 1936 census, must be read with these reservations in mind. This census was based on the reports from individual churches, not from denominational or other central bodies. The data therefore include only expenditures made by the churches themselves on a local basis. Presumably these expenditures are a measure of the total receipts of these churches for the same period, though this would not be true of many individual churches; and certain direct giving to denominational and nonsectarian agencies would not be included at all.

According to this record, the average church spent close to 40 per cent on salaries, a like amount on the building and other current expenses, and some 20 per cent on benevolences, missions, and miscellaneous. The Roman Catholic Church had a vastly higher expenditure per church, but its churches usually served a larger membership than the average for all churches. The general membership average was 280 per church, or 541 for urban churches, 133 for rural. The Roman Catholic average (which, however, included children under 13) was 1,939 urban, 382 rural.

The census also reported the value of church edifices, which were defined as "any building used mainly for religious services and owned wholly or in part by the church." A total of 179,742 such buildings were included, valued at $3.4 billion, but with a debt of $510 million, which affected slightly more than a quarter of these buildings. The value per church averaged $19,636, but ranged from an average of over $300,000 for one small denomina-

[1] Bureau of the Census, *Religious Bodies: 1936.* Government Printing Office, Washington, 1941.

tion (the Society for Ethical Culture) to less than $1,000 per building for another. The average value for the Roman Catholic churches was $47,304. This total of $3.4 billion compared with $3.8 billion in 1926, and $1.7 billion in 1916.

Value of parsonages was reported by only 71,235 churches, at a total of $345 million.

TABLE 37. CHURCH EXPENDITURES AS REPORTED BY THE CENSUS OF RELIGIOUS BODIES, 1936

Amounts, except average per church, in thousands

Item	All churches		Roman Catholic churches		Jewish congregations		Other churches (chiefly Protestant)	
	Amount	Per cent	Amount	Per cent	Amount	Per cent	Amount	Per cent
Pastor's salary	$126,907	24	$ 11,817	8	$ 2,560	18	$112,530	31
All other salaries	73,848	14	29,128	21	3,084	21	41,636	11
Repairs and improvements	45,423	9	16,167	12	787	5	28,469	8
Payment on church debt[a]	43,303	8	14,711	10	830	6	27,762	8
Other current expenses[b]	127,574	25	46,791	33	4,174	29	76,609	21
Local relief and charity	16,073	3	5,108	4	375	3	10,590	3
Home missions	9,515	2	1,158	1	135	1	8,222	2
Foreign missions	9,495	2	744	1	147	1	8,604	2
To general headquarters	35,996	7	3,844	3	..	..	32,152	9
All other purposes	30,820	6	9,605	7	2,312[c]	16	18,903	5
Total	$518,954	100	$139,073	100	$14,404	100	$365,477	100
Churches reporting	188,766		15,720		2,159		170,887	
Average per church	$2,749		$8,847		$6,672		$2,139	

[a] Excluding interest.   [b] Including interest.
[c] Includes $1,600 expenses not classified.
SOURCE: *Census of Religious Bodies: 1936.* Table 15

With revision to reflect the inadequacy of the 1936 census, construction since that time, and the sharp increase in prices, and with addition of nonecclesiastical buildings (such as schools, children's institutions, and hospitals), it seems probable that property owned by churches in the United States may have been worth in 1949 prices not less than $10 billion. The use of this property, which is tax exempt, constitutes a considerable legacy from the past.

Table 38 presents two earlier estimates on giving for religious purposes, with a current estimate by the author based on membership data, the per member amounts reported by the United

TABLE 38. CONTRIBUTIONS TO RELIGIOUS BODIES, 1909–1949, ACCORDING TO THREE ESTIMATES
In millions

Year	Twentieth Century Fund estimate	Edward C. Jenkins estimate	Author's estimate
1909	$300	..	..
1919	613	..	..
1920	..	..	$ 618
1921	613	..	603
1922	..	..	733
1923	684	..	867
1924	..	$ 720	919
1925	778	741	858
1926	..	769	982
1927	833	800	1,028
1928	..	844	954
1929	912	824	915
1930	893	812	1,023
1931	837	902	1,007
1932	743	760	861
1933	665	629	756
1934	641	548	617
1935	627	555	650
1936	621	578	630
1937	638	621	691
1938	651	641	749
1939	659	664	747
1940	662	632	712
1941	652	651	833
1942	662	732	861
1943	695	795	872
1944	750	881	951
1945	783	1,029	1,091
1946	816	1,239	1,293
1947	884	1,276	1,445
1948	910	1,378	1,582
1949	..	..	1,894

SOURCES: The Twentieth Century Fund estimate is from *America's Needs and Resources* by J. Frederic Dewhurst and Associates, Twentieth Century Fund, 1947, with addition for earlier and revision for later years furnished March, 1950, by the Fund for a new edition now in preparation. The Jenkins estimate is from *Philanthropy in America* by Edward C. Jenkins, pp. 172–173. The author's estimate is a composite of membership data, per capita figures from the United Stewardship Council, census information, and data developed independently in this chapter. (includes Y's etc see p. 18?)

Stewardship Council, census information, and weighted for other factors developed in this study. It includes estimates for the support of the numerous national interdenominational church agencies, and state and city councils of churches, and also for certain independent religious agencies. Among the latter are the Young Men's Christian Associations (YMCA), which reported $19.8 million in contributions in 1949, the Young Women's Christian Associations (YWCA) with $14 million as the total on which quotas to the national organization are based, the National Woman's Christian Temperance Union (WCTU), and the American Bible Society.

This estimated total of $1.9 billion in 1949 may constitute more than 50 per cent of our total philanthropic giving. A large part of it, about 40 per cent, goes for salaries; but in nearly all the churches salaries remain at pitifully low levels, and much of the work is done through services wholly volunteered. Most communities could be more effectively served by fewer churches, which presumably could be better financed, but sectarian differences are difficult to overcome and church union proceeds only slowly.

Current contributions through religious agencies of nearly $2 billion may seem substantial, particularly in comparison with other items in the philanthropic budget. But for the three decades here examined, religious giving has not increased in proportion to the increase in national income, nor does the total compare favorably with our spending for many luxuries.

The Department of Commerce estimated November and December retail business for the nation at $21.1 billion in 1949, and leading department stores count 30 per cent of these sales as Christmas buying. This estimate probably includes some family necessities which appear under the tree in Christmas wrappings, and it may be inaccurate. But it seems probable that our 1949 Christmas expenditures were about $6 billion. Christmas, it has been widely forgotten, is a religious holiday. To celebrate the birth of the founder of Christianity we give in presents to one another three times as much as we give to all religious causes during the whole year.

CHAPTER 11

Education and the Arts

EDUCATION has long been a favored form of philanthropy. It admirably places within reach, in Andrew Carnegie's colorful words, "ladders upon which the aspiring can rise." Where giving to relieve physical want has sometimes had the disastrous effect of destroying initiative, educational aid has usually spurred the individual to greater activity and higher achievement.

Giving to education may take a variety of forms. It may pay for a building, books, or other equipment, subsidizing "plant." It may be applied to instruction, through endowing a professorship, contributing to current salaries, assisting in teacher-training, or improving the status of teaching. It may support research. It may directly assist the needy student through scholarships, fellowships, or student loans. Finally, it may finance study of education itself, its content or its procedures.

Any of these programs may be conducted on a local or on a wider front. The gift may be either for current expenditure or in the form of endowment. The field of education offers rich opportunities to givers over a wide variety of special interests.

Some Backgrounds

Philanthropic support is now largely confined to higher education, except for religious schools. This was not always so. An earlier chapter has pointed out that the battle for free elementary schools was won only about a century ago; in many states, par-

188

ticularly in the South, free schools were not plentiful until after the Civil War. Now public education, usually through high school, is available everywhere in the United States.

We spent $4.3 billion for these public elementary and secondary schools in the school year 1947–1948, averaging $179.43 apiece for the nearly 24 million pupils enrolled. This money was raised by taxes, 53 per cent coming from local funds, 5 per cent county, 39 per cent state, and 3 per cent federal.[1]

In addition, three million pupils were receiving education in private elementary and secondary schools, numbering about 13,000, and chiefly under religious auspices. These schools are usually supported in part by direct assessment on parents, in part by philanthropy. The philanthropic contribution has been discussed under religious giving.

Beyond the secondary level, tax-supported schools are becoming more numerous. The President's Commission on Higher Education in its 1948 report, *Higher Education for American Democracy*, included among its recommendations the establishment of free, two-year community colleges and a program of government subsidies for higher education to facilitate doubling the present college enrollment by 1960. Tax-supported junior colleges already exist in a number of cities, their 1948 total being 242. The numerous state universities and a few municipal colleges offer four-year courses and some graduate study, and there has been a tremendous recent peak in government funds for scholarships (under the GI Bill of Rights) and large increases for research programs, which support education at both the college and the postgraduate levels.

Early Support of Higher Education

All our earliest colleges were founded and largely supported by philanthropists, and were usually under religious auspices. Harvard College, oldest of them all, was established in 1636 with a grant of £400 from the General Court and a gift of £779 together with a library from the Reverend John Harvard. Its

---

[1] Blose, David T., *State School Systems:* Statistical Summary for 1947–1948. Office of Education, Circular 270, Government Printing Office, Washington, 1950.

charter, not granted until 1650, acknowledged further gifts, reporting that "many well devoted persons have been, and daily
are moved, and stirred up, to give and bestow, sundry gifts,
legacies, lands, and revenues, for the advancement of all good
literature, arts, and sciences in Harvard College." These gifts
were generally small, and were not always in money. At Harvard
they included:

> . . . a number of sheep bequeathed by one man, a quantity of
> cotton cloth worth nine shillings presented by another, a pewter
> flagon worth ten shillings by a third, a fruit-dish, a sugar-spoon,
> a silver-tipt jug, one great salt, and one small trecher salt, by others.[1]

Student aid was often necessary, but it might take primitive
forms. Wrote Eleazar Wheelock, founder and first president of
Dartmouth: "I have, with the assistance of a number of those who
have contributed their old put-off clothing, supported them [the
scholars] along hitherto." But costs were low. Up to 1659 the
total expense for Harvard graduates, including four years'
residence in the college, ran from $100 to $200.

Later, substantial sums began to be given. Jesse B. Sears compiled from yearbook and almanac sources fairly comprehensive
lists of gifts and bequests of $5,000 or more for the years 1893
through 1916, divided into these categories: education, charity,
religious purposes, museums and public improvements, libraries.[2]
During these twenty-four years education received amounts
varying from $12 million (in 1897) to $91 million (in 1914),
getting 34 per cent of the total amount of these larger gifts for the
whole period—43 per cent if one excludes 1916, which because of
the European war recorded such large totals for "charity" that
averages for the whole table were affected. "Charity is education's great competitor," says the author, "and we may be fairly
sure that wars, famines, earthquakes, and other great disasters
which appeal to human sympathy for help will be costly to
education."

[1] Pierce, Benjamin, *History of Harvard University from Its Foundation.* Brown, Shat-
tuck and Co., Cambridge, 1833, p. 17.
[2] *Philanthropy in the History of American Higher Education.* Bureau of Education,
Bulletin No. 26, Government Printing Office, Washington, 1922, p. 60.

Throughout this period these recorded gifts of $5,000 or more must have constituted a very large portion of the total income of higher education—just how large cannot be determined since higher education was not singled out from "all forms of education." Table 39 compares these benefactions with the reported total income of higher education by three-year periods.

TABLE 39. GIFTS AND BEQUESTS OF $5,000 OR MORE FOR ALL EDUCATION COMPARED WITH RE-PORTED TOTAL INCOME OF HIGHER EDU-CATION BY THREE-YEAR PERIODS, 1893–1916

In millions

Period	Benefactions of $5,000 or more for all forms of education	Total income of higher education
1893–1895	$ 44	$ 67
1896–1898	47	79
1899–1901	139	113
1902–1904	130	122
1905–1907	190	171
1908–1910	144	224
1911–1913	155	309
1914–1916	199	373
Total	$1,048	$1,458

SOURCE: Adapted from *Philanthropy in the History of American Higher Education* by Jesse B. Sears, pp. 61–62.

Higher Education Today

In the period between the two world wars the problem of higher education mushroomed. From 1918 to 1940 the total population of the country increased from 104 to 132 million, a mere 27 per cent; but in the same period students enrolled in higher education increased from 440,742 to 1,494,203—an increase of 239 per cent! Table 40 presents by decades this remarkable expansion in higher education.

The data for 1946 and 1948 are to be taken with some caution; they represent aftereffects of the war. The tremendous enrollment of more than two and a half million in 1947–1948, for example, included more than one million veterans, many of whom would not have been in college that year under normal circumstances, or might never have gone except for government aid. This table therefore reflects both the accelerating prewar growth in higher education which was already straining normal resources, and the extraordinary situation just after the war.

TABLE 40. POPULATION 18 TO 21 YEARS, STUDENTS IN INSTITU-
TIONS OF HIGHER EDUCATION, AND NUMBER OF SUCH
INSTITUTIONS, 1900–1948

Year	Population 18 to 21 years (thousands)	Students in institutions of higher education (thousands)	Students as per cent of population	Institutions of higher education		
				Public	Private	Total
1900	5,931	238	4	..	..	969
1910	7,335	355	5	..	..	866
1920	7,344	598	8	414	627	1,041
1930	8,899	1,101	12	519	890	1,409
1940	9,691	1,494	15	610	1,141	1,751
1946	9,354[a]	1,677	18	624	1,144	1,768
1948	9,410[a]	2,616	28[b]	630	1,158	1,788

[a] Estimated.

[b] Percentage not comparable because of inclusion of many veterans from older age groups.

SOURCE: *Biennial Survey of Education, 1944–1946,* and Circular 263, November, 1949, Office of Education.

A comprehensive view of present support for higher education is given by Table 41, but again allowance must be made for the fact that this table represents the school year 1947–1948, with exaggeration of some of its items because of the large veteran contingent still within the colleges.

Public and private institutions of higher education are nearly in equilibrium. While there are almost twice as many private schools as public, most private schools are smaller; in the two groups, the numbers of students and of faculty are nearly equal,

Notes to Table 41

[a] Organized activities related to instructional departments, as dairy products, etc.

[b] Residence and dining halls, intercollegiate athletics, printing and other industrial plants, etc.

[c] Includes student aid, prizes, promotion, interest on debt.

[d] Almost wholly for endowment.

SOURCE: Circulars 263 and 268, November, 1949 and February, 1950, Office of Education.

TABLE 41. FINANCIAL DATA FOR INSTITUTIONS OF HIGHER EDUCATION, SCHOOL YEAR 1947–1948

Dollar figures in millions

	Public institutions		Private institutions		All institutions	
	Number	Per cent of all institutions	Number	Per cent of all institutions	Number	Per cent of all institutions
Number of institutions	630	35	1,158	65	1,788	100
Students (thousands)	1,326	51	1,290	49	2,616	100
Faculty (thousands)	110	49	114	51	224	100
	Amount	Per cent of receipts	Amount	Per cent of receipts	Amount	Per cent of receipts
Receipts for current operation:						
Student fees	$ 85	8	$ 220	23	$ 305	15
Federal government	254	24	272	28	526	26
State governments	332	31	20	2	352	17
Local governments	48	5	..	..	48	2
Endowment earnings	8	1	79	8	87	4
Private benefactions	14	1	77	8	91	5
Organized activities[a]	53	5	40	4	93	5
Miscellaneous sources	17	2	19	2	36	2
Auxiliary enterprises[b]	229	22	236	24	465	23
Other noneducational income	11	1	13	1	24	1
Total receipts	$1,051	100	$ 976	100	$2,027	100
	Amount	Per cent of expenditures	Amount	Per cent of expenditures	Amount	Per cent of expenditures
Expenditures for current operation:						
Administration and general expense	$ 66	7	$ 106	11	$ 172	9
Resident instruction	340	36	318	34	658	35
Libraries	21	2	24	3	45	2
Plant operation and maintenance	95	10	107	12	202	11
Organized activities[a]	46	5	39	4	85	5
Organized research	83	9	76	8	159	8
Extension	62	6	9	1	71	4
Auxiliary enterprises[b]	222	23	217	23	439	23
Other noneducational expenditures[c]	17	2	36	4	53	3
Total expenditures	$ 952	100	$ 932	100	$1,884	100
	Amount	Per cent of all institutions	Amount	Per cent of all institutions	Amount	Per cent of all institutions
Receipts for plant expansion	$ 248	68	$ 117	32	$ 365	100
Expenditures for plant expansion	183	60	123	40	306	100
Private gifts and grants for nonexpendable funds[d]	11	14	65	86	76	100
Property:						
Physical plant and plant funds	2,135	53	1,861	47	3,996	100
Endowment funds	325	14	2,060	86	2,385	100
Annuity funds	16	23	53	77	69	100
Student loan funds	13	30	31	70	44	100
Total property	$2,489	38	$4,005	62	$6,494	100

as are current income and expenditures. Public institutions have a slightly more valuable physical plant, and it is increasing more rapidly; private institutions have almost all of the available endowment.

For the first time in American history, higher education has passed the $2 billion mark. Current income exceeded $2 billion, and if receipts for plant expansion and for nonexpendable funds (chiefly additions to endowment) are included, total income approximated $2.5 billion for the year. Expenditures, including those for plant expansion, amounted to about $2.2 billion.

In meeting this enormous budget, direct fees from students have dropped to a mere 15 per cent. Students also pay most of the "auxiliary enterprises" income (largely residence and dining halls), which accounts for 23 per cent.

Nearly half—46 per cent—of current income in this year was received from government at its three levels. Of the $526 million given by the federal government in the year of record, $364.7 million was for veterans' education, and presumably is a temporary item. Most of the state tax funds and substantially all the local went to publicly controlled institutions, so that the total governmental support amounted to 60 per cent of current income for public institutions of higher education, as against 30 per cent for private colleges and universities.

Philanthropy contributes a smaller portion of current funds of colleges and universities than most people have supposed, only about 9 per cent of their current income. Not quite half of this—the $87 million income from endowment funds—is from past philanthropy.

Private gifts and grants were $91 million in 1948—a large increase from $17 million in 1926, but not a large portion of present required income. However, nearly all of these philanthropic contributions go to the private colleges and universities, where their share in the annual budget is substantial. In addition, philanthropy has built up the $2 billion endowment of private colleges and universities, has contributed most of their current plant worth of nearly $2 billion, and shares in various other forms of educational aid.

The present picture of higher education is of a facility which has grown faster than its usual means of support. Tax-supported institutions are accommodating an increasing proportion of students. Tax funds also represent, at least temporarily, a large portion of the current income of private colleges and universities. Implications of these changes need to be examined from viewpoints other than sheer finance.

The Plight of the Private College

Private colleges and universities are suffering from a disastrous success. Though the highest peak of the postwar enrollment is past, few colleges are able to accept all the qualified students who apply. In most businesses, such an excess of demand would result in higher prices and prosperity. In the colleges, additional students usually increase the operating deficit,[1] which must be made up out of higher student fees, increased earnings from endowment, larger current gifts, or subsidies from government.

Student fees are already at a level where lower- and middle-income families find difficulty in financing higher education for their children, even when the student helps by working part of his way. "Private colleges will soon be forced to admit only the economically privileged," warns one authority,[2] unless government subsidies or additional funds from private donors become available.

Many colleges have endeavored to increase their own incomes through shifting to investments offering somewhat less security but higher yields. Some of them have taken over business enterprises, directly or through subsidiaries, with the expectation of applying their tax-exempt status to the profits of these companies. Both the United States Treasury Department and private business raised vigorous objections, and the 81st Congress in the Revenue Act of 1950 strictly limited this practice. For most tax-exempt organizations, including universities, income over $1,000 of a business enterprise not "substantially related" to the organization's tax-free activities has become subject to income taxes.[3]

[1] Not true for many colleges during and just after World War II, when large classes and other substandard (but economical) conditions were tolerated.

[2] Hollis, Ernest V., "Federal Aid for Higher Education," *School and Society*, January 8, 1949, p. 20.

[3] See pp. 294–301 for a summary of these provisions.

Special campaigns have brought larger current gifts to many colleges, but these will scarcely compensate for the withdrawals of government funds as the GI program closes.

Will colleges follow the pattern of secondary schools, with public, tax-supported education predominating, with survival of only a few of the stronger private schools and those supported for specifically religious purposes? This, many educators believe, would be undesirable and dangerous in a democracy. Acknowledging the contributions of the state universities and other tax-supported institutions of higher education, they insist that the training of the intellectual leadership of the nation requires the diversity and freedom possible only under the stimulus of colleges and universities independent of political controls.

For this reason educators in the private colleges regard the possibility of federal aid as a doubtful solution to their financial difficulties. They point out that such aid has often involved degrees of control. For example, the Morrill Land-Grant Act, donating public lands to the states and territories for agricultural colleges, was passed in its first form in 1862 during a war; it made the offering of military training compulsory in land-grant colleges. This has been interpreted as a compulsion upon the student and currently (nearly ninety years later) all land-grant colleges except the University of Minnesota have compulsory military training, usually for the first two years.

A Tennessee college refused even to accept some surplus potatoes offered by the government. It shortly received a private gift of $10,000, with a note of thanks, saying, "It is gratifying to know that your small college realizes that freedom is no small potatoes."

Since many of the private colleges are under religious auspices, direct federal aid raises the further problem of proper separation of church and state. To avoid this religious difficulty and to ensure independence, some groups of educators recommend that federal aid take the form of scholarship grants, the student to be left to choose his school.

The Association of American Universities has received a grant of $450,000 from the Rockefeller Foundation and the Carnegie

Corporation of New York for a three-year study by a special Commission on Financing Higher Education, which should shed light on this difficult problem.

Endowment Funds

A college endowment may be defined as "a fund, the principal of which is invested and kept inviolate and only the income used for the general support of the college, or for some specific object in connection with it."[1]

The immediate needs of colleges were at first so great that few contributions to permanent endowment were made. Early endowments were not large, and did not accumulate rapidly. The first substantial gift of securities to an American college is said to have been George Washington's gift of $50,000 in stock of the James River Company to Liberty Hall Academy (later Washington and Lee University) made in 1796; over $400,000 in income has been received from this fund, which is still intact. Charles F. Thwing estimated that in 1800 total college endowment was not more than $500,000. By 1900 it was about $165 million.[2]

Then came the great foundations, several of which were devoted wholly to education. They observed that in 1900 income from endowment supplied about 20 per cent of the total operating costs of higher education; it seemed feasible to solve the whole problem by simply doubling or trebling the existing endowments. The Carnegie Foundation for the Advancement of Teaching greatly stimulated drives for endowment among smaller colleges by making one of the requirements for participation in the Carnegie pension fund for professors the possession by private colleges of an endowment fund of at least $200,000—after 1921, $500,000. By 1925 the General Education Board was able to report that it had itself contributed $60 million to the endowment of 291 colleges and universities,[3] and under "matching" provisions that would mean the addition of $200 million to such funds.

[1] Arnett, Trevor, *College and University Finance*. General Education Board, New York, 1922, p. 24.

[2] Hollis, Ernest V., *Philanthropic Foundations and Higher Education*. Columbia University Press, New York, 1938, p. 200.

[3] Not including its large contributions for endowment of medical schools.

But in its report for 1925–1926 the General Education Board acknowledged that higher education had less per student than "a quarter of a century ago," when measured in purchasing power. The Board had already abandoned contributions to endowment as a general policy, and in 1932 and in 1937 progressively removed restrictions from funds originally contributed for permanent endowment, so that both the General Education Board and the Rockefeller Foundation permit endowment principal to be diverted to other uses on a four-fifths vote of the trustees of the institution concerned.

But endowment funds continued to accumulate from other foundations, from special campaigns, and from bequests, and they still do. A very few colleges, such as Cooper Union in New York City, have endowments large enough to support substantially their whole operation. Others are assured of meeting a large portion of their expenses from endowment income, provided the size of the student body is restricted. But endowment is notoriously uneven in distribution. Two-thirds of the total endowment of the thousand private colleges and universities is said to be held by only 50 of these institutions, which enroll less than 15 per cent of college students.

The principle of permanent endowment for educational institutions has sometimes been questioned. Adam Smith in his *Wealth of Nations* maintained that endowments diminished the necessity of application by the teachers and enabled the older and richer colleges to cling longer to useless and outworn curricula. More recent commentators have pointed to present low yields on conservative investments as making endowment less worthwhile, and to the dangers of fixed endowment losing values through price inflation, as has recently occurred. Moreover, economists ask whether profitable investments can continue to be found for the mounting sums involved in college endowments, foundations, life insurance, and the vast new "pension funds" appearing in industry.

Future prospects aside, college endowment funds are substantial. They were recorded in 1948 at $2,253 million, with an additional $132 million in "funds temporarily functioning as endowment." They added $87 million to college income that year, which was a mere 4 per cent of this income. But since most of this endowment was concentrated in the private colleges, the contribution for this group was more substantial—about 8 per cent of their current income.

The General Education Board had thought colleges would reach a sound footing if from 40 to 60 per cent of their current operating cost were supplied from endowment earnings. Using the lower figure and applying it only to the 1948 current expenditures of the private institutions ($715 million after deduction of the self-liquidating item for auxiliary enterprises), then to raise the required 40 per cent, or $286 million, at the current interest rate for college funds of about 3.65 per cent, an endowment of approximately $8 billion would be required—more than three times the endowment accumulated by these colleges in the past two hundred years.

Fixed endowment may be the answer to the financial problems of a very few wealthy colleges, or to special programs within colleges, and doubtless administrators of all colleges will continue to welcome such sums. But it makes little sense as an answer to the total problem of currently financing private colleges and universities. The problem has grown too big.

Contributions for Buildings

Needed college buildings[1] are a close equivalent to endowment, with the advantage that the whole gift is put to immediate use, and it continues to pay a dividend in service so long as the building stands. In the present period of rapidly expanding student bodies many colleges have centered their drives for funds—whether in a general campaign or in individual approach to large givers—on specific building needs, or on a developmental program in which new buildings are a prominent part.

Early in 1950 Columbia University started a drive to raise $12 million for an engineering research center. The University of Michigan is campaigning for $6.5 million for an atomic research

---

[1] But unessential ones, unless endowed, are so heavy a drain on income that colleges sometimes refuse them.

center as a memorial to the dead of World War II, not more than $2 million to be devoted to building and the remainder to a program directed toward the beneficial and humanitarian application of atomic energy to the peacetime economy and social life of the nation. Syracuse University is conducting a $15 million drive for building and development. The University of Notre Dame recently acknowledged a single gift of $1 million, three-quarters of which is to be used to construct a dormitory, the remainder for a student loan fund. Indeed, nearly all institutions of higher education, public and private, are expanding plant, and most of the private institutions are energetically seeking funds for that purpose.

The United States Office of Education reported receipts of $365 million for plant expansion in 1948, with expenditure of $306 million. But 68 per cent of the receipts and 60 per cent of the expenditures were for public institutions, substantially all of it from tax funds. Private colleges and universities received $117 million for plant expansion, and spent slightly more than that. A *New York Times* survey conducted by Benjamin Fine in 1949 reported "A huge building program, totaling more than two and one-half billion dollars, is now under way. . . . The liberal arts institutions will spend just about two billion dollars on the construction of new buildings during the next few years. Much of this work has begun."

Funds for Professorships and Special Courses

Endowments are frequently given colleges for specific purposes. Indeed, large parts of the existing endowments of most colleges are committed to purposes dictated by the donors. Where this commitment is something the college would normally have supported itself, it releases funds for another need. Where a desirable but not essential service is endowed, the college program is enriched but the budgetary burden for essential services is not lightened. In some instances donors have so tightly conditioned their gifts that with the passage of time they have become useless; colleges have refused conditioned gifts more frequently than is generally known.

Many donors desire to endow special studies in which they have an interest. This may be done by setting up a fund for a lecture course, a chair, a professorship, a department, or even a whole school. The fund or the endowed chair sometimes bears the name of the donor, a relative, or perhaps a revered teacher.

Among gifts of this type announced in 1949 or 1950 are these. Columbia University received $11,000 to set up a lecture series dedicated to international peace. An anonymous industrialist gave Washington and Lee University $91,000 to endow the chair of philosophy. Princeton has announced that a professorship in economics would be endowed with a $300,000 fund as a memorial to Gordon S. Rentschler, alumnus and trustee, the fund to be raised by friends of Mr. Rentschler. Brandeis University received $150,000 from the Richter Memorial Foundation for establishment of the Max Richter Chair of Political Science, the gift being announced at the convocation marking the end of the University's first academic year.

The Old Dominion Foundation gave $2 million to Yale University to expand its program of psychiatric guidance for students, and the same amount to Vassar College for a program of academic and personal counseling for students. Northwestern University received an anonymous gift of $750,000 for a professorship and an assistant professorship in the medical school. To establish the first graduate school of industrial administration, the Carnegie Institute of Technology has received $6 million from the W. L. and May T. Mellon Foundation, with about $1 million to be spent for a building and the remainder to endow the new school.

Sometimes the gift is not in the form of endowment, but supports a special activity for a given period. For example, in 1949 the Carnegie Corporation of New York gave Columbia College $100,000 covering a five-year period to permit the College to introduce survey courses on Asiatic peoples and civilizations.

Scholarships and Fellowships

Aid to the student himself has made a special appeal to many philanthropists interested in education. Such aid may be offered as a scholarship, based on a competitive examination or other selective device; a fellowship, awarded usually to scholars of proved ability; or a student loan, with the expectation that the principal, usually with interest, will be repaid. The aid may come from the individual college, out of its own funds or funds set up for the purpose; from the government, under a variety of current programs; from one of the foundations, a number of which were established solely to aid needy students; from organizations such as Rotary International, the General Federation of Women's Clubs, alumni associations, business organizations; or from individuals.

The benefiting student is selected on a variety of bases. Financial need and scholarship are common criteria, but by no means universal. In New York State competitive examinations are held among high-school pupils, and the State awards ten times as many scholarships as there are assembly districts in each county and some special scholarships; in 1949 the total reached 3,204. The LaVerne Noyes scholarships are awarded to descendants of veterans of World War I; a University of Chicago survey disclosed that 62 per cent of holders of these scholarships at that University had scholastic standings below the general undergraduate average, while 90 per cent of the holders of other endowed scholarships were above this average.

A taxicab company in New York offers two scholarships annually to sons of taxi drivers. William Stanislaus Murphy of Boston established a Murphy Scholarship for any young man named Murphy who deserves encouragement. Numerous scholarships are available for persons who live in or near Lithopolis, Ohio. The Westinghouse Educational Foundation offers a major scholarship and a number of lesser ones to high-school students who are selected by its annual science-talent search. Scholarships for Argentine students have been established at Duke University; for "deserving young men of Chinese extraction" at Columbia— and Columbia students themselves are raising money for a World Student Service Fund, with half its proceeds earmarked to help students of the new Free University of Berlin. A New York boy, dying of leukemia, asked his parents to help his friends as they would have helped him; they set up a memorial scholarship fund for deserving students of the Bronx High School of Science. Numerous scholarships exist for the blind and other handicapped persons.

Sometimes the donor of scholarships has in mind purposes beyond helping the needy student. Cecil Rhodes, British empire maker, set up in his will the famous Oxford scholarships for British colonials, for Americans (two from each state constantly in residence), and for five German students. His objects for the American scholars included his "desire to encourage and foster an appreciation of the advantages which . . . will result from the union of the English-speaking people throughout the world." His will set up these principles for the selection of Rhodes Scholars:

> My desire being that the students who shall be elected to the scholarships shall not be merely bookworms, I direct that in the election of a student to a scholarship regard shall be had to
>
> (1) his literary and scholastic attainments;
>
> (2) his fondness for and success in manly outdoor sports such as cricket, football and the like;
>
> (3) his qualities of manhood, truth, courage, devotion to duty, sympathy for and protection of the weak, kindliness, unselfishness and fellowship; and
>
> (4) his exhibition during school days of moral force of character and of instincts to lead and to take an interest in his schoolmates, for those latter attributes will be likely in after life to guide him to esteem the performance of public duties as his highest aim.

Neither the number of scholarships now available in American higher education nor the funds represented are known, even approximately. In 1936 the United States Office of Education reported 72,505 scholarships and fellowships worth $11.4 million "available at institutions of higher education," and the Office is now engaged in a new survey. But even the new tabulation will not include many of the scholarships offered by outside organizations or individuals.

The federal government is contributing heavily. The whole $365 million given in 1947–1948 for veterans' education may be regarded as a scholarship fund. The fellowship programs of the Atomic Energy Commission and the Public Health Service were budgeted for 1949 at $3.4 million and $900,000 respectively, and these and other government agencies finance extensive research in the colleges and universities, often involving fellowship grants or their equivalent.

The Fulbright Act was passed in 1946, authorizing the use of foreign currencies and credits realized from the sale of American surplus property outside continental United States "for sending Americans abroad and maintaining foreigners at American educational institutions abroad and for financing travel for nationals of other countries to the United States for study here."[1] Where sufficient credits exist and suitable agreements can be made with foreign governments, as much as $1 million a year for twenty years may be utilized in these exchanges. In practice, a United States Educational Foundation is set up in each participating country to handle funds and recommend details of the program. For the 1950 program, 648 fellowships for Americans were made available in the 12 countries now in the program. A similar number of nationals of these countries could have their expenses paid to the United States, but since no U. S. dollars are involved in the program, their maintenance at American institutions must be otherwise provided. A further extension of scholarly exchange with federal funds was made possible when the Congress passed the Smith-Mundt Act in 1948, giving the Department of State authority to carry on various kinds of educational, scientific, and cultural exchanges.

The President's Commission on Higher Education recommended in 1948, as a means toward "equality of opportunity for a college education," a broad program of federal grants-in-aid to provide scholarships for some 20 per cent of (nonveteran) undergraduates, based primarily on individual need, and a further plan for fellowships for graduate study. This scholarship plan, for which a first-year cost of $135 million was estimated, has not been enacted. The Association of American Colleges endorsed this

---

[1] *Educational Exchanges Under the Fulbright Act.* Government Printing Office, Washington, 1948, p. 1.

portion of the Commission's recommendations "provided that educational standards be maintained."

Foundations continue to support scholarship programs extensively. Our 1946 tabulation,[1] with additions from the Raymond Rich Associates list[2] and other recent sources, indicates that such foundations and funds now total not fewer than 178, though some of these confine their activities to loans rather than outright scholarships. Many of these programs are highly individualistic in the kinds of study encouraged or the classes of students supported.

A strong recent emphasis has been the promotion of international cultural exchange. The American-Scandinavian Foundation, established in 1911, was the first foundation to concentrate in this field. International exchange of scholars, financed by government, foundations, and various other agencies, has grown to large dimensions. It was reported in 1949 that about 50,000 students and teachers were exchanged between the United States and the rest of the world. Nearly 27,000 foreign students were enrolled in 1,115 American colleges and universities; they came from 151 countries and dependencies and represented 152 faiths. At the same time some 16,000 American students and teachers were studying or teaching abroad and another 10,000 scientists, research workers, and other specialists were working abroad. The Institute of International Education coordinates many of these exchange programs and is a central source of information on foreign scholarships.

If mention of these many and diverse scholarships leaves the impression that this need is now adequately met, that impression should be corrected. Total figures are not available, but the 1950 situation of students in one private college, which may be reasonably representative, is at least illustrative:

> Even without scholarship aid a student in Oberlin College pays about one-half the actual cost of his academic education. . . .

[1] Harrison, Shelby M. and F. Emerson Andrews, *American Foundations for Social Welfare*. Russell Sage Foundation, New York, 1946, pp. 196–197.

[2] "Foundations Granting Fellowships and Awards" in *American Foundations and Their Fields*. Raymond Rich Associates, New York, 1948, pp. 146 ff.

About 530 students, or 25 per cent of the total student body, are receiving scholarship aid from special scholarship funds or from general college income. About 15 per cent of the total tuition of all students in the College is covered by scholarships.

In addition over 700 students, or about 30 per cent of the student body, are working their way through college in whole or in part, through part-time jobs in dining halls, dormitories, laboratories, etc., averaging over $200 each per year from such work.[1]

Student Loan Funds

Student aid is sometimes offered in the form of loans to students instead of scholarships. Arguments for this form of aid include the consideration that money goes further, since usually it is returned (sometimes with interest) and can be used again, and the contention that it avoids pauperizing the student through receipt of a gift, gives the undergraduate training in business practice and ethics, and is a reasonable charge against the higher earning power his education will presumably ensure.

Substantial funds are available for such loans, both within the colleges themselves and from a wide variety of outside organizations. The colleges reported to the United States Office of Education a total of $44 million in existing student loan funds in 1948, of which 70 per cent was held by private institutions. In that fiscal year additional gifts for nonexpendable loan funds totaled more than a million dollars.

Terms under which these loans are available to students vary greatly. Loans may be limited to girls only, or boys, or the completion of the last year of school, or graduate education, or persons majoring in a given subject, or with "first consideration to Cincinnati residents." Interest varies from zero to 6 per cent; frequently it is charged only from maturity of the note, which may be set for two years after graduation, or may begin upon gainful employment. Some loan funds require the borrower to carry a term life-insurance policy to ensure payment in event of his death. The funds may be deposited with the college for administration, or held and wholly managed by the contributing

---

[1] Statement on behalf of Oberlin College before the House of Representatives Ways and Means Committee, February 10, 1950.

organization or individual. The entire fund may be used for loans, with the expectation that interest will compensate for losses and perhaps augment the principal; or only income from the fund may be used, which will greatly reduce the amount available, but protect the principal.

Experience with loan funds has varied with individuals and with the economic cycle. For a substantial period the Harmon Foundation reported its losses at less than 2 per cent. But in 1934 the American Bankers Association, which supported a loan fund in its Foundation for Education and possessed unequaled experience in loan management, reported that "even with the best of judgment it has not always been possible to estimate correctly either the desire or the ability of the student to repay his obligation to the Foundation." During the depression many graduates found no jobs available, and loans were widely defaulted. During World War II so few men students went to college that large portions of many loan funds remained unused.

It is probable that the amount of funds for student loans is now adequate. It is less certain that all such funds are strategically placed, or well managed; and they are not popular with students. For obvious reasons they prefer scholarships, which do not need to be repaid, and many of them elect to combine work with study rather than mortgage their future. Any further giving of loan funds should at least include provision for other appropriate use of the money if it proves not to be needed for loans.

General Fund-Raising

Under present financial stresses, nearly all colleges and universities engage in virtually continuous financial campaigns. In the 1947–1948 year higher education reported receipts of $91 million from private benefactions available for current use; $76 million in gifts and grants for nonexpendable funds such as endowment and student loan funds; and $365 million[1] from all

---

[1] This item included tax funds allocated to publicly controlled universities, borrowings, and other nongift items. The gifts and grants totaled $57 million, but many colleges known to have received such gifts failed to fill out this portion of the questionnaire.

sources for plant expansion. It is probable that receipts from private gifts and grants did not exceed $300 million in that year.

A *New York Times* survey by Benjamin Fine reported in late 1949 that of 630 colleges replying to questionnaires, slightly more than half were currently engaged in fund-raising campaigns. The sum of their goals was $551 million and they had thus far raised $222 million. It was "harder to raise money now than a year or so ago," according to 96.4 per cent of these colleges. These sums are large and would be larger if the nonreplying institutions could be included; but they do not support the $2 billion figure sometimes publicized in recent years as the over-all goal of drives for colleges.

Many private colleges are owned by, or closely affiliated with, religious groups. They sometimes receive funds directly from the church treasuries. Special collections are taken for the colleges from the church membership. The United Lutheran Church in America announced plans for a six-day collection drive in 1950 to raise $6 million for the improvement and expansion of its 23 colleges and theological seminaries. The Methodist Church held in 1949 a special conference on fund-raising for its colleges. The National Protestant Council on Higher Education has recommended that a National Christian College Day be established, suggesting the second Sunday after Easter.

Aside from occasional group drives for colleges belonging to the same religious denomination, the only federated fund for colleges is the United Negro College Fund. It raised $1,156,000 in 1949, to be distributed among 31 accredited colleges in 13 states.

A college's own alumni are a fruitful source of contributions, especially for current needs. Some 200 colleges and universities now operate alumni funds seeking annual contributions. The name "living endowment" has been applied to many of these funds, suggesting that a reliable annual income of a given amount is as useful to the college as an addition to endowment some thirty times as large, at current rates of interest. Income from such funds has greatly increased in recent years. Complete figures are not known, but the American Alumni Council reports for 1949 the receipt of $12 million by 189 colleges and universities, counting only alumni contributions expected to be made on an annual, recurring basis. A similar report in 1939 totaled only $2.8 million from alumni fund plans. Harvard University reported 1949–1950 receipts from its alumni campaign of $770,182, and in this, "the most amazing year in Harvard's history," its total receipts from gifts, grants, and bequests were $25.8 million. Dartmouth College claims the highest percentage of contributors —64 per cent of all Dartmouth alumni.

Libraries and Museums

Funds may usefully be devoted to many educational and cultural enterprises outside the formal school and college programs, for educational growth is a lifelong process. Libraries and museums have long been favored objects of philanthropy.

The "public" library—there are now some 7,500 public and an additional 4,000 school and special libraries in the United States—is seldom built and wholly supported by taxes, like the public school. Andrew Carnegie alone, by the time of his death in 1919, had given a total of 2,811 library buildings at a cost of $60 million. He made these gifts, however, on condition that the community itself should furnish a suitable site, and should guarantee an annual support for the library of not less than 10 per cent of the cost of the building. Probably most of the library buildings in smaller communities are private gifts, memorials, or the result of a special subscription.

Some of the library collection has usually been donated, and often an endowment partially supports it. Even the tax-supported libraries of the largest cities frequently receive special gifts. A former fruit peddler, who used the Boston Public Library to educate himself, recently gave it trust funds which will total $3.5 million. The New York Public Library, suffering from severe drains on its capital funds to meet current deficits, conducted a drive for funds in 1949. The Library of Congress received $100,000 in 1949 from Serge Koussevitzky to establish a special music collection; it has acquired more than $2 million in special endowments since the Congress passed a law in 1925 permitting such receipts.

Of course, most of the funds for running expenses and purchase of current books are supplied from tax funds, in the case of free public libraries, or from general educational income if the library is part of an educational institution. Expenditures for libraries are estimated at $100 million annually, excluding capital outlay.[1]

Library needs are still great. The American Library Association estimated $500 million in 1948 as the needed capital outlay for public library buildings. Gifts for book purchase funds, special collections, and the promotion of cooperative library service were urged.

Some recent gifts illustrate opportunities in this field. Mrs. Woodrow Wilson gave the Library of Congress a Woodrow Wilson Room containing the personal library of the twenty-eighth President. The family of Ernie Pyle gave his home for a branch library to the Albuquerque Public Library. The Libby-Owens-Ford Glass Company gave Rossford, Ohio, $50,000 toward a new public library in recognition of the cooperative relationship between the community and the Company. The Rockefeller Foundation granted $10,000 to Swarthmore College Library for cataloguing the Jane Addams peace library. An organization of Greek ship operators presented 1,500 volumes of Greek classics in English to the Columbia University libraries. The Georgia Home Demonstration Council had a demonstration bookmobile built for the Georgia State Department of Education in "appreciation of farm boys and girls of World War II."

There are about 3,000 museums in the United States, of which nearly half are historical, and one-third devoted to science; the remaining sixth includes the art museums, which are among the largest and most heavily endowed. Museums may serve a wide variety of interests, from the broad collections of the American Museum of National History to the specialized National Baseball Hall of Fame and Museum in Cooperstown, New York. Most of them are set up by an original gift or bequest and are maintained largely through income from endowment, current gifts, or membership fees. A few receive support from local government.

[1] For detailed data, see *The Public Library in the United States* by Robert D. Leigh. The Public Library Inquiry, Columbia University Press, New York, 1950.

Gifts and bequests to museums are substantial, though complete data do not exist. Gifts and bequests to 12 large museums were tabulated at $63 million over the twenty-seven-year period 1920 through 1946,[1] or at an annual rate of about $2.3 million. But of this total the Metropolitan Museum of Art in New York City alone received $23 million, the American Museum of Natural History $18 million.

THE ARTS

Twenty centuries ago a wealthy Roman by the name of Gaius Maecenas, recognizing that the arts seldom bring their practitioners an adequate income, devoted some of his fortune to the support of literary dark horses. Two of his farm-boy protégés, Quintus Horatius Flaccus and Publius Vergilius Maro, gained such resounding fame in the unlikely field of poetry that their patron's name has become the symbol of such giving.

The arts are still economically hazardous, and they are often supported by gifts. Many foundations devote their incomes wholly or largely to painting, writing, music, drama, or other arts, and individuals have also been liberal patrons.

One example in the Maecenas pattern is the John Simon Guggenheim Memorial Foundation, established in 1925 by former Senator and Mrs. Simon Guggenheim in memory of a son who died just as he was ready to enter college, with the hope that "this foundation will advance human achievement by aiding students to push forward the boundaries of understanding, and will enrich human life by aiding them in the cultivation of beauty and taste." In 1950 it made grants to 158 persons totaling $500,000. These grants were for study, usually looking toward publication, in a wide variety of fields, only a few of which, however, were in the arts. But Thomas Wolfe had an earlier Guggenheim fellowship while *Look Homeward, Angel* was awaiting publication; Stephen Vincent Benet's *John Brown's Body*, Countee Cullen's *The Black Christ*, and many other notable literary productions were written on such fellowships.

[1] By Sidney Oviatt in the *Yearbook of Philanthropy, 1947–1948*, edited by John Price Jones. Inter-River Press, New York, 1948, p. 83.

Art as painting is fostered by the Bache Foundation, Solomon R. Guggenheim Foundation, Nelson Trust, and Louis Comfort Tiffany Foundation. Music is the province of the Griffith Music Foundation, Juilliard Musical Foundation, Kathryn Long Trust. Several publishing houses have set up literary fellowships. Prizes are sometimes offered to stimulate artistic production. Art scholarships, the financing of musical debuts, public contributions for the support of the opera and philharmonic orchestras are other forms of philanthropic support of the arts.

Expansion is not the only note. The Rachmaninoff Fund, founded to provide career opportunities for young musicians, was abandoned in 1949 for lack of funds. The ailing theater failed in an attempt to get $1 million in federal funds as part of an educational appropriation. Beauty remains a commodity in scarce supply and ill-rewarded, but the role of Maecenas, to be successful, requires an extraordinary combination of artistic taste and hard sense.

CHAPTER 12

Financing Research

THE GENIUS of the twentieth century has been scientific research, and its results have transformed the material world in which we live. Applied research in the natural sciences, geared up with big business and lubricated with substantial funds, has compressed the energy of rivers into thin wires, put civilization on wheels and on wings, hurled the human voice around the world, and finally, in the convulsive efforts of war, extracted from the atom one of the ultimate sources of power.

But though we travel faster, we have not outdistanced poverty nor always caught up with human happiness. We have a powerful new tool, but control over materials is not enough. Even in the field of technical advance, human factors need to be considered. Dr. Albert Einstein warned us two decades ago that "concern for the man himself and his fate must always form the chief interest of all technical endeavors."

Research and Human Welfare

The methods of scientific research which have brought such spectacular results in the physical sciences can also be applied to the study of man himself and his relationships. Outstanding achievements have already been made in the biological sciences, particularly in the conquest of disease and the lengthening of human life. But the social sciences have not kept pace, and even their announced findings have often turned into centers of controversy. The increasing gap between our skill in handling materials and our ability to deal with human relationships is a cultural lag which threatens catastrophe.

Several causes exist for this disastrous lag. One of these is financial. Social discovery rarely results in a patentable device from which a profit can be made, so that there is little direct financial inducement for business and industry to subsidize social research; moreover, the results are often in fields of such controversy and conflicting pressures that government funds cannot be made available. Much of the financing must come from purely philanthropic sources.

Also, the data of social science are frequently more difficult to isolate and to manipulate than those of the natural sciences. Facts in physics are the residue after human desires, emotions, ideas, and ideals have been rigorously excluded; social facts, dealing with human interrelations, are often properly the aggregate of precisely such human factors.

Types of Research

Scientific research may be divided for convenience into two main types, pure and applied; and into two large fields, the natural sciences and the social sciences. Society supports research in the humanities to a lesser extent. Since the problems of financial support are quite different in these varied areas, a brief description is desirable.

Pure research is the attempt to uncover new facts (e.g., Is an atom divisible?) without immediate concern for their use. Applied research takes a known fact (atomic fission) and tries to put it to practical use (building an electric power plant), or else it takes a specific problem (the water shortage in New York City) and tries to solve it by a variety of controlled experiments (inducing rain by seeding clouds, or popular propaganda for "thirsty Thursdays").

In the United States the major emphasis has been on applied research. Business and industry have poured out vast sums for contract research in universities and for maintenance of their own research laboratories, with the expectation of profitable discoveries. The government spent $2 billion developing the atomic bomb. Philanthropists willingly give millions for research for specific purposes, such as a cure for cancer. Paul V. Bacon, textbook publisher who suffered acutely from colds, bequeathed $500,000 to the Harvard Medical School for use in seeking a cure for the common cold. It is estimated that about 97 per cent of the research funds available to universities from government and industry are allotted to applied research.[1]

Meanwhile, pure research lags. In a thousand ingenious ways we are "cashing in" on fundamental knowledge already accumulated, much of it by European scientists, but are adding little to the storehouse. Some new discoveries are, of course, made in these attempts to apply existing knowledge, and the need for more pure research is being increasingly recognized. But at present applied research tremendously overshadows pure research in amount of work being done and attractiveness of financial reward for competent scientists.

Research, both pure and applied, may be in either the natural or the social sciences. The natural sciences are those which deal with natural objects, organic and inorganic, and thus include physics, chemistry, geology, metallurgy, and the like, together with biology in all its branches. Social science deals with "the human being as a unit of society, and the societies or groups that human beings form."[2] It includes such disciplines as history, sociology, psychology, social psychology, economics, political science, and anthropology. "The task of the social sciences, most simply stated," says Donald Young,[3] "is the advancement of knowledge of human relations. The goal is the best possible understanding of the problems of living together in the modern world."

Sometimes the borderline is not distinct. Psychology may be a biological science when neuron structure is being studied; it becomes a social science in research on propaganda. Psychosomatic medicine finds the whole man and his environment its

---

[1] By Benjamin Fine, *The New York Times*, December 11, 1949.

[2] *Effective Use of Social Science Research in the Federal Services.* Russell Sage Foundation, New York, 1950, p. 7.

[3] "Limiting Factors in the Development of the Social Sciences," *Proceedings of the American Philosophical Society*, vol. 92, November, 1948, p. 325.

necessary province. But most research projects fall definitely into one or the other of these two fields, and the great majority are in the natural sciences.

Sources of Research Funds

If it is agreed that scientific research, and particularly social research, has large promise for human welfare, its adequate financing is a matter of concern. For although the solitary scientist, working with little equipment, may come upon still other revolutionary discoveries, most modern research requires the handling of mass data, the use of teams of investigators and analysts, and costly equipment. For example, the 1950 census—a necessary bit of data gathering and analysis—employed in its peak period some 173,000 workers and had a first-year budget of $50 million.

The chief sources of research funds are (a) government, at all levels, (b) business and industry, (c) universities, (d) voluntary givers, including foundations, associations, and individuals.

The Government. All levels of government conduct research, usually financed out of taxes. The Board of Education of the Borough of Tenafly, New Jersey, hired a research team from Columbia University to survey its school system—plant, administration, curriculum, with recommendations for the future—at a cost of $7,000. In 1949 New York City signed a seventeen-year contract involving about $400,000 annually, engaging the Public Health Research Institute to conduct research into infectious diseases, mass immunization, and other health problems of New York residents. At least 87 cities are served by bureaus of municipal research, with 35 additional such bureaus located in universities and 17 in chambers of commerce. State governments have extensive research operations of various types.

But the federal government spends research funds (even in non-census years) which greatly exceed those of any other single agency and probably come close to being half of that somewhat mythical figure, the total spent in the United States for scientific research.

One of the important agencies of government research expenditure is the Public Health Service of the Federal Security Agency. Under the Public Health Service Act of 1944 this agency administers an extensive research grants program.

> The purpose of the Public Health Service research grants program is to support research in medical and allied fields for which institutional funds are not adequate or which could not otherwise be conducted. . . . The major objectives are (1) to expand research activities in universities and other institutions, (2) to stimulate the initiation of research in small colleges where previous research programs have been very limited or non-existent, (3) to encourage investigators to undertake research in neglected areas, and (4) to provide training for scientific personnel.[1]

The Public Health Service's large program of research grants is administered through its research arm, the National Institutes of Health, and through four of the Institutes' subdivisions—the National Cancer Institute, National Heart Institute, National Institute of Mental Health, and the National Institute of Dental Research. From the beginning of the program through March, 1950, 4,055 research grants had been made with approved expenditure of $39.6 million. But the program is rapidly expanding. Of the PHS's total budget for fiscal 1950 of $320 million,[2] it was estimated that $13 million would be spent on research grants and $12 million for the construction of research facilities.

The vast research operations of the Atomic Energy Commission are to be classified under present conditions largely as military preparedness. However, the Commission is under civilian control, some of its research is basic, and its discoveries have peacetime applications of tremendous importance, not only as a vast new source of power but in biological research. Its first cancer research center was opened at Oak Ridge early in 1950. The 1950 budget for development and control of atomic energy was $673 million.

The National Military Establishment was estimated to have spent a round $500 million in "research" in 1948; about $7.5

---

[1] *Research Grants and Fellowships.* Government Printing Office, Washington, 1948, p. 1.

[2] Of this figure $178 million is contract authority money for forward financing.

million on various projects in the social sciences, a large sum except in comparison with the stunning totals for weapon research. The Establishment's social research is often done under contract in universities. It includes such items as the Quartermaster Corps' research upon psychological problems in food preferences and ration acceptability; research in personnel selection in many branches of the service; development of tests to increase the efficiency of selection and training of airplane pilots; the Army-wide general research program of the Operations Research Office at Johns Hopkins University; and the Office of Naval Research with programs in psychological and social research.

Statistical services of the government[1] are of wide general use. They include furnishing population data, broken down into many special categories; employment and labor statistics, with wage rates and productivity figures; production statistics— agricultural, manufacturing, and mineral; price statistics, with reports on housing, business, banking, and over-all summaries of national income and national product.

These and still other governmental research programs constitute a fact-finding operation much vaster than is generally known. Because of difficulties in deciding what is, and what is not, true research, dollar signs can be attached to it only with heavy reservations. But Table 42 suggests the general growth in research expenditures for various branches of the government in the decade 1938 to 1948.

If figures for the Atomic Energy Commission and the Military Establishment are omitted from this tabulation, the contrast between the natural and the social science expenditures is not so overwhelming. The totals then become, for 1948, $169.1 million for the natural sciences, $44.7 million for the social sciences— 79 and 21 per cent, respectively.

As the Steelman Report points out, "the scientific activities of the Government have grown piecemeal in response to particular needs and we have never—as most other advanced nations

---

[1] Described in *Statistical Services of the United States Government*. Government Printing Office, Washington, 1947.

have long since done—accorded science a central place in our Governmental structure."[1]

TABLE 42. ESTIMATED EXPENDITURES FOR RESEARCH OF THE FEDERAL GOVERNMENT IN 1938 AND 1948
In thousands

Department or agency	Natural sciences and technology		Social sciences and statistics	
	1938	1948	1938	1948
Agriculture	$17,630	$ 40,700	$ 3,450	$ 9,460
Commerce	1,750	7,360	3,740	13,370
Interior	1,830	31,450	1,620	930
Justice	..	..	80	160
Labor	..	..	1,420	4,500
State	..	620	320	620
Treasury	40	170	1,190	1,770
Federal Security Agency	2,750	22,320	1,890	3,020
Atomic Energy Commission	..	108,530	..	..
National Military Establishment	14,760	492,500	..	7,500
Independent agencies	3,670	66,470	5,240	10,860
Total	$42,430	$770,120	$18,950	$52,190

SOURCES: Estimates for 1938 adapted from *Research: A National Resource*, National Resources Committee, Washington, 1938, pp. 73–74. Estimates for 1948 from Bureau of the Budget and compilations by John W. Riley, Jr.

Efforts to amend this situation through creation of a National Science Foundation have, after many years' delay, reached partial success in the passage in May, 1950 of a bill creating such a Foundation which is "authorized and directed"

(1) to develop and encourage the pursuit of a national policy for the promotion of basic research and education in the sciences;

(2) to initiate and support basic scientific research in the mathematical, physical, medical, biological, engineering, and other sciences, by making contracts or other arrangements (including grants, loans, and other forms of assistance) for the conduct of such basic scientific research and to appraise the impact of research upon industrial development and upon the general welfare;

(3) at the request of the Secretary of Defense, to initiate and support specific scientific research activities in connection with matters relating to the national defense by making contracts or other arrangements (including grants, loans, and other forms of assistance) for the conduct of such scientific research;

[1] Steelman, John R., *Science and Public Policy*, vol. 1. The President's Scientific Research Board, Government Printing Office, Washington, 1947, p. 9.

(4) to award, as provided in section 10, scholarships and graduate fellowships in the mathematical, physical, medical, biological, engineering, and other sciences;

(5) to foster the interchange of scientific information among scientists in the United States and foreign countries;

(6) to evaluate scientific research programs undertaken by agencies of the Federal Government, and to correlate the Foundation's scientific research programs with those undertaken by individuals and by public and private research groups;

(7) to establish such special commissions as the Board may from time to time deem necessary for the purposes of this Act; and

(8) to maintain a register of scientific and technical personnel and in other ways provide a central clearinghouse for information covering all scientific and technical personnel in the United States, including its Territories and possessions.[1]

Instead of sums of the order of $122 million annually as originally proposed for this Foundation by Vannevar Bush in 1945, the present Act limits its expenditures to a maximum of $15 million a year. The social sciences are not mentioned. In early hearings Senator Hart declared, "The fact is that social studies and basic science are not sufficiently alike either to be joined by the same legislation, or to be administered by the same organization."

But many lay witnesses and congressmen disagreed. Said Harold L. Ickes, then Secretary of the Interior:

. . . the results of purely physical research unimplemented by the talents and ingenuity of others, expert in the fields of human relations and behavior, would be both barren and futile. . . . I suspect that applied social science will be of ever-increasing importance to virtually the entire body of the Nation in the years to come.[2]

Said Vannevar Bush, speaking as director of the Office of Scientific Research and Development:

I believe that our strength is also dependent upon the extent of our knowledge of social phenomena and our ability to bring such understanding to bear wisely on the urgent problems confronting us.[3]

---

[1] National Science Foundation Act of 1950, sec. 3.

[2] *Hearings on Science Legislation and Related Bills*, S1297, October 18, 1945, before a subcommittee of the Senate Committee on Military Affairs, p. 341.

[3] *Ibid.*, p. 200.

Business and Industry. Both have long supported research, and with increasing generosity as useful inventions and improved techniques flowed from it with profitable regularity. At first most of the work was in the field of mechanics and materials; more recently vast numbers of projects are in the areas of the applied social sciences; a few can even be classified as pure research, from which immediate profitable use is not anticipated.

In only rare cases, however, does business pay for research projects aimed so directly at human welfare that they might have been a logical charge upon philanthropic funds. The 1947–1948 *Survey of University Business and Economic Research Projects*,[1] for example, briefly describes 1,188 projects: there are 63 studies of public utilities, only 25 of living standards, social security, and population; 54 of marketing, only 6 of business, civic, and religious group influences. However, one newer trend is emphasized in the 133 studies of labor relations.

Broadly based research is occasionally financed by business income. Some 74 food manufacturers, related companies, and individuals have contributed $3.4 million to the Nutrition Foundation for "basic research and education in the science of nutrition," according to the 1949 report of that organization. The Standard Oil Company of California made in 1949 a $250,000 grant to Massachusetts Institute of Technology for its research program, but with certain requests as to fields of research. The University of Chicago recently reported that industry was supporting its several institutes for nuclear studies and related subjects to the amount of $650,000 a year for basic research.

> The industrial support of the Institutes is spectacular, not so much because of the amount, though that is impressive enough, but because of the terms on which it is given. Industrial corporations are used to paying universities to work on projects formulated to answer practical, immediate questions that a corporation has to solve. They are not used to the support of basic research. The grants made to the Institutes are exclusively for such research. The corporations that subscribe do so on the ground that basic research should be continued and that it should not be entirely financed by government.

---

[1] U. S. Dept. of Commerce, Washington, 1949. Covers research in the areas named, but not necessarily financed by business.

They are aware that, though this country has excelled in technology, its ideas have come, on the whole, from abroad. The European universities cannot be expected to resume supplying us with ideas for many years to come.[1]

The Steelman Report estimates contributions to research in the natural sciences from business and industry at about $450 million in 1947; data of the National Resources Committee and other agencies suggest some $27 million in the same year for the social sciences and statistics. Both figures are open to attack on definition of "scientific research," and only a small proportion of the projects in either category bear directly upon fundamental problems of human welfare.

Colleges and Universities. A large part of the scientific research done in the United States is performed by university personnel, and usually in the universities. This follows a historic pattern. When universities started, learning was just beginning to emerge from the stagnation of the Dark Ages. As its branches were organized into ordered sciences, great gaps in knowledge became apparent. Universities adjusted themselves ingeniously to the need for investigation and creative scholarship: they invented the thesis. Every candidate for an advanced degree was required to study intensively some small field of learning, or (especially in the natural sciences) to contribute some item of absolutely new knowledge, as one of the prices of his degree. A steady stream of research was thus stimulated, the students themselves contributing their services and usually paying for publication of the result.

The thesis system still operates, but more creakingly and chiefly for its training values. Advanced degrees awarded in 1950 exceeded 68,900, of which 6,900 were doctorates. It is not easy to pick out 68,900 pieces of original research a year, each simple enough to be handled by an inexperienced worker, with prospect of a worthwhile discovery. In consequence, we have had theses on "The Economic Significance of Extra Ribs in Pigs," and similar subjects—and many colleges have given up the thesis as a re-

[1] Hutchins, Robert M., *The State of the University, 1929–1949.* University of Chicago Press, Chicago, 1949, pp. 20–21.

quirement for the master's degree. Most of the research urgently needed today calls for expensive equipment and frequently teams of workers, some of whom must have had previous training. Beginners in research are not always well adapted to the task.

Of course, continuing research is supposedly a part of nearly every professor's job; but few universities have substantial items in their budgets for the encouragement of this function, or are able to make even rough estimates of actual expenditures for such purposes. One crude estimate of "fluid" university research funds puts the figure at $7 million for 1948, with $1.5 million of this total being in the field of the social sciences.

But universities do possess important advantages as centers for scientific research. Their professors have specialized knowledge, usually some research training, and the advantages of close association with experts in related fields of learning. Needed laboratory equipment is often available. Graduate and sometimes undergraduate students are a reservoir of assistants who can work under direction. Financing is needed, and in recent years this is being increasingly supplied under "contract" arrangements, paid for, usually, by either government or business.

A *New York Times* survey indicated that in the college year 1949–1950 some 200 educational institutions would receive more than $100 million for research purposes from the federal government, and about $25 million from private industry. Preceding sections have discussed the sources, purposes, and limitations of most of these funds. Table 43 presents data on the 18 universities reported as receiving more than half a million dollars from government and industry for the year indicated.

Research funds currently available are nearly five times as great as in the prewar period for the universities listed in the table, and fully that for the total group of colleges and universities in the survey. The study showed, however, heavy concentration of funds in the larger universities and in the applied sciences, with engineering alone receiving more than one-third of the federal grants.

The availability of these vast sums is not an unmixed blessing. They help finance the expansion of research facilities and the training of many research workers. But they so dwarf the free funds these colleges can apply to research that most competent scientists may be drawn into what one university spokesman calls "gadget research," such as developing special weapons, and needed research into the basic problems of our civilization may remain undone.

TABLE 43. FUNDS FOR RESEARCH GRANTED TO 18 UNIVERSITIES BY THE FEDERAL GOVERNMENT AND BY BUSINESS AND INDUSTRY, 1941–1942 AND 1949–1950

In thousands

University	Granted by federal government		Granted by business and industry	
	1941–1942	1949–1950	1941–1942	1949–1950
Arkansas	$ 154	$ 535	$ 15	$ 23
Cincinnati	50	600	25	100
Columbia	1,884	3,336	74	125
Cornell	800	922	51	155
Duke	..	392	87	479
Harvard	550	2,225	97	220
Illinois	353	1,650	230	900
Kansas	..	309	..	457
Michigan	13	5,000	159	800
Minnesota	263	1,901	460	925
Pennsylvania	370	1,201	..[a]	331
Princeton	390	1,157	76	122
Stanford	78	1,383	20	57
Texas	..	1,450	7	100
Tulane	42	577	3	33
Washington[b]	17	799	1	462
Wisconsin	151	731	137	600
Yale	163	767	..[a]	..[a]
Total	$5,278	$24,935	$1,442	$5,889

[a] Data not available.   [b] University of Washington.

SOURCE: Survey conducted by Benjamin Fine, reported in *The New York Times*, December 5, 1949.

The fact that government is the source of most of these funds has sometimes been a further cause for alarm. A group of 26 educators, including Dr. Einstein, issued a report on *Militarism in Education* early in 1950 charging the National Military Establishment with "systematic and well-financed efforts . . . to penetrate and influence the civilian educational life of America."

In recent months Dr. James R. Killian, Jr., president of Massachusetts Institute of Technology, Senator Leverett Saltonstall, and Dr. Linus C. Pauling, former president of the American Chemical Society, independently urged vastly increased support of college research by business or other private sources to avert the threat of government domination of scientific study.

Voluntary Givers, Including Foundations. The special position of foundations as the "venture capital" of philanthropy has already been noticed.[1] Many of these organizations see in research their most promising field of activity, and prosecute it either directly through programs of their own or by making grants to outside organizations, universities, or sometimes individuals. Many others, however, are limited by their charters or by current action of their trustees to programs for relief, for maintenance of specified institutions, or for any of a wide variety of other programs involving treatment of social ills rather than discovery of causes, relationships, and cures. In this complex and rapidly shifting field definite figures cannot be assigned, but if current foundation expenditures are taken as about $133 million a year, probably one-third of this sum is devoted to scientific research.

Boards of trustees of foundations are not immune to the discomforts which turned the Congress away from the controversial social sciences, and a considerable proportion of early foundation funds was devoted—and much still is—to less controversial fields such as medical research. Important discoveries were made, sometimes at small investment, as in the $1,280 Rockefeller grant which aided penicillin development.

But now large funds from other sources are becoming available for nearly all the noncontroversial fields. They are not so freely given by government or business, and are not likely to become so, for the needed deep probings into our social and economic structure and into relations between classes, races, and nations. The past few years have therefore seen a pronounced swing in foundation programs toward social research, as a field where the unique liberty of inquiry and action of the foundation can be of

[1] See p. 103.

special value. One large foundation, the Carnegie Corporation of New York, reported that 73 per cent of the funds voted in 1947–1948 involved the development or utilization of the social sciences as compared with 28 per cent in 1945–1946.

In view of such large shifts, attempts at a definite division for any recent year have little pertinence. But foundations are among the few sources where support for the social sciences is substantial and growing, and is not dwarfed by the natural sciences.

A number of other nonprofit organizations in addition to foundations support research. National health agencies, such as the American Cancer Society, the American Heart Association, the National Foundation for Infantile Paralysis, and the National Tuberculosis Association, all devote substantial sums to research, the third of these reporting $1.9 million for virus research alone in 1948. Various other organizations in the social field, supported by contributions or memberships, either finance or themselves conduct limited research programs in the areas of their special interest.

The Research Budget. Financial support for scientific research has tremendously increased in the past few years, together with popular appreciation of its effectiveness. The total research budget in the United States is largely a mythical figure, depending upon definition of what constitutes "research" and assignment of overhead costs. The President's Scientific Research Board recently reported that $1.1 billion is being spent on research[1] by government, universities, and industry, with about 90 per cent of this going into development of applications of known principles. Other estimates are even higher.

As preceding sections have indicated, however, most of this new wealth goes into contract research on specific problems, many of them relating to national defense. Relatively little pure research is being undertaken. The social sciences remain the stepchild. Funds for the social sciences have increased in the general affluence, but at so slow a rate that social sciences are in a much worse relative position than before, receiving now perhaps 6 per cent of the total research budget.

[1] Not including the social sciences.

But even in the social sciences the primary problems are not financial. They are ineffective allocation of funds and problems of personnel.

Personnel Problems

The Steelman Report estimated that there were in the United States in 1947 about 137,000 "scientists and engineers actually engaged in scientific research, technical development or teaching."[1] Excluded from this count were the social scientists, possibly 30,000. Shortages of first-rate scientists exist in all fields in terms of the greatly increased funds suddenly available to finance research. But since the interests of philanthropy are more closely concerned with the social sciences, the shortages in this field may deserve special examination. Says Dr. Young:

> Today the various arms of government are unable to obtain all the social scientists for whom they have provision in their budgets. The same is true of business, industry, and agriculture. Universities and research agencies are similarly short-handed. The result is that crucial work is left undone or in the hands of unqualified personnel.[2]

So far as work for advanced degrees is a measure of future personnel for research, little evidence exists that the shortage is being made up through the colleges. Of doctoral dissertations accepted by American universities in 1939, 585 (20 per cent) were in the social sciences. By 1948 the number had slightly increased (to 681), but the percentage had dropped to 19. In the natural sciences, in addition to the usual scholarships many new fellowships have become available for the training of workers. It has been noted that the Atomic Energy Commission set up a fellowship program for 1949 with a budget of $3.4 million for the physical sciences, medicine, and biology; similarly the Public Health Service set up fellowships worth $900,000 in the same year. Special funds of such magnitude are not noted for the social sciences.

The existing situation emphasizes the importance of attracting the most competent of present research workers to basic explorations of our fundamental problems in spite of many openings in

[1] Steelman, John R., *Science and Public Policy:* vol. 4, Manpower for Research, p. 9.
[2] *Op. cit.*, p. 325.

"practical" research at inviting salaries, and of recruiting workers for the future, adequate in training and in numbers.

Opportunities in Research

The fact that some areas of research are now financed beyond the present possibilities of efficient work should not be allowed to obscure the primary importance of this field in terms of human welfare, and perhaps even survival. Said Raymond Fosdick:

> The issues of our time and of human destiny will be determined, not at the physical, but at the ethical and social level. Material power and dollars and military ascendancy may preserve us temporarily; but the dynamic tensions of our society can be relieved only by moral and social wisdom, and that kind of wisdom cannot be precipitated in a test tube nor can it be won by the brilliant processes of nuclear physics.[1]

The types of research which concern most deeply "the issues of our time and of human destiny" have little immediate cash value on the market; they will usually have to be financed by philanthropic funds. It is not easy to define precise projects. When the Institute of Human Relations was established in Yale University in 1929 it proposed "to carry on cooperative research in all fields concerned with human behavior in its social milieu." The lists of several hundred different national agencies in the social field suggest something of the variety of fields in which social research is proceeding or is needed. We have developed a few useful tools—the social survey and educational measurement will serve for examples—but we are only on the threshold of the era of social discovery. Preliminary spadework of the most rigidly scientific order needs to be done.

The difficulties are not insuperable. Social scientists are convinced that human affairs and relationships are predictable, can be studied by controlled experiment, and are well within the range of effective scientific research.

> The scientific method does not tell us how things ought to behave, but how they do behave. Clearly there is no reason why the methods should not be applied to the behavior of men as well as to the behavior of electrons. There are social experiments and physical ex-

[1] *Annual Report, 1947, The Rockefeller Foundation.* New York, 1947, p. 10.

periments and the scientific method can be used most advanta-
geously in both. . . . On the level we are discussing there is no difference between social science and natural science. On this level we
define social science once more as *the use of the scientific method to solve
questions of human relations.* "Science" goes with the method, not with
the subject matter.[1]

World War II brought to its highest point public appreciation
of the values of research. The $2 billion project which produced
the atom bomb was by a long margin the most spectacular
achievement, but the social sciences, too, proved their value in
many specific tasks, such as the selection of pilots, preservation
of army morale, economic controls, the devising of a satisfactory
demobilization procedure.[2]

A word of caution is needed, however. Rapid progress in the
physical sciences (ability to handle materials) brought us face to
face with severe problems in personal relations. Rapid progress
in the social sciences (ability to handle personal relationships)
may in turn bring new and acute problems beyond the competence of these sciences. Louis N. Ridenour[3] gives as one frighten-
ing example the increased competence with which mass communication can be managed so as to sway the opinions of almost all
the people, and concludes that "we can only pray that man's
morality is competent to the handling of the tools with which the
social sciences will soon equip him."

But possibilities of research in terms of human welfare are exciting. Research can supply the knowledge for building above
the dangerous cliff of human disaster that fence of prevention of
which an earlier chapter spoke. Social discovery could bring
startling changes in such areas as international relations, labor
relations, control of business cycles, family relationships, and
group living—changes as revolutionary as discoveries in the
physical sciences concerning travel, communication, and power;
or biological discoveries concerning communicable disease,
length of life, and nutrition.

[1] Chase, Stuart, *The Proper Study of Mankind.* Harper and Bros., New York, 1948,
pp. 10–11.

[2] For a more extensive treatment, see *Effective Use of Social Science Research in the
Federal Services.* Russell Sage Foundation, New York, 1950, pp. 14–20.

[3] "The Natural Sciences and Human Relations," *Proceedings of the American
Philosophical Society,* vol. 92, November, 1948, pp. 351 ff.

CHAPTER 13

Taxation Factors

Taxing authorities at all levels of govern-
ment encourage gifts to charitable institutions and causes.
Donations of this sort are exempt from the federal gift tax, and
they are deductible for estate tax purposes. Substantial portions
of current income, where devoted to such causes, may also
escape state and federal income taxes.[1] Likewise, local governments generally exempt from property taxes the land and
buildings used by religious, educational, and charitable organizations.

For government, such encouragement of giving is probably
sound business. In most instances the agencies aided are performing a useful function which, directly or indirectly, reduces
government expenditures. Agencies promoting health, recreation, and character-building presumably diminish damage to
property, lower the costs for police and prisons, and by improving
health and the moral tone, increase national (and taxable)
wealth. Agencies in the educational and relief fields sometimes
perform functions which government would otherwise have to
undertake.

For the individual, the opportunity is offered to give to a self-
selected charity a considerable sum of money much of which
would otherwise have gone to the tax collector. At the 1949
rates, single persons with taxable income after exemptions of

[1] This chapter is based on provisions of the Internal Revenue Code as of January
1, 1950, unless otherwise specified, and deals only with general principles. The more
complicated problems will require the services of a lawyer or tax expert.

$10,000 were able to give to charity $1,000 at a net cost to them of $700.80; the remaining $299.20 is "contributed" by the federal government in taxes forgiven.[1] Whether the Recording Angel sets down as a credit to this individual the whole $1,000 the charity received, or the $700.80 he might have kept for himself, is a matter on which we have no statistical data.

Persons concerned for welfare projects desire to make as large a gift as they can afford. Tax evasion is illegal; but to take full advantage of the provisions written into the tax laws to increase the size of one's gift is perfectly proper.

Income-Tax Deductions

For most individual givers, the chief tax saving with respect to gifts is on personal income tax. In general, gifts to charitable and educational organizations are deductible up to 15 per cent of adjusted gross income. "Gross" is important; for most salaried persons, adjusted gross income is equivalent to total income, making the 15 per cent a much larger permitted item than if net income had been used.

However, for many givers the problem is not whether their gifts exceed 15 per cent of gross income, but whether gifts together with other allowable deductions, such as a proportion of medical expenses, interest on mortgages, certain taxes, and the like, amount to more than the "standard deduction" of $1,000 or 10 per cent of income. If they do not, the taxpayer usually takes advantage of this standard deduction, which is permitted without proof or itemization.

Fund-collecting agencies were apprehensive when a provision for a standard deduction—at first $500—was put into effect in 1944, fearing that contributions would fall off among the smaller givers, who would receive the same tax advantage whether they gave or not. To what extent this actually occurred is unknown. A large majority of the taxpayers did take advantage of the standard deduction, and still do, so that the contributions section of the

[1] As this book went to press, the Revenue Act of 1950 increased income-tax rates beginning with the last quarter of 1950. Under this legislation the tax, and therefore the tax saved through a charitable gift, was increased about 17 per cent, varying somewhat with income level.

income-tax figures can no longer be used as an index of giving.[1] How the rate of giving was affected by the new attempt to simplify income-tax calculation remains debatable.

For all large givers and for any person whose gifts plus other allowable deductions exceed the present standard deduction of $1,000, or 10 per cent of adjusted gross income, whichever is less, in a particular year, provisions as to charitable deductions are still very important.

Organizations to which tax-exempt contributions may be made are defined as those for "religious, charitable, scientific, literary, or educational purposes, or for the prevention of cruelty to children or animals."[2] They include fraternal organizations if the gifts are to be used for charitable, religious, or similar purposes, and veterans' organizations or a governmental agency which will use the gifts for public purposes. The contribution may be made in money or property (not services), with the value of property gifts to be measured by fair market value at the time the contribution was made. Dues or assessments for which the giver receives benefits cannot be deducted, nor can gifts to individuals.

If the contribution is to be deductible, the organization must be set up under the laws of the United States or a state or territory thereof, though its operations may benefit persons abroad; no part of the earnings of the organization may benefit any private shareholder or individual; and no substantial part of its activities may consist in "carrying on propaganda, or otherwise attempting, to influence legislation." Further requirements have been added by the Revenue Act of 1950, summarized in Appendix I.

The provision against legislative propaganda removes from the tax-exempt list many organizations which would otherwise qualify. While doubtless it has salutary effects, it also curbs needed legislative efforts on the part of some organizations which dare not risk their tax-exempt status. Even the World Peace Foundation was challenged in 1925 by the Treasury Department

---

[1] See discussion on pp. 288 ff.

[2] See Appendix B, Section 23 of the Internal Revenue Code, p. 267.

on the ground that its activity in distributing League of Nations publications constituted a dissemination of "partisan propaganda," but three years later was readmitted to the fold of properly "educational" organizations.

Charitable agencies are usually more than willing to inform contributors if they are tax exempt. The Treasury Department has issued a comprehensive roster.[1]

The contribution must be effectively paid within the tax year. Making a pledge or giving a note is not sufficient. Even a dated check may not be enough. It used to be the rule (though it has recently been modified) that the check must be paid, accepted, or certified by the bank within the taxable year for which the deduction is claimed. Delivery of deeds, checks, or even cash to an intermediary within the tax year is not adequate, unless the intermediary is the agent of the organization receiving the gift. These stringent regulations appear to be made to avoid the possibility of recalling a contribution, or juggling the time of payment for tax purposes.

Sometimes these provisions may be applied to the advantage of the giver and his charity. For example, the charity may be in immediate need of funds, but the giver has used up his 15 per cent exemption for the current year and wishes to delay his contribution for some months. He can deliver a personal note payable in the fiscal year suited to his tax problem, but the organization can at once discount the note or borrow against its value.

The net cost of a contribution that falls within the 15 per cent category varies with the tax bracket of the giver. Complete tables are available,[2] but a few examples will indicate the general range.[3] Figures are for unmarried givers. Married givers reach the same brackets only when their combined income is double that of the single giver, under the "income splitting" provision written into the federal income-tax statutes for the first time in 1948.

[1] *Cumulative List of Organizations, 1946.* Separate 1948 Supplement. Government Printing Office, Washington.

[2] These and other useful data are included in *How Tax Laws Make Giving to Charity Easy* by J. K. Lasser. Funk and Wagnalls Co., New York, 1948.

[3] The 1951 rates are higher. See footnote p. 231.

If the giver resides in a state collecting a personal income tax, a further deduction can usually be taken on the state income tax if the gift was made to a charity within that state.

TABLE 44. COST IN 1949 TO SINGLE GIVERS OF CHARI-
TABLE GIFT OF $1,000, AFTER FEDERAL IN-
COME-TAX DEDUCTION

Taxed income	Amount of gift	Tax saved	Net cost
$ 5,000	$1,000	$228.80	$771.20
10,000	1,000	299.20	700.80
50,000	1,000	633.60	366.40
100,000	1,000	765.60	234.40

Individuals are able to make a 100 per cent tax-free contribution to a selected charity under certain conditions. This can be done by refusing compensation for a particular job, with a suggestion as to its other use. The refusal, however, must be absolute, and the suggestion not a qualifying direction, or the individual will be constructively taxed on the income, just as if he had received it.

Gifts made by a partnership are treated as the personal gifts of the individual partners, proportioned in accordance with their interest in the partnership.

Legislative Changes

Efforts are constantly being made to change federal legislation affecting giving, sometimes toward more restriction to prevent abuses, sometimes toward liberalization with a view to stimulating wider giving. Some of the liberalizing proposals would raise the limit on deductible contributions. A bill permitting such deductions up to 20 per cent of the taxpayer's income was introduced into Congress in 1949. It has even been proposed that individuals be permitted to deduct from their income-tax *payments* the whole of their charitable contributions. The effect on the federal budget would be so extreme that there is little likelihood that such a proposal will be seriously considered.

Other proposals are directed toward reducing tax exemption, usually with a view to increasing federal income or preventing abuses. The Revenue Act of 1950 included a series of restrictions on the activities of tax-exempt organizations which may also concern givers. The business income of an enterprise not "substantially related" to the organization's tax-free activities is not tax exempt if it exceeds $1,000. Income from leaseback arrangements is now taxable under many conditions. Other provisions sought to curb the manipulation of trusts and foundations for private benefit. A summary of these provisions is included in Appendix I.

Corporation Contributions

Corporation contributions to charitable agencies are deductible for tax purposes up to 5 per cent of corporate net income.[1] As in the case of individual contributions, the receiving agency must be organized within the United States or its possessions, but may use its funds to benefit foreign welfare causes, if incorporated. If the agency is not incorporated, and uses its funds abroad, it is not in the exempt list for corporations, though it remains so for individuals.

At 1949 and early 1950 rates the normal and surtax for corporations with net income above $50,000 was 38 per cent. The Revenue Act of 1950, retroactive to July 1, 1950, sets up a normal tax on corporations of 25 per cent of net income, with a surtax of 20 per cent on net income in excess of $25,000. For the portion of net income exceeding $25,000 the normal and surtax is therefore 45 per cent, and the cost of gifts only 55 per cent of the amount given, up to the 5 per cent limitation. If an excess-profits tax is passed, corporations subject to this tax will have a further stimulus toward charitable contributions to the limit of the 5 per cent deductibility.

All corporations can deduct the whole of certain "contributions," without regard to the 5 per cent limitation, if they can be classified as a business expense. Examples of such contributions are sums paid to a hospital which agrees to provide certain

[1] Internal Revenue Code, Section 23, q. See pp. 271–272.

definite services to the corporation's employes, or gifts by merchants or a bus company to a charitable agency to enable it to hold a convention in a city where its delegates will help the business of the corporation concerned.

Giving Appreciated Assets

Large tax savings can be achieved by giving securities, real estate, or other property which has increased in value while in the giver's possession. The saving results from the fact that the donor may take credit for his gift at its present fair market value without ever having paid a capital gains tax on its increase in value.

Tax specialists are fond of citing extreme cases in which the donor is actually wealthier as a result of his gift than if it had not been made. To accomplish this an individual in a high tax bracket gives a security which has quadrupled or more in value. The saving he makes on his income tax through credit for this gift at present market value is greater than the amount he could realize by selling the security itself and deducting the capital gains tax.

Such cases are rare, but givers in any bracket who own appreciated assets can increase their gifts, or make the same gift at less cost to themselves, by giving the appreciated asset instead of cash. Such an asset need not be a negotiable security; it can be property of any kind, including real estate, a painting, a rare book.

Life Insurance and Annuities as Gifts

In the 1920's and early 1930's giving by means of insurance was extensively promoted by both the benefiting agencies and insurance companies. The Equitable Life Assurance Society set aside a special week in 1926, during which all its agents encouraged the writing of insurance with charitable organizations as beneficiaries. Many colleges put heavy pressure upon graduating classes to take out insurance policies in favor of the college, thereby assuring, as they thought, annual contributions from these graduates which would later mount into substantial endowments. Social agencies, such as the American Bible Society and the Salvation Army, set up endowment and annuity plans under which individuals would make a lump-sum contribution, and be promised a stated monthly income, beginning at a certain age and continuing for the rest of their lives.

These insurance plans did not prove the great boon to philanthropy that their early proponents had anticipated. Insurance companies discovered that, instead of opening up a vast new field, they were now involved in a double selling job—selling first the merits of a social agency and then selling insurance; most of their agents preferred to return to selling insurance with the stronger motivation of benefit to the prospect himself or his immediate family.

As for colleges, the young graduates too often found their rosy hopes for immediate high-paying jobs fading and under pressure of their financial problems lapsed their policies; sometimes they expressed resentment over the attempt to capitalize on their inexperience and the emotional loyalties of the graduation period. Most colleges have abandoned the plan and at least one large insurance company refuses to write policies naming a college as beneficiary on student groups until they have been out of college a minimum of five years.

Of the annuity plans, some survive, but they are not the charitable gold mines that the volume of business handled might suggest. Organizations that use such plans generally take out for themselves a small amount of the original sum and reinsure the annuitant in a commercial company with the remainder. If the annuities they offer are to be attractive, about equaling those commercially available, it follows that their income from the transaction is not large—about the equivalent of an agent's commission. In a few instances the agency qualifies under the insurance laws of its state to handle the annuity policies itself; the Salvation Army is a notable example. Persons who take out such annuities may count as a contribution the excess of their payment over the value of the annuity as determined by actuarial tables.

In some situations insurance is a useful means of making a charitable gift. For instance, a giver wishes to make a substantial gift of definite amount to a building or endowment fund, but finds it undesirable to make an immediate lump-sum contribution, either because he does not have the money available or wishes to keep within the 15 per cent deductible rate for contributions. He can take out a life-insurance policy and irrevocably assign it to the desired charitable agency. His annual premium payments are deductible for tax purposes in the year they are paid, but the beneficiary is assured of the whole amount of his intended gift from the moment the policy is accepted—provided his payments are continued. The policy can be so written that it will be fully paid up within a fixed term of years.

It sometimes happens that a life-insurance policy, taken out for the protection of children or other dependents, is no longer needed for that purpose. In such cases a very substantial gift can be made at no cash outlay, and with tax advantages.

> Mr. T. J. Jones took out a $10,000 straight life policy at the age of 26 when his first child was born. Mr. Jones is now 65, his children are all grown and have substantial incomes, and his wife has died. In another year Mr. Jones will be retired by his company, and will find it difficult to continue payments on this policy he no longer needs. Mr. Jones' present income is $12,000.
>
> Mr. Jones assigns his policy irrevocably to Alma Mater College. The college has three choices. It can turn the policy in for its cash surrender value, which is approximately $5,455.[1] It can elect to stop further premium payments but keep the policy in force until Mr. Jones' death, when it will receive the present paid-up value of $7,930. Or, having heard that Mr. Jones' health is regrettably poor, it may decide to continue regular payments, and receive on his death the full face value of $10,000.
>
> Whatever the college's decision, Mr. Jones is entitled immediately to a deductible contribution equal to the terminal reserve, and any prepaid premiums, on his policy. At his age the terminal reserve is equal to the cash surrender value, or $5,455. Since his income is only $12,000, he claims $1,800 (15 per cent of his income) as a charitable deduction, and saves in taxes $601.92.

[1] These figures apply to a policy Mr. Jones took out in the early 1900's on the American Experience Table at 3½ per cent interest rate. For policies issued on basis of more recent mortality tables and lower interest rates, premium rates and policy values would be different.

Had his income been in the $50,000 class, he could have claimed the whole amount as deduction, and in his bracket would have saved in taxes $3,456.48.

The Treasury Department rules that for tax-deduction purposes the value of a premium paying policy, such as that of Mr. Jones', is its terminal reserve at the time the gift was made, plus any prepaid premiums. On a fully paid-up policy, the value is its full replacement value at the time of the gift.

Tax Aspects of Foundations[1]

The general values of foundations as a channel for larger gifts have been discussed in Chapter 6. Tax advantages which these organizations possess remain to be examined.

Once the exempt status of the foundation has been established, gifts to it are deductible contributions under the regulations already discussed, and the foundation itself is exempt from federal taxes on income. The exempt status may be forfeited under certain circumstances.

By channeling their gifts through a foundation, individuals do not increase their exemption ceiling of 15 per cent of gross income, but they do acquire certain advantages. Gifts may be made at convenient times, with no need to decide immediately on ultimate recipients. Gifts may be proportioned to the tax advantages of lush and lean years, and leveled off within the foundation to a regular rate of contribution. Gifts may conveniently be made in the form of appreciated assets, with the saving in capital gains tax and other advantages already noted.

The foundation is also advantageous to donors with respect to certain state laws. For instance, many states permit deduction of charitable contributions only when made to agencies within that state. By organizing a foundation under the laws of his own state, a donor may secure exemption for all his contributions to that foundation, even though organizations outside the state are the ultimate recipients.

[1] For a fuller treatment, see "Charitable Foundations, Tax Avoidance and Business Expediency" by Berrien C. Eaton, Jr., *Virginia Law Review*, vol. 35, November and December, 1949.

Under present laws both donations and the income from previous donations may be accumulated.[1] This offers the possibility of building up substantial foundations out of the annual contributions of individuals or families, perhaps comparable in size and service with some of the other foundations which were built up from individual estates.

Accumulation may also offer certain business advantages which have little or nothing to do with philanthropy. In a closely held corporation, an owner can make annual contributions of stock to a foundation of his own creation, of which he and his family or associates are trustees. He secures a charitable deduction for the value of this stock. He and his fellow trustees, however, continue to vote this stock. Ownership is partially surrendered, and some dividends; but control is retained.

Similarly, if the owner of a business bequeaths the larger part of the stock to the family foundation, the estate taxes are reduced to manageable limits and the family, as foundation trustees, may still vote the stock.

Such arrangements may result in large and useful funds added eventually to philanthropy, or they may represent abuses of the tax privilege, reacting to the disadvantage of all foundations and requiring correction. It would seem possible, for example, for trustees of such a foundation, voting as stockholders, to maintain themselves in key positions in the controlled company, voting themselves substantial salaries, or in other ways transferring profits and even assets of the company into their own pockets. Severe abuse, however, might lead to denial of exemption to the foundation or legal proceedings against the trustees by the attorney general or the beneficiaries. Certain earlier abuses will now be prevented by the provisions concerning accumulations and prohibited transactions in the Revenue Act of 1950.

Philanthropy in Business

In recent years of heavy business taxation, foundations, universities, churches, and other philanthropic organizations have

[1] The Revenue Act of 1950 sets up certain restrictions on accumulations, designed to prevent abuses. See p. 300.

received invitations to take over the real-estate holdings or all the assets of business enterprises; and some have done so.[1] In a few cases the business enterprise itself has been reorganized as a foundation, with income irrevocably assigned to a charitable use.

According to an early decision of the Supreme Court, the deciding factor in tax exemption was the use of funds, and not their source. Accordingly, businesses run by philanthropies, or operated in their behalf, claimed exemption from corporation taxes. In a few instances exemption from local real-estate taxes has also been claimed and obtained, though more frequently such exemption is restricted to real estate used only for the philanthropic purposes of the institution, and not for producing income.

This saving of the corporation tax proved so attractive that for some years philanthropies were besieged with offers to take over businesses, from factories to chain stores. The practice was widely attacked as constituting unfair competition for other business enterprises, and as opening the way to serious abuses. One element in the charge of unfair competition was the possibility that a foundation, operating as a business, could accumulate the whole of its income without paying any taxes, and devote this accumulation to rapid expansion of the business, instead of paying any portion of it over to the eventual beneficiary.

Leasebacks are a variation of the "philanthropy in business" pattern, which has grown into wide use in the past half-dozen years. They involve a double operation, a sale of real estate by its owner with a simultaneous leasing back of the same property to the original owner for an extended period. In the typical transaction, the original owner is a business concern; the property is a store, factory, apartment house, or other income-producing holding; the sale is made to a university, foundation, or other tax-exempt organization; the lessee agrees to pay all taxes, insurance, maintenance, and repairs.[2]

Extravagant claims have been made both for and against this complicated device. For the business concern, its most obvious

---

[1] For a discussion of colleges and business enterprises, see p. 195.

[2] See "Some Economic and Legal Aspects of Leaseback Transactions," *Virginia Law Review*, Notes, vol. 34, August, 1948, pp. 686 ff. for an extended discussion.

advantage is as a device for expanding effective capital without increasing apparent debt. The company builds a factory to its own specifications, and then sells it at cost to a tax-exempt organization, leasing it back for twenty or forty years, with attendant further options. It has a building under terms of practical permanence, its capital has been returned, and it can repeat the process again and again. No debt shows on the books, as it would if a mortgage had been taken, though the rental payments are substantially the equivalent of mortgage payments for amortization and interest. Through juggling of terms and the time element, the business concern may sometimes effect substantial tax savings; this phase is being investigated.

For the philanthropy, leasebacks generally yield a somewhat higher relative return than do the more traditional investments such as mortgages. The usual cares of the landlord (repairs, taxes, insurance) are customarily mitigated. Income is promised at a regular rate, and if for any reason rental payments cease, ownership of the property probably represents reasonable security.

The Revenue Act of 1950 endeavored to correct many of the inequities and abuses which occurred, or were suspected, in some of these transactions, with doubtless a further eye upon an increase of some $60 million in federal revenue. Its provisions are summarized in Appendix I. In general, they deny tax exemption on income in excess of $1,000 of a business enterprise not "substantially related" to the organization's tax-free activities, and impose the regular corporate income tax (individual rates apply on trusts) on certain previously exempt organizations which are in the nature of business corporations but devote their income to a philanthropic purpose. New regulations apply to long-term leases, taxing the income from such leases as "unrelated business income" under certain conditions. Tax exemption is forfeited if the organization engages in certain "prohibited transactions," including transactions in which it

(1) lends any part of its income or corpus without adequate security or at an unreasonable rate of interest to donors (including testators), members of their families, or a corporation which they control,

(2) pays any compensation to such persons in excess of a reasonable allowance for personal services actually rendered,

(3) makes any part of its services available to such persons on a preferential basis,

(4) makes any substantial purchase of securities or other property from such persons for more than adequate consideration,

(5) sells any substantial part of its securities or other property to such persons without adequate consideration, or

(6) engages in any other transaction which results in a substantial diversion of its income or corpus to such persons.

Tax exemption is also lost if the income accumulated in current and prior years is found to be unreasonably large, or held for an unreasonable period of time, in view of the exempt purposes for which the funds are intended; or used to a substantial degree for purposes other than the organization's exempt purpose; or invested in such a manner as to entail risk that the funds will be lost.

Life Interests

Sometimes a giver may find it advantageous to make a charitable gift but reserve a life interest, either for himself—

Mr. John Johnson, aged 50 and a resident of New Jersey, possessed bonds worth $10,000 which he desired to bequeath to Faith Church but felt he needed to reserve the income as long as he lived. He was certain he would never require the principal.

Instead of entering the item in his will, he made an immediate gift of the bonds to Faith Church, reserving to himself the income during the period of his own life. In that year he was able to deduct from income tax a charitable contribution representing the remainder interest of the Church in this gift, which at his age was $4,819.10. At the time of his death Faith Church avoided payment of $250, since in New Jersey only the first $5,000 of a charitable contribution is exempt from estate tax, and the remainder is taxable at 5 per cent.

—or for the life of another:

Mr. Jack Jameson and his wife were childless, and wished to will their home to the Red Cross for a local chapter house. They deeded the house to the Red Cross at once, subject to life tenancy of both or either of them. They were able to claim a charitable contribution equal to the remainder value of the house and avoided any involvement of this asset in the estate settlement.

Gifts with life interest attached are recognized as charitable only if they are made irrevocable, and if the purpose—though not necessarily the agency—is clearly stated and within the scope of tax-exempt provisions. It would be possible to make the gift to a named committee later to select the agency to receive the gift.

Foundations may be set up with life interests. Contributions to community trusts are often so encumbered.

Trusts

Sometimes a donor is willing to forego the income from an asset during his lifetime, or for a definite term, but wishes the asset then to return to him or his estate. A trust may be the desirable instrument. A trust is a legal entity separate from both the grantor and the beneficiary. If a contributor's gifts exceed the deductible 15 per cent, he can set up a trust for a given term of years, with its income irrevocably assigned to a chosen charity. Such a trust need not claim exemption under Section 101 (6), but can file under Section 162 (a). By this means the contributor removes for the stated period from his own income the income of the assets he transfers to the trust, lowering his income bracket and contributing to the desired charity without invading the 15 per cent he may need for other contributions.

Under some circumstances the income of a trust will, however, be taxed to its creator. This may occur if the trust is for a short term, or if he keeps substantial administrative control, such as voting the stock or closely controlling investment, or if power to revest principal or income to the grantor remains in the hands of the grantor or of any person not having a "substantial adverse interest." Legal advice should be sought on these complicated questions.

Bequests

The great but varying income which is annually channeled to charity through bequests has already been roughly estimated.[1]

[1] See pp. 68–69.

Such bequests are free from federal estate taxes if the beneficiary falls within the charitable definition. Sometimes, however, a larger gift might have been made at the same cost, or the same gift with advantages to the giver, if foresight had been exercised.

When a man's estate reaches $1,000,000, the federal tax rate is 39 per cent; at the $10,000,000 level, it rises to 77 per cent; and gift-tax rates (75 per cent of estate taxes) tend to prevent wealthy persons from dodging the death duty by earlier transfers. When the man dies, moreover, the tax collector wants cash, and he wants it promptly. In cases of estates containing hard-to-sell assets, this situation may result in serious difficulty. But by skillful employment of the exemption provisions, wealthy persons can at once minimize these problems and make socially beneficial contributions to charity.

The inheritance tax situation is more involved on the state level. Here the amount given to charity may have an absolute limit, as in New York State, where not more than 50 per cent of an estate may be willed to charitable agencies as against very close relatives such as the wife and child; or charitable contributions may be exempt only within certain limits, as in New Jersey where such bequests are taxable at 5 per cent if they exceed $5,000. Estate taxes may apply only to those who die resident within the state, or they may also apply to property within the state owned by deceased nonresidents. The local laws affecting charitable contributions with regard to estate and inheritance taxes should be consulted for the particular state or states in which property is held or residence maintained.

The Recipient and the Donor

To TURN about an old adage, "It is less blessed to receive than to give."

Some givers doubt this pronouncement. They assume that it must be very pleasant indeed to be on the receiving end, to get something for nothing. But many recipients—individuals in personal need, scholars and creative artists, officials of churches, colleges, and welfare organizations—know the bitter unblessedness of receiving: the loss of status, the need to suit one's manners and sometimes even one's program to the desires of the benefactor, the need to appear grateful, the need to report and be scrutinized.

The gift is desired, needed, appreciated; but the manner of giving may have impaired its usefulness. If giving is to be fully effective, attitudes of the recipient require consideration.

Gifts Between Nations

Many Americans traveling in Europe after World War I were shocked at the attitude of Europeans toward this country. We had given, we thought generously, to the relief of Belgian children, to the repair of French cities, and we had lent their national governments, their cities, and some of their private companies many billions of dollars for reconstruction—"loans" which, it soon appeared, were the equivalent of gifts, for they would never be repaid. Instead of gratitude these travelers found resentment and hostility. Benevolent Uncle Sam was caricatured as Uncle Shylock.

We are again engaged in tremendous programs for relief and reconstruction abroad. This time, somewhat greater care has been given to the attitude of the recipients. Marshall Plan aid is for the most part outright, without repayment strings attached. We have admitted that our motives are not pure benevolence. Aid is given partly as a matter of national policy, and to save our own skins.

At the present stage, with most of the programs in full operation, expressions of appreciation predominate. At the close of the Marshall Plan's first year nearly all the assisted countries sent official thanks. In London, Prime Minister Attlee called the Foreign Assistance Act "hope and help when most we needed it." In Paris, Finance Minister Petsche called grateful attention to the acquiescence of United States citizens in having their "taxes increased by 10 per cent to assure the salvation of our country." Other government leaders spoke similarly. The Lord Mayor of London recently opened a drive for a £2 million National Thanksgiving Fund to be devoted to construction of living quarters for students from Commonwealth countries and the United States as an expression of appreciation for the £80 million worth of food given to Britain since the beginning of the war from these countries.

But other notes intrude, and may become more frequent as aid is reduced or cut off. In late 1949 Poland ordered CARE to end its work and ousted the world Red Cross. A Girl Scout leader from Great Britain warned that American generosity would turn Girl Scouts in foreign lands into "poor relations" unless the foreign children were allowed to do things in return, and suggested a reciprocal exchange of trinkets and letters.

A recent international incident may illustrate that we also are not always gracious recipients, when the tables are turned. The Children's Aid Society in Washington, D.C., made a pre-Christmas appeal for clothing for needy children. One of the appeal letters happened to reach an individual in the Argentine Embassy. Shortly the Society received six crates of clothing, containing 500 complete outfits for children, from the Fundación de Ayuda Social María Eva Duarte de Perón, established by the wife of the President of Argentina. A tremendous furor ensued. If we accepted foreign aid, would we not be acknowledging we were unable to take care of our own poor children? Moreover, some of the policies of the Perón government were disapproved. A member of the Society's advisory board resigned in protest. A number of contributors telephoned, warning that they would no longer contribute if this gift were accepted. The Society at first refused to receive the gift "because of all the complications," but later, on suggestion of the State Department, did accept it and sent a letter of thanks.

It *is* more blessed to give than to receive.

Individuals as Recipients

When an individual is the recipient, emotional and psychological factors deserve great consideration. Unfortunately, very few studies on the attitude of recipients have been made. Public opinion surveys and other studies report what the general public, or higher-income groups, or physicians, or businessmen think about expansion of government services, or contributing to the community chest, or about any of a wide variety of topics bearing on philanthropy. On the critical question of what the recipient thinks of the help he receives—its form, its adequacy, the way in which it is given, how it affects him—the evidence is only fragmentary.

Mass Christmas parties for children are a gay and gaudy way of giving, attractive to many givers but often harmful to individual children. The Christmas Bureau of the Council of Social Agencies of Rochester, New York, reported on fourteen years of experience with such parties:

> For years a large fraternal organization entertained some 2,000 youngsters in a public building, with an entertainment, lollipops, a band, and presents of wearing apparel. . . . These parties became smaller and smaller and finally were discontinued; a few small public parties still remain, but we continue to hope.[1]

[1] Danstedt, Rudolph T., *Christmas Giving*. Family Welfare Association of America, New York, 1937, p. 5.

In 1949 in Milwaukee the superintendents of children's institutions and the Community Welfare Council worked out a folder offering suggestions on Christmas giving, "as a result of concern with the damaging aspects of parties planned by well-meaning groups."

The Family Service Association of America's booklet on Christmas giving, already quoted, stresses the desirability of giving money rather than things to needy families:

> *Social Welfare Council, Atlanta, Ga.:* Make it possible for the mother to plan the Christmas dinner . . . for then it is "our Christmas dinner" and not a basket handed in by a stranger.

> *Family Welfare Association, Baltimore, Md.:* Most of us want to help. Can we do it best by sending a basket to a family or by taking a dozen children to a Christmas party or by packing fifty stockings with candy or nuts? Or can we do it best in a way which brings a less obvious personal satisfaction—by a contribution of money which can be given to parents so that they may provide in as normal a way as possible these things which will give their own children the most pleasure?

During the depression a controversy arose between advocates of the commissary system (which permitted the economies of quantity purchasing and presumably made it certain the relief client could not chisel for luxuries) and advocates of cash relief. In most communities cash relief won, and there was never any doubt as to how recipients felt on this subject. One college-bred wife of a jobless professional man wrote:

> We received through the mail cash to cover food, fuel, lighting, a little for ice, fresh milk and so on. Cash to be applied to our grocery bill and other debts as we saw fit. Yes, my husband bought a can of tobacco. . . . Gone is the humiliation of taking a printed slip to a grocery store. If the parents think that cod-liver oil is more important than prunes in a particular child's diet, with cash they may shop in any store they choose. . . . It is the person that has never had to ask for aid who assumes the attitude that cash given to the unemployed man is a deteriorating factor.[1]

Wrote a man relief client during the 1930's:

> I got a check for $4.66 and I can tell you truly it was the best two weeks I lived since I've been on the Relief. I got about twice as much

[1] "Charity Bread," by A Recipient, *The Family*, May, 1935, p. 83.

groceries for that money as I could get on a grocery order and besides I felt a different man. . . . In the last two weeks I always had a nickel or a dime to put in it [the church collection box] when it came around. I tell you it made me feel good, that I was living like a man once more. And besides, I could buy myself some razor blades and little things I wanted and still have money left.[1]

The source of the aid, as well as its form, may be important. Is the individual more likely to feel he has failed or is inadequate if his aid comes from a voluntary agency, or from government? (After all, we are all recipients of philanthropic aid, if we go to college, use a public library, or attend an endowed museum.) But will he take aid from government too complacently?

Aid to individuals is by no means limited to those in physical want. Indeed, in these days when government services cover most of the elemental needs, private philanthropy may rise to a more creative role, for many kinds of persons. Aid may usefully be extended to students, or to graduates for professional education or particular research projects; to writers and creative workers in all the arts; or for a wide variety of other purposes which promise advancement to the individual and benefit to society.

Here again, a cooperative attitude in the recipient is essential to success. This is not to say that his expressed wishes should always be granted. The panhandler would like to have his "dime for a cup of coffee" given freely with no aftercheck, and panhandlers operate in all levels of society. The problem is to know well enough the attitude of the recipient so that the gift will not sap effort or confirm a feeling of inadequacy, but stimulate him to renewed activity on his own behalf; or, in the more creative kind of giving, open for him a door of opportunity for work on a higher, more useful plane.

The problems of giving to individuals resemble in many respects problems industry faces with workers. Personnel management is only beginning to learn that even in work for wages one of the most important factors in stimulating production is atten-

1 Colcord, Joanna C., *Cash Relief*. Russell Sage Foundation, New York, 1936, p. 230.

tion to the wage-earner as an individual person. Social casework makes careful studies of the recipient as an individual, his total situation, and endeavors to secure his participation in the formation and the execution of plans for his welfare. But philanthropy in general has only begun to consider attitudes of the recipient as a key to more effective giving.

Organizations as Recipients

Organizations, whether they are churches, colleges, hospitals, or welfare societies of many varied types, seldom share the reluctance of many individuals to accept outside aid. Indeed, most of them survive solely through such aid, which they solicit vigorously. But the manner of the giving is important, as is the attitude of the receiving agency.

Recently Lafayette College rejected a bequest of $140,000; it would have provided scholarships for American-born students, "Jews and Catholics excepted." Frequently colleges and similar institutions have received gifts of buildings, laboratories, or other expansion of facilities which they have afterward found difficult to maintain. The gift of a large foundation to a small society or association may boomerang into a financial disaster; regular contributors to that cause conclude that its needs are being adequately met by the big giver, and strike it from their lists. When the foundation gifts stop, the gap is not easily filled.

The recipient may even regard the gift as harmful in itself. Alcoholics Anonymous Intergroup Association of New York rejected a $10,000 legacy left by one of its own members for fear that the handling of money or property would divert members from their primary task of helping drinkers:

> Members have discovered they cannot mix money and its management with the spiritual nature of the work they are trying to do. So, like the fellow at the end of the bar who has learned the hard way what's best for him, they too have said "no" to this offer of "one on the house."

Gifts to an organization for a special service or a research project should usually be outright, in an amount regarded as adequate for the project even though not all paid at once. The giver's right of choice is exercised in his original selection of the type of project and the organization to conduct it. Attempts at continuing control through making the first grant inadequate, insisting on board membership, or similar devices are likely to impair operating efficiency or, in research projects, to result in biased findings. Even under the freest conditions, recipient organizations may be influenced by the probability that they will request other grants. What has been elsewhere said with respect to foundation giving has general application:

> Some foundations expect board or committee membership in the assisted organization or project; they require detailed reports, and expect to be consulted from time to time on policy and future program. This is done with a view to achieving a more effective program as the foundation sees it; but possibly no foundation policy has aroused more public criticism or ill-will on the part of grantees than this, which could easily take the form of continuing control. Many of the more experienced foundations have adopted a strictly "hands off" policy after the grant has been made.
>
> There is a very nice line of distinction, however, to be drawn between the desire to avoid anything resembling dictation of policy or program through the gifts of funds, and follow-up attention to grants. This seems a necessary part of the foundation's responsibility in determining whether the funds were spent for the purposes intended, and as a check by the foundation on its own judgment in choosing projects. The tendency in present foundation policy is to exercise as much care as possible in making decisions on projects to be aided or supported, and then to trust those in whose hands the grants fall to carry out the purposes faithfully and efficiently. This is an extension of the principle of academic freedom to the operations of organizations and research bodies supported by foundation grants.[1]

Harold Coffman once tabulated the opinions of 60 givers (in this case foundation executives) and 60 recipients (executives of child welfare agencies) on an identical set of questions bearing on policies in giving. On many points there was an approach to unanimity—for instance, 57 recipients and 55 givers favored

---

[1] Harrison, Shelby M. and F. Emerson Andrews, *American Foundations for Social Welfare*. Russell Sage Foundation, New York, 1946, p. 52.

giving to "preventive and constructive projects"—but the questions on which the two groups diverged are sometimes significant[1]:

"Foundations should make grants to the operating budgets of welfare organizations." Yes, said 30 prospective recipients; only 22 givers agreed. [In this and further questions, the remainder of the 120 were undecided, disapproved, or in a few instances failed to vote.]

"Foundations should center support on a single enterprise." Only 8 recipients agreed; 24 foundation executives approved.

"Foundations should assume administration or advisory responsibility for projects to which grants are made." Seventeen recipients agreed, as compared with 33 foundation executives.

"Foundations should spend only income, conserving principal." No, said 31 recipients; 23 givers agreed with them.

"Foundation grants should be on a decreasing scale when covering a period longer than a year." Fourteen recipients objected, but only 6 foundation executives.

"Foundation grants should be determined by the outlook or underlying 'philosophy' of the director." Fourteen recipients approved, with none in the "strongly" column; 25 foundation executives approved, 4 of them "strongly."

"Foundation grants should be determined by the requests from applicants seeking assistance." Twenty recipients favored; but only 11 foundation executives.

"Foundations should control the work their funds support." Here there was strong opposing sentiment, 47 recipients and 34 givers; but while only 2 recipients weakly approved, 8 foundation executives approved, 2 of them strongly.

Seeing Problems Whole

Philanthropy will seldom be effective without careful consideration of the recipient—his needs, his desires, his capacity to help himself, his whole self. This is true whether the recipient is an individual, an organization, or society. Giving remains an art, but in the complicated world of today it can often use the tools of science, and its work must sometimes be done through cooperative groups, associations, organizations.

[1] Coffman, Harold Coe, *American Foundations:* A Study of Their Role in the Child Welfare Movement. General Board of the Y.M.C.A., New York, 1936, pp. 164–167.

As in medicine, the techniques are more difficult. We cannot dispense one pink pill to fit all ills. The recipient is an individual, and it is necessary to know not only his physical needs, but the state of his mind—a psychosomatic philanthropy.

The Donor

Happiness, it is said, is seldom found by those who seek it, and never by those who seek it for themselves. Like happiness, philanthropy was born a twin. The giving that proceeds from a desire for personal credit or satisfaction may be tax-deductible, but it is scarcely philanthropy. The deep rewards of giving go to those who give out of a concern for others, and take pains to see that their giving is done wisely, to meet real needs or seize promising opportunities.

How Much Shall We Give?

Advice on the amount we should give ranges from the poet's

> Give all thou canst; high Heaven rejects the lore
> Of nicely-calculated less or more.[1]

and admonitions to "Give until it hurts" to detailed plans for proportioning giving to income, including the Biblical tithe. In Detroit, employes were urged to give to their community chest five hours' pay. An earlier chapter reports specific schedules for corporation contributions. In professionally organized campaigns the larger contributor is seldom left in doubt as to the amount expected from him; a special-gifts committee has examined his income, proportioned it to the proposed goal, and put the desired amount on the card given to the person chosen to solicit him.

Some of the older commentators left no doubt as to the desired amounts. Said Maimonides (twelfth century):

> *He who giveth* a fifth-part of his means, obeyeth the Precept in the highest degree; he who giveth a tenth-part of his means, *obeyeth the*

[1] Wordsworth, William, *Ecclesiastical Sonnets*. Part 3, no. 43.

Precept in a medium degree; he who giveth less than a tenth-part is a man of an evil eye.[1]

Truly creative giving, however, is not done by formula. Such methods have their place, as in support of communitywide needs which for one reason or another we are not willing to maintain as public services with the tax collector as our fund-gatherer. But when it comes to support of agencies or causes which represent opportunities rather than duties, then the amount we give should be related to certain other considerations.

One of these is the "free money" the individual has. Two men work side by side, at the same hourly wage. John is unmarried and has no dependents; for him, five hours' wages to the community chest may be niggardly. Tom has four children and two indigent old people to support; for him, five hours' wages might be more than generous; it might be vicious, depriving his own family of necessities. For many professional people, in the past decade increased taxes and higher prices have more than absorbed increased income, so that the margin for philanthropy is less than it was in 1940.

A second factor is the urgency of the cause. If my neighbor's house burns down on a winter night, he may have half mine; but I do not regularly devote half my house to that third of a nation known to be ill-housed. Seneca put the matter in ultimate terms:

> I must help him who is perishing, yet so that I do not perish myself, unless by so doing I can save a great man or a great cause.[2]

The wise giver will not contribute to the cause or institution whose product is doubtful; such generosity may do more harm than good. He will regulate the amount he gives by the free money he has available, related to the urgency of the causes which come to his attention; but he has responsibilities toward

---

[1] *The Laws of the Hebrews*, Relating to the Poor and the Stranger, from the "Mischna-Hathora" of the Rabbi Maimonides. Translated by James W. Peppercorne. Pelham Richardson, London, 1840, p. 46.

[2] *On Benefits*. Translated by Aubrey Stewart. George Bell and Sons, London, 1887, p. 32.

discovering those opportunities. In her book, *How Much Shall I Give?*[1] Miss Lilian Brandt put the matter forthrightly:

> The first duty, then, of the man who gives money to philanthropic purposes, is to inform himself on the social problems of the day and to reach an independent judgment on the value of the social work which he is asked to support. If he does that, the amount of his contribution may safely be left to take care of itself.

Are Americans Generous?

Headline writers sometimes praise Americans as the most generous people the world has seen, pointing to the many millions and sometimes billions poured out for a multitude of causes, and at other times castigate us as a niggardly people, who give only about 2 cents of the dollar received. Praise and blame are based on the same statistics.

The question itself has little meaning. We are individuals, and we do not contribute by averages. Some Americans are by any standard exceedingly generous. Others find it expedient to head contributors' lists and for various other selfish reasons are statistically counted among the large givers. Some would be generous if they were not confused by the new era giving has entered, unable to find causes that vitally challenge them. Some live so close to the subsistence margin that they cannot give without endangering their own families. And some have margin enough in their finances, but none in their sympathies.[2]

The use of averages to show trends in presumed generosity is hedged with further statistical briers. When social security was adopted in 1935, and later expanded, it transferred one large and important segment of charitable need from voluntary agencies, seeking gifts, to government, levying taxes. These taxes are personal philanthropy only in the remote sense that we elect the lawmakers who do these things at our presumed wish, but added taxes are a drain on precisely that margin between income and fixed expenditures from which philanthropy usually comes.

[1] Frontier Press, New York, 1921, p. 139.

[2] In 1946 only 8,753,000 persons itemized their deductions on income-tax reports. Even of these, 955,000 (11 per cent) claimed no charitable contributions whatever. On the unitemized returns, the percentage of nongivers was probably higher.

Using merely statistical averages from the Bureau of the Census and income and contribution data from Table 46,[1] the picture for an average family of four, two children and two adults, looks like this for certain years:

Year	Gross income	Charitable contributions	Rate per cent
1930	$2,104	$30.36	1.44
1940	2,010	32.44	1.61
1949	5,004	96.89	1.94

The 1930 family was just entering the depression. National income was still high, however, and the contribution rate had not yet received the spur of great drives for the starving unemployed, which the next year materially increased the rate from those still able to give.

The 1940 family had an almost identical income, from which it gave an increased charitable contribution at a better rate, though this family was beginning to pay substantial taxes for support of the aged and other groups covered by social security.

The 1949 family had a tremendously increased money income, and in spite of much higher prices and very heavy taxes, it raised its charitable contribution to nearly $97 at a rate close to 2 per cent. While this family was giving a total of $97 to all voluntary welfare agencies, including its church, in the United States, it was contributing by way of taxes $120 to the Marshall Plan, chiefly to aid European recovery, and $58 for Social Security payments to the needy aged, dependent children, the blind, and general assistance. Giving for welfare purposes, if we include the obligatory "giving" by way of taxation, has greatly increased for the 1949 family as compared with its 1930 predecessor.

It is not yet impressive in comparison with certain other expenditures. The 1949 family spent $111 for tobacco and $218 for alcoholic beverages within the year, and its federal tax bill for national defense was about $376.

[1] Dividing the population of the indicated years by 4, and assuming the adjusted personal income (column 2 of Table 46 on page 291) to be evenly divided among all these standardized families.

How Shall We Give?

Dr. Robert J. McCracken asserts that a literal rendering of II Corinthians 9:7 would make its closing clause read: "God loves a hilarious giver." Certainly the creative giving we have in mind should be free, willing, and glad; not the performance of a duty, but the acceptance of an opportunity. For such giving there can be no commandments or fixed rules. A few suggestions may be offered.

1. Give to your own community, where you are most likely to know about needs and services; but remember also poorer communities, which have greater needs and fewer able to help.
2. Give nationally and internationally, for we need to be one world.
3. Give to relieve physical need, in an emergency or when relief from the constituted agencies is for some good reason inappropriate or impossible.
4. Give in such ways that the gift will not sap effort or confirm a feeling of inadequacy, but will stimulate the recipient to renewed activity on his own behalf.
5. Give toward rehabilitation rather than relief.
6. Give toward cure rather than treatment.
7. Still better, give toward prevention.
8. Seek no personal credit[1] for your gift and do not expect gratitude.
9. Give to no organization unknown to you, without investigation.
10. Avoid giving to organizations which unnecessarily duplicate work already being efficiently done.
11. Avoid giving to organizations whose collection costs are high or methods doubtful.
12. When you give, give absolutely, with no expectation of control over the recipient.
13. Give while living, that you may see your gifts in action and learn the art of giving.
14. Give in ways that will stimulate larger giving from others.
15. Give in order to open doors of opportunity for the talented, and to make possible for others that greatest gift, their personal service.
16. Give adequately for the need, but not lavishly.

[1] Except, of course, from the Bureau of Internal Revenue.

17. Give toward research and discovery, and especially toward discovery of the conditions of health and well-being.

18. Give toward demonstrations of useful new services and ideas, and when these have proved themselves, withdraw support and let them be maintained by the users or the community.

19. If you give substantial amounts or for the long future, give under provisions which will permit changing the purpose of your gift.

20. Finally, in all your giving, give thought. "Somebody must sweat blood with gift money," said Henry S. Pritchett when president of the Carnegie Foundation, "if its effect is not to do more harm than good." But with thoughtful giving even small sums may accomplish great purposes.

The philanthropist of the past looked about him with a keen eye and a sympathetic heart, and gave to meet the needs he saw. The philanthropist of today must also look ahead with an informed mind and a warm imagination, and with new tools help build the world that is to be.

APPENDICES

APPENDIX A

SECTION 101 OF THE INTERNAL REVENUE CODE

[*The following is a direct quotation of Section 101 as it existed on January 1, 1950. The Revenue Act of 1950, summarized in Appendix I of this volume, affects Section 101 directly and indirectly by (a) taxing certain organizations exempt under (1), (6), (7), and (14), but not churches, upon their "unrelated business income," including rentals from certain leaseback transactions; (b) depriving certain 101 (6) organizations of tax exemption if they engage in certain "prohibited transactions"; (c) depriving certain 101 (6) organizations of tax exemption if they unreasonably or improperly accumulate their income; and (d) requiring certain 101 (6) organizations to file annual information returns.*]

The following organizations shall be exempt from taxation under this chapter—

(1) Labor, agricultural, or horticultural organizations;

(2) Mutual savings banks not having a capital stock represented by shares;

(3) Fraternal beneficiary societies, orders, or associations, (A) operating under the lodge system or for the exclusive benefit of the members of a fraternity itself operating under the lodge system; and (B) providing for the payment of life, sick, accident, or other benefits to the members of such society, order, or association or their dependents;

(4) Domestic building and loan associations substantially all the business of which is confined to making loans to members; and cooperative banks without capital stock organized and operated for mutual purposes and without profit;

(5) Cemetery companies owned and operated exclusively for the benefit of their members or which are not operated for profit; and any corporation chartered solely for burial purposes as a cemetery corporation and not permitted by its charter to engage in any business not necessarily incident to that purpose, no part of the net earnings of which inures to the benefit of any private shareholder or individual;

(6) Corporations, and any community chest, fund, or foundation, organized and operated exclusively for religious, charitable, scientific, literary, or educational purposes, or for the prevention of cruelty to children or animals, no part of the net earnings of which inures to the benefit of any private shareholder or individual, and no substantial

part of the activities of which is carrying on propaganda, or otherwise attempting, to influence legislation;

(7) Business leagues, chambers of commerce, real-estate boards, or boards of trade, not organized for profit and no part of the net earnings of which inures to the benefit of any private shareholder or individual;

(8) Civic leagues or organizations not organized for profit but operated exclusively for the promotion of social welfare, or local associations of employees, the membership of which is limited to the employees of a designated person or persons in a particular municipality, and the net earnings of which are devoted exclusively to charitable, educational, or recreational purposes;

(9) Clubs organized and operated exclusively for pleasure, recreation, and other nonprofitable purposes, no part of the net earnings of which inures to the benefit of any private shareholder;

(10) Benevolent life insurance associations of a purely local character, mutual ditch or irrigation companies, mutual or cooperative telephone companies, or like organizations; but only if 85 per centum or more of the income consists of amounts collected from members for the sole purpose of meeting losses and expenses;

(11) Mutual insurance companies or associations other than life or marine (including interinsurers and reciprocal underwriters) if the gross amount received during the taxable year from interest, dividends, rents, and premiums (including deposits and assessments) does not exceed $75,000;

(12) Farmers', fruit growers', or like associations organized and operated on a cooperative basis (a) for the purpose of marketing the products of members or other producers, and turning back to them, the proceeds of sales, less the necessary marketing expenses, on the basis of either the quantity or the value of the products furnished by them, or (b) for the purpose of purchasing supplies and equipment for the use of members or other persons, and turning over such supplies and equipment to them at actual cost, plus necessary expenses. Exemption shall not be denied any such association because it has capital stock, if the dividend rate of such stock is fixed at not to exceed the legal rate of interest in the State of incorporation or 8 per centum per annum, whichever is greater, on the value of the consideration for which the stock was issued, and if substantially all such stock (other than nonvoting preferred stock, the owners of which are not entitled or permitted to participate, directly or indirectly, in the profits of the association upon dissolution or otherwise, beyond the fixed dividends) is owned by producers who market their products or purchase their supplies and equipment through the association; nor shall exemption be denied any such

association because there is accumulated and maintained by it a reserve required by State law or a reasonable reserve for any necessary purpose. Such an association may market the products of nonmembers in an amount the value of which does not exceed the value of the products marketed for members, and may purchase supplies and equipment for nonmembers in an amount the value of which does not exceed the value of the supplies and equipment purchased for members, provided the value of the purchases made for persons who are neither members nor producers does not exceed 15 per centum of the value of all its purchases. Business done for the United States or any of its agencies shall be disregarded in determining the right to exemption under this paragraph;

(13) Corporations organized by an association exempt under the provisions of paragraph (12), or members thereof, for the purpose of financing the ordinary crop operations of such members or other producers, and operated in conjunction with such association. Exemption shall not be denied any such corporation because it has capital stock, if the dividend rate of such stock is fixed at not to exceed the legal rate of interest in the State of incorporation or 8 per centum per annum, whichever is greater, on the value of the consideration for which the stock was issued, and if substantially all such stock (other than nonvoting preferred stock, the owners of which are not entitled or permitted to participate, directly or indirectly, in the profits of the corporation, upon dissolution or otherwise, beyond the fixed dividends) is owned by such association, or members thereof; nor shall exemption be denied any such corporation because there is accumulated and maintained by it a reserve required by State law or a reasonable reserve for any necessary purpose;

(14) Corporations organized for the exclusive purpose of holding title to property, collecting income therefrom, and turning over the entire amount thereof, less expenses, to an organization which itself is exempt from the tax imposed by this chapter;

(15) Corporations organized under Act of Congress, if such corporations are instrumentalities of the United States and if, under such Act, as amended and supplemented, such corporations are exempt from Federal income taxes;

(16) Voluntary employees' beneficiary associations providing for the payment of life, sick, accident, or other benefits to the members of such association or their dependents, if (A) no part of their net earnings inures (other than through such payments) to the benefit of any private shareholder or individual, and (B) 85 per centum or more of the income consists of amounts collected from members and amounts contributed

to the association by the employer of the members for the sole purpose of making such payments and meeting expenses;

(17) Teachers' retirement fund associations of a purely local character, if (A) no part of their net earnings inures (other than through payment of retirement benefits) to the benefit of any private shareholder or individual, and (B) the income consists solely of amounts received from public taxation, amounts received from assessments upon the teaching salaries of members, and income in respect of investments;

(18) Religious or apostolic associations of corporations, if such associations or corporations have a common treasury or community treasury, even if such associations or corporations engage in business for the common benefit of the members, but only if the members thereof include (at the time of filing their returns) in their gross income their entire pro-rata shares, whether distributed or not, of the net income of the association or corporation for such year. Any amount so included in the gross income of a member shall be treated as a dividend received.

(19) Voluntary employees' beneficiary associations providing for the payment of life, sick, accident, or other benefits to the members of such association or their dependents or their designated beneficiaries, if (A) admission to membership in such association is limited to individuals who are officers or employees of the United States Government, and (B) no part of the net earnings of such association inures (other than through such payments) to the benefit of any private shareholder or individual.

APPENDIX B

SECTION 23 OF THE INTERNAL REVENUE CODE

[*The following is a direct quotation from Section 23 as it existed on January 1, 1950. The Revenue Act of 1950, summarized in Appendix I of this volume, affects Section 23 by providing that no deduction can be taken for gifts to certain 101 (6) and 162 (a) organizations which engage in "prohibited transactions."*]

In computing net income there shall be allowed as deductions: * * *.

(o) *Charitable and other contributions.* In the case of an individual, contributions or gifts payment of which is made within the taxable year to or for the use of:

(1) The United States, any State, Territory, or any political subdivision thereof or the District of Columbia, or any possession of the United States, for exclusively public purposes;

(2) A corporation, trust, or community chest, fund, or foundation, created or organized in the United States or in any possession thereof or under the law of the United States or of any State or Territory or of any possession of the United States, organized and operated exclusively for religious, charitable, scientific, literary, or educational purposes, or for the prevention of cruelty to children or animals, no part of the net earnings of which inures to the benefit of any private shareholder or individual, and no substantial part of the activities of which is carrying on propaganda, or otherwise attempting, to influence legislation;

(3) the special fund for vocational rehabilitation authorized by section 12 of the World War Veterans' Act, 1924, 43 Stat. 611 (U. S. C., Title 38, § 440);

(4) posts or organizations of war veterans, or auxiliary units or societies of any such posts or organizations, if such posts, organizations, units, or societies are organized in the United States or any of its possessions, and if no part of their net earnings inures to the benefit of any private shareholder or individual;

(5) a domestic fraternal society, order, or association, operating under the lodge system, but only if such contributions or gifts are to be used exclusively for religious, charitable, scientific, literary, or educational purposes, or for the prevention of cruelty to children or animals; or

267

(6) the United Nations, but only if such contributions or gifts (A) are to be used exclusively for the acquisition of a site in the city of New York for its headquarters, and (B) are made after December 1, 1946, and before December 2, 1947;

to an amount which in all the above cases combined does not exceed 15 per centum of the taxpayer's adjusted gross income. Such contributions or gifts shall be allowable as deductions only if verified under rules and regulations prescribed by the Commissioner, with the approval of the Secretary.

(p) *Contributions of an employer to an employee's trust or annuity plan and compensation under a deferred-payment plan.*

(1) *General rule.* If contributions are paid by an employer to or under a stock bonus, pension, profit-sharing, or annuity plan, or if compensation is paid or accrued on account of any employee under a plan deferring the receipt of such compensation, such contributions or compensation shall not be deductible under subsection (a) but shall be deductible, if deductible under subsection (a) without regard to this subsection, under this subsection but only to the following extent:

(A) In the taxable year when paid, if the contributions are paid into a pension trust, and if such taxable year ends within or with a taxable year of the trust for which the trust is exempt under section 165(a), in an amount determined as follows:

(i) an amount not in excess of 5 per centum of the compensation otherwise paid or accrued during the taxable year to all the employees under the trust, but such amount may be reduced for future years if found by the Commissioner upon periodical examinations at not less than five-year intervals to be more than the amount reasonably necessary to provide the remaining unfunded cost of past and current service credits of all employees under the plan, plus

(ii) any excess over the amount allowable under clause (i) necessary to provide with respect to all of the employees under the trust the remaining unfunded cost of their past and current service credits distributed as a level amount, or a level percentage of compensation, over the remaining future service of each such employee, as determined under regulations prescribed by the Commissioner with the approval of the Secretary, but if such remaining unfunded cost with respect to any three individuals is more than 50 per centum of such remaining unfunded cost, the amount of such unfunded cost attributable to such individuals shall be distributed over a period of at least 5 taxable years, or

(iii) in lieu of the amounts allowable under (i) and (ii) above, an amount equal to the normal cost of the plan, as determined under regulations prescribed by the Commissioner with the approval of the Secretary, plus, if past service or other supplementary pension or annuity credits are provided by the plan, an amount not in excess of 10 per centum of the cost which would be required to completely fund or purchase such pension or annuity credits as of the date when they are included in the plan, as determined under regulations prescribed by the Commissioner with the approval of the Secretary, except that in no case shall a deduction be allowed for any amount (other than the normal cost) paid in after such pension or annuity credits are completely funded or purchased.

(iv) Any amount paid in a taxable year in excess of the amount deductible in such year under the foregoing limitations shall be deductible in the succeeding taxable years in order of time to the extent of the difference between the amount paid and deductible in each such succeeding year and the maximum amount deductible for such year in accordance with the foregoing limitations.

(B) In the taxable year when paid, in an amount determined in accordance with subparagraph (A) of this paragraph, if the contributions are paid toward the purchase of retirement annuities and such purchase is a part of a plan which meets the requirements of section 165(a), (3), (4), (5), and (6), and if refunds of premiums, if any, are applied within the current taxable year or next succeeding taxable year towards the purchase of such retirement annuities.

(C) In the taxable year when paid, if the contributions are paid into a stock bonus or profit-sharing trust, and if such taxable year ends within or with a taxable year of the trust with respect to which the trust is exempt under section 165(a), in an amount not in excess of 15 per centum of the compensation otherwise paid or accrued during the taxable year to all employees under the stock bonus or profit-sharing plan. If in any taxable year beginning after December 31, 1941, there is paid into the trust, or a similar trust then in effect, amounts less than the amounts deductible under the preceding sentence, the excess, or if no amount is paid, the amounts deductible, shall be carried forward and be deductible when paid in the succeeding taxable years in order of time, but the amount so deductible under this sentence in any such succeeding taxable year shall not exceed 15 per centum of the compensation otherwise paid or accrued during such succeeding taxable year to the beneficiaries under the plan. In addition, any amount paid into the trust in a taxable year beginning after December 31, 1941, in excess of the amount allowable with respect to such year under the preceding provisions of this subparagraph shall be deductible in the succeeding taxable years in order of time, but the amount so deductible under this sentence in any one such succeeding taxable year together with the amount allowable under the first sentence of this subparagraph shall not exceed 15 per centum of the compensation otherwise paid or accrued during such taxable year to the beneficiaries under the plan. The term "stock bonus or profit-sharing trust," as used in this subparagraph, shall not include any trust designed to provide benefits upon retirement and covering a period of years, if under the plan the amounts to be contributed by the employer can be determined actuarily as provided in subparagraph (A). If the contributions are made to two or more stock bonus or profit-sharing trusts, such trusts shall be considered a single trust for the purposes of applying the limitations in this subparagraph.

(D) In the taxable year when paid, if the plan is not one included in paragraphs (A), (B), or (C), if the employees' rights to or derived from such employer's contribution or such compensation are nonforfeitable at the time the contribution or compensation is paid.

(E) For the purposes of subparagraphs (A), (B), and (C), a taxpayer on the accrual basis shall be deemed to have made a payment on the last day of the year of accrual if the payment is on account of such taxable year and is made within sixty days after the close of the taxable year of accrual.

(F) If amounts are deductible under subparagraphs (A) and (C), or (B) and (C), or (A), (B), and (C), in connection with two or more trusts, or one or more trusts and an annuity plan, the total amount deductible in a taxable year under such trusts and plans shall not exceed 25 per centum of the compensation otherwise paid or accrued during the taxable year to the persons who are the beneficiaries of the trusts or plans. In addition, any amount paid into such trust or under such annuity plans in a taxable year beginning after December 31, 1941, in excess of the amount allowable with respect to such year under the preceding provisions of this subparagraph shall be deductible in the succeeding taxable years in order of time, but the amount so deductible under this sentence in any one such succeeding taxable year together with the amount allowable under the first sentence of this subparagraph shall not exceed 30 per centum of the compensation otherwise paid or accrued during such taxable years to the beneficiaries under the trusts or plans. This subparagraph shall not have the effect of reducing the amount otherwise deductible under subparagraphs (A), (B), and (C), if no employee is a beneficiary under more than one trust, or a trust and an annuity plan.

If there is no plan but a method of employer contributions or compensation has the effect of a stock bonus, pension, profit-sharing, or annuity plan, or similar plan deferring the receipt of compensation, this paragraph shall apply as if there were such a plan.

(2) *Deductions under prior income tax acts.* Any deduction allowable under section 23(q) of the Revenue Act of 1928 (45 Stat. 802), or the Revenue Act of 1932 (47 Stat. 182), or the Revenue Act of 1934 (48 Stat. 691), under section 23(p) of the Revenue Act of 1936 (49 Stat. 1661), or the Revenue Act of 1938 (52 Stat. 464), or the Internal Revenue Code for a taxable year beginning before January 1, 1942, which under such section was apportioned to any taxable year beginning after December 31, 1941, shall be allowed as a deduction for the years to which so apportioned to the extent allowable under such section if it had remained in force with respect to such year.

(3) *Exemption of trust under section 165.* The provisions of paragraphs (1) and (2) of this subsection shall be subject to the qualification that the deduction under either paragraph shall be allowable only with respect to a taxable year (whether the year of the transfer or payment or a subsequent year) of the employer ending within or with a taxable year of the trust with respect to which the trust is exempt from tax under section 165.

(q) *Charitable and other contributions by corporations.* In the case of a corporation, contributions or gifts payment of which is made within the taxable year to or for the use of:

(1) The United States, any State, Territory, or any political subdivision thereof or the District of Columbia, or any possession of the United States, for exclusively public purposes; or

(2) A corporation, trust, or community chest, fund, or foundation, created or organized in the United States or in any possession thereof or under the law of the United States, or of any State or Territory, or of the District of Columbia, or of any possession of the United States, organized and operated exclusively for religious, charitable, scientific, veteran rehabilitation service, literary, or educational purposes or for the prevention of cruelty to children (but in the case of contributions or gift to a trust, chest, fund, or foundation, payment of which is made within a taxable year beginning after December 31, 1948, only if such contributions or gifts are to be used within the United States or any of its possessions exclusively for such purposes), no part of the net earnings of which inures to the benefit of any private shareholder or individual, and no substantial part of the activities of which is carrying on propaganda, or otherwise attempting, to influence legislation; or

(3) Posts or organizations of war veterans, or auxiliary units of, or trusts or foundations for, any such posts or organizations, if such posts,

organizations, units, trusts, or foundations are organized in the United States or any of its possessions, and if no part of their net earnings inure to the benefit of any private shareholder or individual; or

(4) the United Nations, but only if such contributions or gifts (A) are to be used exclusively for the acquisition of a site in the city of New York for its headquarters, and (B) are made after December 1, 1946, and before December 2, 1947;

to an amount which does not exceed 5 per centum of the taxpayer's net income as computed without the benefits of this subsection. Such contributions or gifts shall be allowable as deductions only if verified under rules and regulations prescribed by the Commissioner, with the approval of the Secretary. * * *.

APPENDIX C

REGULATION OF ORGANIZATIONS AND INDIVIDUALS SOLICITING PUBLIC ALMS IN NORTH CAROLINA

N. C. Gen. Stat. of 1943 (Supp. 1947)

§ *108–80. Regulation of solicitation of public aid for charitable, etc., purposes.*— Except as hereinafter provided in G. S. § 108–84, no person, organization, corporation, institution, association, agency or co-partnership except in accordance with provisions of this article shall solicit the public whether by mail, or through agents or representatives or other means for donations, gifts or subscriptions of money and/or of gifts of goods, wares, merchandise or other things of value or to sell or offer for sale or distribute to the public anything or object whatever to raise money or to sell memberships, periodicals, books or advertising space or to secure or attempt to secure money or donations or other property by promoting any public bazaar, sale, entertainment or exhibition or by any similar means for any charitable, benevolent, health, educational, religious, patriotic or other similar public cause or for the purpose of relieving suffering of animals unless the solicitation is authorized by and the money or other goods or property is to be given to an organization, corporation, institution, association, agency or co-partnership holding a valid license for such purpose from the state board of public welfare, issued as herein provided. (*1939, c. 144, s. 1; 1947, c. 572.*)

§ *108–81. Application for license to solicit public aid.*—Any person, organization, corporation, institution, association, agency or co-partnership wishing to secure a license from the state board of public welfare for the purpose of soliciting the public for any of the aforenamed causes shall file a written application with the state board of public welfare on a form furnished by the said board setting forth proof of the worthiness of the cause, chartered responsibility, the existence of an adequate and responsible governing board to administer receipts and disbursements of funds, goods, or other property sought, the need of public solicitation, proposed use of funds sought, and a verified report of the operation of such organization, corporation, institution, association, agency or co-partnership for a fiscal period determined by the said state board, said verified report to show reserve funds and endowment funds as well as receipts and disbursements. (*1939, c. 144, s. 1; 1947, c. 572.*)

§ *108–82. Issuance of license by state board of public welfare.*—If the state board of public welfare after full investigation and careful study of the purpose and functioning of an organization, corporation, institution, association, agency, or co-partnership filing an application for a license to solicit deems such organization, corporation, institution, association, agency or co-partnership a proper one and not inimical to the public welfare and its proposed solicitations to be truly for the purpose set forth in its application and provided for in this article, it shall issue to such organization, corporation, institution, association, agency or co-partnership a license to solicit for its purposes and program for a period not to exceed one year, unless revoked for cause.

The state board of public welfare shall not issue a license to solicit to any such organization, corporation, institution, association, agency or co-partnership which pays or agrees to pay to any individual, corporation, co-partnership or association an unreasonable or exorbitant amount of the funds collected as compensation.

In the event the said board refuses to issue said license, the organization, corporation, institution, association, agency or co-partnership shall be entitled to a hearing before said board provided written request therefor is made within fifteen days after notice of refusal is delivered or mailed to the applicant. All such hearings shall be held in the offices of said board and shall be open to the public. Decisions of said board shall be mailed to the interested parties within ten days after the hearing.

The state board of public welfare before granting or refusing a license as herein provided shall call upon the state commission for the blind, the division of vocational rehabilitation and other divisions of the state department of public instruction, the bureau of labor for the deaf, and the state board of health for advice in any situation or cause in which any of the several state agencies named has an interest or responsibility. (*1939, c. 144, s. 1; 1947, c. 572.*)

§ *108–83. Solicitors and collectors must have evidence of authority to show same on request.*—No person shall solicit or collect any contribution in money or other property for any of the purposes set forth in this article without a written authorization, pledge card, receipt form, or other evidence of authority to solicit for a duly licensed organization, corporation, institution, association, agency, or co-partnership for which the donation or contribution is made and said evidence of authority must be shown to any person on request. Said evidence of authority must be provided by the organization, corporation, institution, association, agency or co-partnership for which the donation or contribution is solicited or by the agency through which the donation or contribution is collected and distributed. (*1939, c. 144, s. 2; 1947, c. 572.*)

§ *108–84. Organizations, etc., exempted from article.*—The provisions of this article shall not apply to any solicitation or appeal made by any church, or religious organization, school or college, fraternal or patriotic organization, or civic club located in this state when such appeal or solicitation is confined to its membership nor shall the provisions of this article apply to any locally indigenous organization, institution, association or agency having its own office, managing board, committee or trustees or chief executive offices located in or residing in a city or county from publicly soliciting donations or contributions within a city and the county or counties in which said city is located or within the county in which such an organization, institution, association or agency is located and operates; provided that nothing in this article shall apply to any solicitation or appeal by any church for the construction, upkeep, or maintenance of the church and its established organization or for the support of its clergy. (*1939, c. 144, s. 2a; 1947, c. 572.*)

§ *108–85. Regulations and licensing of solicitation of alms for individual livelihood.*—It shall be unlawful for an individual to engage in the business of soliciting alms or begging charity for his or her own livelihood or for the livelihood of another individual upon the streets or highways of this state or through door to door solicitations without first securing a license to solicit for this purpose from the state board of public welfare.

Any individual desiring to engage in the business of soliciting alms or begging charity for his or her own livelihood or for the livelihood of another individual as set forth in the first paragraph of this section shall file a written application for a license on a form or forms furnished by the said board, setting forth his or her own true name and address, his or her correct address or addresses for the past five years, the purpose for which he or she desires to solicit alms, the reason why public solicitation is considered a necessary means to obtain a livelihood or relief from suffering rather than the pursuit of a legitimate trade or the acceptance of benefits provided through the social security measures and funds administered by the federal, state and county governments and any other information which the said board may deem necessary to carry out the provisions of this article. A copy of the license must be carried by the solicitor while soliciting and must be shown upon request.

The carrying and offering for sale of merchandise by the individual soliciting alms or begging charity shall not exempt the individual so soliciting from the provisions of this article. The state board of public welfare shall call upon the several state agencies named in § 108–82 for advice in issuing a license to an individual in accordance with the provisions of this article. (*1947, c. 572.*)

§ *108–86. Punishment for violation of article; misapplication of funds collected.*—Any person who, or any organization, corporation, institution,

APPENDIX D

TRUST AGREEMENT FOR THE BENEFIT OF AN EDUCATIONAL INSTITUTION

* * * * * *

TRUST AGREEMENT

THIS AGREEMENT made this .... day of ...., A.D. 1950, and executed in quadruplicate, by and between John Doe of the City of ...., County of ...., State of ...., hereinafter referred to as the Donor, and John Doe, Richard Roe, and William Jones, all of the City of ...., County of ...., State of ...., and John Smith of the City of ...., County of ...., State of ...., hereinafter referred to as the Trustees, Witnesseth:

WHEREAS the Donor desires to create a trust of certain personal property for certain educational uses and purposes, and particularly for such purposes in connection with .... College, a corporation organized under the State of ....

Now THEREFORE in consideration of the premises and the sum of One Dollar ($1.00) lawful money of the United States by each of the Trustees to the Donor paid at or before the ensealing and delivery of these presents, the Donor has sold, assigned, transferred and set over, and by these presents does sell, assign, transfer and set over unto the Trustees and their successors with proper supplemental transfers where necessary to pass title, the property described in Schedule "A" hereto annexed and signed by the parties hereto and by specific reference made a part hereof—

To HAVE AND To HOLD the said property, and such as shall be added thereto, in trust for the uses and purposes hereinafter set forth, as follows:

FIRST: To pay or expend the entire net income derived from said property to and/or for the benefit of said College and/or any other educational institution which the Trustees in their sole and uncontrolled discretion shall select and/or for scholarships in said College or said other educational institution and to make said payments upon such conditions, trusts, and limitations as the Trustees in their sole and uncontrolled discretion shall determine.

277

SECOND: To form or cause to be formed, and/or to operate or cause to be operated, in the furtherance of the aforementioned purposes, one or more charitable, scientific, or educational corporations or unincorporated trusts, or any other charitable, scientific, or educational organization, if the Trustees in their sole and uncontrolled discretion shall deem it so advisable.

THIRD: From and after the .... day of ...., A.D. 1950, to expend any part or all of the property and principal of this trust for the uses and purposes hereinbefore described.

FOURTH: (A more explicit statement of the powers of the Trustees is necessary, and should probably include specific delegation of investment powers and a prohibition against using the principal or income of the trust for purposes not meeting the requirements of the Internal Revenue Code. An example of such a prohibition is contained in Appendix E.)

FIFTH: (A provision for the designation of substitute Trustees is also desirable.)

IN WITNESS WHEREOF, the parties hereto have hereunto set their hands and seals on the day and year first above written.

* * * * * *

This example of a trust agreement is submitted with the caveat that it is *only an example*. The form and content of any particular trust agreement must necessarily differ widely with the jurisdiction and the particular circumstances.

A P P E N D I X   E

FOUNDATION CHARTER AND ANNOTATION OF STATE
LAWS GOVERNING THE CREATION OF CHARITABLE
CORPORATIONS

* * * * *

CERTIFICATE OF INCORPORATION
OF
THE X CORPORATION

(Pursuant to Membership Corporation Law)

We, the undersigned, desiring to form a membership corporation
pursuant to the Membership Corporation Law of the State of New
York, do hereby make, sign and acknowledge this certificate as follows:

First: The name of this corporation shall be THE X CORPORA-
TION.

Second: The purposes for which this corporation is to be formed
are as follows:

To make donations for charitable, scientific and educational
purposes, and particularly to initiate, promote, subsidize and/or
carry on research in man's relationships with his fellow men, the
components of those relationships and means of modifying those
components to the advantage of the individual and/or society; to
grant educational scholarships and/or fellowships in any art or
science.

In furtherance of the said purposes, to accept, receive, hold, invest, reinvest, manage and administer gifts, legacies, bequests,
devises, funds, trusts, benefits of trusts, and property of any sort or
nature, without limitation as to amount or value, and to use, apply,
employ, expend, disburse and/or donate income and/or principal
thereof for, and/or devote the same to, exclusively charitable,
scientific or educational purposes, in accordance with the specific
terms and purposes defined or limited by any will or other written
instrument by which any property is conveyed to this corporation.

Either directly or indirectly, either alone or in conjunction or cooperation with others, whether such others be persons or organizations of any sort or nature, such as firms, associations, trusts, partner-

279

ships, foundations, syndicates, institutions or agencies, to do any and all lawful acts and things, to engage in any and all lawful activities, which may be necessary, useful, suitable, desirable or proper for the furtherance, accomplishment, fostering or attainment of any or all of the foregoing purposes; and, among other things, to initiate, promote, subsidize, foster and/or carry on research, knowledge or training in any and all fields relating to the purposes of this corporation, to disseminate the findings of such research, to publish or cause to be published, or to assist in the publication of, books, pamphlets, magazines, articles, papers and other publications in furtherance of, or relating to, or connected with, any of the foregoing purposes, and to establish, maintain, operate, aid, and/or assist institutions or organizations of any sort, the activities of which shall be such as to further, accomplish, foster or attain any of the purposes for which this corporation is organized, *provided* that such institutions and organizations shall be organized and operated exclusively for charitable, scientific or educational purposes.

In all events and under all circumstances, including, but not limited to, merger, reorganization, termination, dissolution or winding up of this corporation, voluntary or involuntary or by operation of law, or amendment of the articles of this corporation—

(a) No part of the activities of this corporation shall consist of carrying on propaganda, or otherwise attempting, to influence legislation; nor shall it engage in any activities which are unlawful under the laws of the United States of America, or the State of New York, or any other state where such activities are carried on; nor shall it engage in any transaction defined at the time as "prohibited" under the internal revenue laws (codified or otherwise) of the United States of America.

(b) This corporation shall never be operated for the primary purpose of carrying on a trade or business for profit. Neither the whole nor any part or portion of the assets or net income of this corporation shall be used, nor shall this corporation ever be organized or operated, for objects or purposes which are not exclusively religious, charitable, scientific, literary or educational under the laws of both the United States of America and the State of New York.

(c) No compensation or payment shall ever be paid or made to any member, officer, director, trustee, creator or organizer of this corporation, except as a reasonable allowance for actual expenditures or services actually rendered; and neither the whole nor any part or portion of the assets or net income, current or accumulated, of this corporation shall ever be distributed to or divided among any such persons; provided, further, that neither the whole nor any part or portion of such assets or net income shall ever be used for, accrue to, or inure to the benefit of, any private individual within the meaning of the tax-exemption requirements or the laws of both the United States of America and the State of New York.

THIRD: The territory in which the operations of this corporation are principally to be conducted is the United States of America, but the corporation may do any one or more of the acts or things herein set forth as its purposes outside of the United States of America, and in territories and dependencies of the United States of America, and in foreign countries.

FOURTH: The principal office of this corporation is to be located at .... Street, in the Borough of Manhattan, City, County, and State of New York.

FIFTH: The number of directors of this corporation shall be not less than three (3) nor more than nine (9), as shall be provided in the by-laws.

SIXTH: The names and places of residence of the persons to be its directors until the first annual meeting are as follows:

Name	*Address*
....	....
....	....

SEVENTH: All of the subscribers to this Certificate are of full age, at least two-thirds of them are citizens of the United States of America, and at least one of them is a resident of the State of New York. Of the persons named as directors, at least one is a citizen of the United States of America and a resident of the State of New York.

IN WITNESS WHEREOF, we have hereunto set our hands and seals this .... day of ...., 1950.

* * * * * * *

Whereas some foundations exist as unincorporated charitable trusts or associations, most foundations are set up as corporations, and it is in the latter sense that they are commonly understood. Several corporate foundations have been established by special acts of Congress; and a few others have been chartered both by Congress and under state laws. The great majority, however, are simply chartered under the laws of a particular state and are usually of the non-stock variety.

State laws, of course, differ widely in their provisions for creating charitable and kindred corporations. Some state statutes have separate provisions for creating them, depending upon their particular purposes; whereas other statutes place all such corporations together under a single provision. Moreover, some states make it possible to organize foundations in different corporate forms, notably as stock or non-stock corporations; whereas other states provide a single method of organization. Only three state statutes specifically refer to "foundations" as such. IND. ANN. STAT. §1101 (Burns Supp. 1948); MICH. STAT. ANN. §21.164 (Henderson, 1937); *cf.* S. C. CODE ANN. §8173 (1942) ("Masonic foundation").

The provisions in each state under which an ordinary charitable foundation (*e.g.*, "for the welfare of mankind") may be incorporated are as follows: ALA. CODE, tit. 10, §124 (1941); ARIZ. CODE ANN. §53–408 (1939); ARK. DIG. STAT. §2252 (1937); CAL. CORP. CODE §§9200, 10200 (1948); COLO. STAT. ANN., c. 41, §172 (1935); CONN. GEN. STAT. §3498 (1930), *as amended*, CONN. GEN. STAT. §1402c (1935); DEL. REV. CODE §§2033, 2037 (1935); D. C. CODE, tit. 29, §601 (1940); FLA. STAT. ANN. 617.01 (1944); GA. CODE ANN. §22–413 (1933); Act. No. 259 of GA. LAWS 1937–1938 (Extra Session) §42, p. 245, *as amended*, Act. No. 220 of GA. LAWS 1949 p. 953; IDAHO CODE §29–1101 (Supp. 1940); ILL. STAT. ANN. §32.256 (4, 28) (Supp., Jones, 1947); IND. STAT. ANN. §§521, 1101 (Burns, 1948); IOWA CODE §504.1 (1946); KAN. GEN. STAT. ANN., c. 17, §§201, 1701 (1935); KY. REV. STAT. §§273.020, 273.160 (4th ed. 1948); LA. GEN. STAT. ANN. §1260 (1939); ME. REV. STAT., c. 50, §1 (1944); MD. ANN. CODE GEN. LAWS art. 23, §2 (1939); MASS. ANN. LAWS, c. 3, §7 (1944); *id.*, c. 180, §1 (1933); MICH. STAT. ANN. §§21.149, 21.164 (Henderson, 1937); *id.* §21.118 (Supp., Reis, 1947); MINN. STAT. ANN. §309.01 (West 1945); MISS. CODE ANN. §5310 (Supp. 1946); MO. REV. STAT. ANN. §5436 (1939); MONT. REV. CODES §§5905, 5906, 6454 (1935); *id.* §6453 (Supp., 1947); NEB. REV. STAT. §§21–102, 21–601, 21–1501 (1943); NEV. COMP. LAWS ANN. §§1853, 3215 (Supp. 1947); N. H. REV. LAWS, c. 272, §1 (1942); N. J. REV. STAT. §15:1–1 (1937); N. M. STAT. ANN. 54–1306 (1941); N. Y. MEMBERSHIP CORPS. LAW §10; N. C. GEN. STAT. ANN. §55–2 (Supp. 1948); N. D. REV. CODE, §10–0801 (1943); OHIO GEN. CODE ANN. §§8623–97, 10085 (1938); OKLA. STAT., tit. 18, §§12, 541 (1941); ORE. COMP. LAWS ANN. §77–401 (Supp. 1943); PA. STAT. ANN., tit. 15, §§2851–201, 2851–212, 2851–213 (1938); R. I. GEN. LAWS, c. 116, §72 (1938); S. C. CODE ANN. §8158 (1942); S. D. CODE §§11.0201, 11.1401 (1939); TENN. CODE ANN. §4146 (Williams, 1934); TEX. STAT. REV., civ. arts. 1302, art. 1396 (1945) (Cum. Supp. 1948); UTAH CODE ANN. §18–6–1 (1943); VER. STAT. §5754 (1947); VA. CODE ANN. §3872 (1942); WASH. REV. STAT. ANN. §§3863, 3872, 3892 (1932); W. VA. CODE ANN. §3016 (1943); WIS. STAT. §180.01 (1947); WYO. COMP. STAT. ANN. §§44–101, 44–1001, 44–1015 (1945).

It should be noted, in this regard, that the vast majority of states have specific constitutional provisions requiring that all corporations be organized under general laws. ALA. CONST. Art. XII, §229, *as amended*, AMEND. XXVII; ARIZ. CONST. Art. XIV, §2; CALIF. CONST. Art. XII, §1; FLA. CONST. Art. III, §25; IDAHO CONST. Art. III, §19; IND. CONST. Art. XI, §13; IOWA CONST. Art. VIII, §1; KAN. CONST. Art. XI, §1; KY. CONST. §59 (17); LA. CONST. Art. IV, §4 [though Code specifically refers to charitable corporation formed under special acts, LA. GEN. STAT. ANN. §1306 (1939)]; MICH. CONST. Art. XII, §1; MINN. CONST. Art. IV, §33; *id.* Art. X, §2; MISS. CONST. Art. IV, §§87, 88; *id.* Art. VII, §178; MO. CONST. Art. IV, §53 (25); *id.* Art. XII, §2; N. J. CONST. Art. IV, §7, para. 11; N. M. CONST. Art. IV, §24; *id.* Art. XI, §13; OHIO CONST. Art. XIII, §1; OKLA. CONST. Art. IX, §38; ORE. CONST. Art. XI, §2; TENN. CONST. Art. XI, §8; TEX. CONST. Art. XII, §1; UTAH CONST. Art. XII, §1; VA. CONST. Art. IV, §63 (17); *id.* Art. XII, §154; WASH. CONST. Art. II, §28 (6); *id.* Art. XII, §1; W. VA. CONST. Art. XI, §1; *cf.* GA. CONST. Art. I, §4 (1); MD. CONST. Art. III, §48; NEV. CONST. Art. VIII, §1; PA. CONST. Art. III, §7; *id.* Art. XVI, §10; R. I. CONST. Art. IV, §17, *as amended*, AMEND. IX; WIS. CONST. Art. IV, §31 (7); WYO. CONST. Art. III, §27; *id.* Art. X, §1. Eleven states, however, permit the granting of special charters to state-controlled charities; ARK. CONST. Art. XII, §2; COLO. CONST. Art. XV, §2; DEL. CONST. Art. IX, §1; ILL. CONST. Art. XI, §1; MONT. CONST. Art. XV, §2; NEB. CONST. Art. XII, §1; N. C. CONST. Art. VIII, §1; N. D. CONST. Art. VII, §131; S. C. CONST. Art. IX, §2; *id.* Art. III, §34; S. D. CONST. Art. XVII, §1; VER. CONST. c. 11, §65; a few states permit such charters where the purposes of the corporation would not be otherwise attainable; *e.g.*, ME. CONST. Art. IV, pt. 3, §14; N. Y. CONST. Art. X, §1; WIS. CONST. Art. XI, §1; and one state permits special charters where they are proposed by a two-thirds vote of both Houses. S. C. CONST. Art. IX, §2. In states where no pertinent constitutional provision exists, special charters are presumably available. *I.e.*, Conn., Mass., N. H.; *cf.* D. C.

APPENDIX F

BEQUEST TO CHARITIES

I hereby give, devise and bequeath, free and clear of all inheritance taxes, as follows: To the .... Home for Old Ladies of ...., the sum of .... Dollars ($); to the .... Hospital of ...., a corporation organized and existing under the laws of the State of ...., the sum of .... Dollars ($); to the American National Red Cross, ... Chapter, the sum of .... Dollars ($); and to .... Trust Company, Trustee of .... Community Trust, the sum of .... Dollars ($) for the purposes and upon the conditions named in the (resolution, agreement, or charter, describing it more fully if necessary) creating said .... Community Trust.

* * * * *

This example of a bequest to several charities is suitable for insertion as an independent clause in any ordinary will. It must, of course, be altered to fit the particular circumstances.

APPENDIX G

GEOGRAPHICAL LIST OF COMMUNITY TRUSTS
(Limited to community trusts in the United States reporting assets of at least $50,000)

California

California Community Foundation
Security-First National Bank of Los Angeles
Terminal Annex—Box 2097
Los Angeles 54, Calif.

Alameda County Community Foundation
c/o Mr. D. L. Anderson, Sec.
Central Bank
Oakland, Calif.

Santa Barbara Foundation
11 East Carrillo St.
Santa Barbara, Calif.

Colorado

Colorado Springs Community Trust Fund
28 East Boulder St.
Colorado Springs, Colo.

Denver Foundation
First National Bank Bldg.
Denver 2, Colo.

Connecticut

Hartford Foundation for Public Giving
c/o Gross, Hyde & Williams
49 Pearl St.
Hartford 3, Conn.

New Haven Foundation
Box 1936
New Haven 9, Conn.

Connecticut, continued

Waterbury Foundation
Waterbury Savings Bank
P. O. Drawer 2060
Waterbury 20, Conn.

Illinois

Centralia Foundation
Old National Bank
Centralia, Ill.

Chicago Community Trust
10 South La Salle St.
Chicago 3, Ill.

Indiana

Indianapolis Foundation
1012 Hume Mansur Bldg.
Indianapolis 4, Ind.

Massachusetts

Permanent Charity Fund, Committee of the
100 Franklin St.
Boston 10, Mass.

Cambridge Foundation
Harvard Trust Co.
Cambridge 38, Mass.

Michigan

Detroit Community Trust
Detroit Trust Co.
201 Fort St., W.
Detroit 31, Mich.

Michigan, continued

Grand Rapids Foundation
201 Michigan Trust Bldg.
Grand Rapids 2, Mich.

Kalamazoo Foundation
First National Bank & Trust Co.
104 East Michigan Ave.
Kalamazoo 4, Mich.

Minnesota

Minneapolis Foundation
115 South Fifth St.
Minneapolis 2, Minn.

New Jersey

Plainfield Foundation
202 Park Ave.
Plainfield, N. J.

New York

Buffalo Foundation
232 Delaware Ave.
Buffalo 2, N. Y.

Glens Falls Foundation
c/o The First National Bank
of Glens Falls
Glens Falls, N. Y.

New York Community Trust
250 Park Ave.
New York 17, N. Y.

Rochester Community Chest, Inc.
70 North Water St.
Rochester 4, N. Y.

Watertown Foundation, Inc.
118 Washington St.
Watertown, N. Y.

North Carolina

Durham Foundation
Durham Bank & Trust Company
Durham, N. C.

North Carolina, continued

Winston-Salem Foundation
Wachovia Bank & Trust Co.
P. O. Box 3099
Winston-Salem 1, N. C.

Ohio

Cleveland Foundation
1338 Terminal Tower Bldg.
Cleveland 13, Ohio

Columbus Foundation
400 South Front St.
Columbus 15, Ohio

Dayton Foundation
403 West First St.
Dayton 2, Ohio

Mount Vernon Community Trust
Mount Vernon
Ohio

Toledo Foundation
The Ohio Citizens Trust Co.
Toledo, Ohio

Youngstown Foundation
c/o The Dollar Savings & Trust
Co.
Youngstown, Ohio

Oklahoma

Tulsa Permanent Community
Trust Fund
First National Bank & Trust Co.
Box 2240
Tulsa 2, Okla.

Pennsylvania

Lancaster Community Trust
Chamber of Commerce Bldg.
45 East Orange St.
Lancaster, Pa.

Philadelphia Foundation
135 South Broad St.
Philadelphia 9, Pa.

Pennsylvania, continued

Pittsburgh Foundation
1002 Farmers Bank Bldg.
Pittsburgh 22, Pa.

Williamsport Foundation
102 West Fourth St.
Williamsport 2, Pa.

Rhode Island

Rhode Island Foundation
15 Westminster St.
Providence 3, R. I.

South Carolina

Spartanburg County Foundation
906 Montgomery Bldg.
Spartanburg, S. C.

Texas

Dallas Foundation
City State Bank of Dallas
Dallas 2, Texas

Virginia

Richmond Foundation
Virginia Trust Co.
821 East Main St.
Richmond 14, Va.

Washington

Seattle Foundation
Meals & Co.
1411 Fourth Ave.
Seattle 1, Wash.

Wisconsin

Madison Community Trust Fund
The First National Bank
1 South Pinckney St.
Madison 1, Wis.

Milwaukee Foundation
First Wisconsin Trust Co.
Box 2054
Milwaukee 1, Wis.

APPENDIX H

DERIVATION OF ESTIMATES OF INDIVIDUAL GIVING

Income-tax reports of individuals, which until recent years included charitable contributions on all reports as a separate item, would seem an appropriate source for comprehensive and comparative data on individual giving, and they have frequently been so used. Unfortunately they are neither comprehensive nor closely comparable. A workable estimate requires cautious use of these figures, and their supplementation from other sources.

The requirements for filing income-tax reports have varied greatly, but have never reached into the very lowest brackets of wage-earners and income recipients.[1] A few examples from the period covered in our study will illustrate these variations. In 1929, returns were required of married persons living with husband or wife only if net income was $3,500 or more, or gross income reached $5,000; of single individuals, if net income was $1,500, or gross income $5,000. For income years 1932 through 1939 married persons with net income of $2,500 or more and single persons with net income of $1,000 were required to file returns; the gross income requirement remained at $5,000. Beginning with 1940, net income was no longer a criterion, and the gross income requirement became $2,000 for married persons and $800 for single persons. In the next two years successive tightenings of the law reduced the filing requirements by 1942 to $1,200 gross income for married persons and $500 for single persons. Currently, everyone with a gross income of $600 or more is required to file a return.

It is obvious that widely varying proportions of the personal income of the country are represented in income-tax returns under these varying provisions. Any attempt at comprehensive or comparative figures must allow for the omitted groups.

Throughout the period a deduction from taxable income was permitted for charitable contributions up to 15 per cent of income—but the word "income" was defined first as net income, and later as adjusted gross income. In neither case would the tabulations of contributions from the Bureau of Internal Revenue show any contributions in excess of 15 per cent of income, even if the taxpayer had itemized them on his return. But since the over-all contribution rate has usually been less

---

[1] A summary of the filing provisions of the various acts appears in the Bureau of Internal Revenue's *Statistics of Income for 1943*, Part 1, p. 344.

288

than 2 per cent, it is believed that the number of persons who contributed more than 15 per cent of income to philanthropy in any year is not large, and the sums here omitted are not a significant part of the total.

It is probable that taxpayers in some instances overstated their charitable contributions to secure a larger exemption; in some cases they may have understated them through oversight or lack of knowledge of their privileges under the law. No way exists for estimating either error, though one suspects the former considerably exceeds the latter.

It is known that many taxpayers understate their income. In earlier years the Bureau of Internal Revenue investigated many separate returns, chiefly those on which doubt was felt, but these findings were a selected sample and could not be applied percentagewise to total reported income. In 1948 an attempt at random sampling was made. Only preliminary findings are available, but these have been used as a guide in our tabulations.

Such understatement of income has two effects. The gap between actual total personal income in the United States and the total reported by persons filing returns is not so large as the figures indicate, and the contribution *rate*, being based on under-reported income, appears higher than in fact it was. We think neither of these factors seriously affects the ratios computed and recorded in this volume, but both have been given some weight in our total estimates.

The more serious problem is to determine accurately the gap between total personal income and the portion of that income represented in income-tax returns itemizing contributions. In earlier years minimum filing provisions were so high that less than half, and sometimes less than a third, of personal income was represented in income-tax reports. In the 1940's this minimum was drastically lowered; in 1943, for example, income-tax returns covered total income of more than $106 billion out of an estimated personal income for that year of $115 billion. But from 1941 through 1943 a new provision had come into effect under which persons with incomes below $3,000 were permitted to file a short form 1040A with a standard deduction in place of itemization of contributions. This reduced by $31 billion, in 1943, the amount of income on which contributions were reported. However, for these years some opportunity was offered to study the contribution rates of the low-income givers who did itemize their reports, and results of this study are presented in Chapter 4.

In 1944 a further change in the law greatly widened the opportunity for taking a standard deduction; persons with gross income of less than $5,000 could deduct 10 per cent without itemizing, and persons with larger incomes could deduct a maximum of $500 without itemizing. From that year on, fewer than one taxpayer in five itemized contributions. Most of those who did itemize had either very large incomes or had in that year unusually heavy deductible items, among which may have been contributions. It had become manifestly unsafe to use these reported contributions, either in their totals or in proportion to income, as an index of giving. Table 45 presents this situation with respect to 1946 reports.

TABLE 45. INDIVIDUAL INCOME-TAX RETURNS AS RELATED TO STANDARD AND ITEMIZED DEDUCTIONS, BY ADJUSTED GROSS INCOME CLASSES, 1946

Gross income class	Returns			Gross income			Contributions	
	Standard deduction (millions)	Itemized deduction	Per cent itemized[a]	Standard deduction (billions)	Itemized deduction	Per cent itemized[a]	Amount (millions)	Per cent of gross income[a]
Under $5,000	42.3	7.2	14.5	$80.6	$17.7	18.0	$843	4.8
$5,000 under $10,000	1.4	.9	39.1	9.2	6.1	39.9	240	3.9
$10,000 and over	.4	.6	67.5	4.8	15.8	76.8	556	3.5

[a] Percentages were derived from nonrounded figures.
SOURCE: *Statistics of Income for 1946*, Treasury Department.

For years earlier than 1944, however, considerable information is available on contributions from incomes representing a substantial part of total personal income. The problem is to determine year by year the gap between income reported and total personal income, and estimate the contribution from the unreported income on a sound basis.

This has been attempted in Table 46, which presents in its first column the Department of Commerce estimates of total personal income[1] from 1929 through 1949. The definition of personal income used by the Department of Commerce, however, is not comparable with that of the Bureau of Internal Revenue. A government interdepartmental committee has been working on reconciliation of these two series, and its findings have been heavily relied upon in arriving at the figures in Column 2, which adjusts the Department of Commerce estimates to the Bureau of Internal Revenue (BIR) concept of income.

Among the more important items involved in this adjustment are these. The Commerce figure should be reduced by the amount of transfer payments, such as benefits from social insurance, direct relief, military pensions, and disability payments. Certain "labor income" items, such as compensation for injuries and employer contributions to private pension funds, should be deducted. Personal income in kind,

[1] From *Survey of Current Business*, July, 1949, p. 10; *Ibid.*, February, 1950, p. 8.

TABLE 46. ESTIMATES OF PHILANTHROPIC CONTRIBUTIONS FROM PERSONAL INCOME, 1929–1949

Dollar figures in millions

Year	Total personal income		Persons reporting contributions			Persons not reporting contributions			Total contributions	
	1 Dept. of Commerce estimates	2 Adjusted to BIR definition	3 Income	4 Contributions	5 Per cent of income	6 Income (col. 2 minus 3)	7 Estimated contribution rate	8 Estimated contributions	9 Total contributions	10 Per cent of total income
1929	$ 85,127	$ 72,393	$30,747	$ 540	1.76	$ 41,646	1.23	$ 512	$1,052	1.45
1930	76,195	64,574	24,524	434	1.77	40,050	1.24	497	931	1.44
1931	64,835	53,752	15,568	354	2.27	38,184	1.59	607	961	1.79
1932	49,274	39,960	15,224	317	2.08	24,736	1.46	361	678	1.70
1933	46,629	38,181	14,120	282	2.00	24,061	1.40	337	619	1.62
1934	53,230	44,567	15,437	280	1.81	29,130	1.27	370	650	1.46
1935	59,861	50,558	17,605	310	1.76	32,953	1.23	405	715	1.41
1936	68,353	57,200	22,137	390	1.76	35,063	1.23	431	821	1.44
1937	73,976	63,776	24,248	445	1.84	39,528	1.29	510	955	1.50
1938	68,327	57,865	22,868	414	1.81	34,997	1.27	444	858	1.48
1939	72,607	61,708	26,045	499	1.92	35,663	1.34	478	977	1.58
1940	78,347	66,167	40,517	740	1.83	25,650	1.28	328	1,068	1.61
1941	95,308	81,968	46,574	1,002	2.15	35,394	1.51	534	1,536	1.87
1942	122,721	98,232	60,341	1,450	2.40	37,891	1.68	637	2,087	2.12
1943	150,286	115,019	75,699	1,836	2.43	39,320	1.70	668	2,504	2.18
1944	165,892	124,886	32,694	1,258	3.85	92,192	1.54	1,420	2,678	2.14
1945	171,927	126,051	34,955	1,450	4.15	91,096	1.45	1,321	2,771	2.20
1946	176,908	142,362	39,569	1,639	4.14	102,793	1.24	1,275	2,914	2.05
1947	193,508	166,920	45,862[a]	1,974[a]	4.30	121,058	1.07	1,295	3,269	1.96
1948	211,900	188,227	50,000[b]	2,150[b]	4.30[b]	138,227	1.07	1,479	3,629	1.93
1949	209,800	186,400	50,000[b]	2,150[b]	4.30[b]	136,400	1.07	1,459	3,609	1.94

[a] Preliminary. [b] Estimated.

SOURCES: Column 1, *Survey of Current Business*, Department of Commerce; columns 3 and 4, *Statistics of Income*, Bureau of Internal Revenue.

such as food furnished by government or employer, lodging furnished by employer, should be deducted, as should also the value of food and fuel consumed on farms. For the war years radical adjustment is needed to take out income of the armed forces (which was not reported for income-tax purposes until after the war, and most of it was tax exempt) and some adjustment for civilian pay for parts of those years when the civilian entered service or died during the year. On the other side, employe contributions for social insurance are counted as income by the Bureau of Internal Revenue but are not represented in the Commerce total, and must therefore be added instead of subtracted. Finally, for purposes of arriving at the gap for this table, the estimated understatement of income in income-tax reports was deducted from the Department of Commerce total.

The differences between Column 2, adjusted personal income, and Column 3, income of persons reporting contributions on income-tax returns, result in Column 6, believed to represent a fair estimate of the "gap" of personal money income on which contributions were not reported on income-tax returns.

After careful study of the data for many individual years and the giving of selected income classes in those years, a contribution rate of .7 of the reported rate for each year was estimated for this "gap" through 1943. This does not mean that the "gap" income, most of it representing very low-income givers, is assumed to have contributed at a rate equal to only seven-tenths of that shown for the reported incomes; it also includes a correction allowance for the probably too-high rate for reported incomes.

It is likely that the resulting estimates are inaccurate for certain years because of special problems. For example, early in the depression of the 1930's many persons, both in the high and moderate income groups, reported capital losses which canceled their tax liability on income from salaries and other sources. These persons were usually still receiving substantial money income from which they doubtless contributed to philanthropic causes—possibly even increasing their giving because of the emergency drives of those difficult days. But these contributions could be reflected in Bureau of Internal Revenue figures only up to "15 per cent of the net income"—and many of these persons had no net income. Even though it is probable that the estimates of individual giving for these years are considerably below the actual amounts, they have been let stand so that Table 46 may consistently reflect data available from income-tax sources.

Beginning in 1944, the rate for reported contributions shot sharply up; with the new standard deduction provision, a much larger proportion of the itemized returns came from large-income brackets, where the rate of contribution has always been higher, and there is reason to believe that the lower-income groups who did itemize their reports probably did so because, for that year, their deductions including contributions were abnormally high. For these reasons, for 1944 only .4 of the reported rate is assumed for the income on which contributions are not reported; for 1945, 3.5; for 1946, .3; and for the remaining years, .25. On evidence of the resulting over-all rate, it is believed that this is realistic though possibly conservative; but after 1943 any contribution totals derived from income-tax data must rely on judgment for such large segments of personal income that reliability cannot be expected.

Some estimates of contributions from living donors have included gift-tax reports of charitable donations. Since 1932 gifts to persons or organizations of substantial size (the amount is now $3,000 or more to any one beneficiary) must be reported on special gift-tax forms. From these reports we have record of charitable contributions ranging in various years from $42 million to over $100 million. But the givers could also report these same gifts on their income-tax returns, and receive credit for them up to 15 per cent of gross income. It is not known to what extent this is done, but it seems so probable a practice that we have entirely omitted gift-tax records in this summary. The charitable contributions there recorded which do not duplicate those in income-tax returns are possibly an appropriate offset to the equally unverifiable overreporting of contributions.

Finally, the contributions reported by income-tax payers (Column 4 of Table 46) and the contributions estimated for the remainder of personal income (Column 8) are totaled to form Column 9, our estimate of philanthropic contributions from living donors for each of the years 1929 through 1949. This is the estimate used in Chapter 4, and appearing in the first column of Table 13 in that chapter. The derivation of the estimate has been presented in some detail because of the magnitude and importance of the totals involved, and the severe complications of the underlying data.

APPENDIX I

SUMMARY OF TITLE III, THE REVENUE ACT OF 1950

[*The following is a direct quotation of* Summary of H. R. 8920, "The Revenue Act of 1950," as Agreed to by the Conferees. *Government Printing Office, Washington, 1950, pp. 23–29. This Act was passed in September, 1950.*]

TITLE III. TREATMENT OF INCOME OF, AND GIFTS AND BEQUESTS TO, CERTAIN TRUSTS AND TAX-EXEMPT ORGANIZATIONS

The bill as agreed to in conference includes a series of provisions which, under specified conditions, result in the imposition of taxes in the case of educational, charitable, and certain other tax-exempt organizations, foundations, and trusts; the denial of charitable deductions under section 162 (a) to nonexempt trusts; and the denial of deductions for income, estate, and gift tax purposes to donors to these organizations. It is estimated that these provisions in a full year of operation will increase the revenues by about $60,000,000.

A. *Unrelated business income (sec. 301 and the part of sec. 321 which inserts sec. 162 (g) (1) into the code)*

The bill imposes the regular corporate income tax on certain tax-exempt organizations which are in the nature of corporations, and the individual income tax on tax-exempt trusts, with respect to so much of their income as arises from active business enterprises which are unrelated to the exempt purposes of the organizations. Trusts claiming the charitable, etc., deduction under section 162 (a) of the code also are denied this deduction with respect to their business income. The tax in the case of exempt organizations applies to the unrelated business income of the labor, agricultural, and horticultural organizations exempt under section 101 (1) of the code; the literary, scientific, religious (other than churches), educational, and charitable organizations, including hospitals and foundations, exempt under section 101 (6); and the business and trade associations exempt under section 101 (7). The tax does not apply to income of this type received by a church (or association or convention of churches) even though the church is held in the name of a bishop or other church official. However, the tax does apply to other exempt institutions operating under the auspices of a church.

The tax on unrelated business income also applies to the so-called investment subsidiaries now exempt under section 101 (14) if their income is payable to section 101 (1), (6), or (7) organizations. However,

294

since these organizations are presently limited to holding title to property, collecting income from it and turning the proceeds over to other exempt organizations, the only trade or business in which they can engage is the rental of property. Consequently the tax on unrelated business income can only apply to their rental income from the type of leases described under (2) below. The tax on unrelated business income is applicable with respect to taxable years beginning after December 31, 1950.

(1) *Income from an Unrelated Trade or Business other than the Rental of Property.*—Under the bill a tax is imposed on income derived from a trade or business "regularly carried on" by a tax-exempt organization if the business is not "substantially related" to the performance of the functions upon which the organization's exemption is based. However, the tax does not apply if substantially all the work done in the trade or business is performed without compensation, or if, in the case of a section 101 (6) organization, the trade or business is carried on primarily for the convenience of the members, students, patients, officers or employees of the tax-exempt organization.

Athletic activities of schools are substantially related to their educational functions. For example, a university would not be taxable on income derived from a basketball tournament sponsored by it, even where the teams were composed of students of other schools.

In the case of an educational institution, income from dining halls, restaurants, and dormitories operated for the convenience of the students would be considered related income and, therefore, would not be taxable. Income from a university press would be exempt in the ordinary case since it would be derived from an activity that is "substantially related" to the purposes of the university.

The bill also exempts from tax income derived from the sale of merchandise by tax-exempt organizations when substantially all the merchandise is acquired by gift. This is intended to exclude "thrift shops" run by tax-exempt organizations where those desiring to benefit the exempt organization contribute old clothes, books, etc., to be sold with the proceeds going to the exempt organization.

The bill specifically exempts from tax income derived from research for the United States or any of its agencies, and for State and local governments.

A special exemption is provided in the case of colleges, universities, and hospitals for income received from research done for anyone. Income derived from research is also exempted in the case of other nonprofit research organizations if they are operated primarily to carry on fundamental research which is freely available to the general public.

The bill also includes a specific exemption of $1,000. This, in addition to the requirement that such businesses must be carried on "regularly" to be taxable, will dispose of most of the nuisance cases. In applying the tax, the bill provides for the consolidation of all of an organization's income from its various unrelated trade or business activities.

The tax on unrelated business income does not apply to dividends, interest, royalties, and rents (other than certain rents on property acquired with borrowed funds). The bill indicates that for this purpose the term "royalties" includes overriding royalties and includes royalties whether measured by production or by gross or net income from the property.

The bill also provides that the tax on unrelated business income does not apply to gains or losses from the sale of any property (including standing timber) other than stock in trade, property held for sale to customers, or timber cut by the organization.

(2) *Rentals from certain long-term leases.*—The bill taxes as unrelated business income certain income received from the lease of real property and personal property leased in connection with it. The organizations covered by this portion of the bill are the same ones which are subjected to tax on their other unrelated business income.

The tax applies only when the property owned by the organization is leased for a period of more than 5 years, or when the period of the lease plus options is more than 5 years. It applies only where borrowed funds are used to finance the purchase or improvement of the property. The amount of rents included in gross income is restricted to the same proportion of the rents as the borrowed funds used to finance the purchase or improvement bear to the adjusted basis of such property. This restricts the tax to the income which does not result from a simple investment of the trust or organization's capital funds. The tax applies whether or not the vendor and the lessee are the same person.

Four exclusions from the application of this tax are provided. The first excludes from the tax "related" leases even though the lessee is a taxable organization. "Related" is defined in a similar fashion as in the case of a related trade or business and is, for example, intended to exclude from the application of this tax leases by tax-exempt hospitals of part of the hospital facilities to doctors' associations for use as clinics.

The second of these exclusions relates to property which was acquired by gift, bequest or devise before July 1, 1950, and at the time of acquisition was already subject to a mortgage or was under a lease requiring improvements. This exclusion also applies to investment subsidiaries exempt under section 101 (14) where one-third of the stock in the subsidiary was acquired by gift and all of the stock was acquired prior to July 1, 1950. In the case of such subsidiaries and their parent organizations, indebtedness incurred prior to July 1, 1950, or indebtedness incurred after such date in improving property as required by a lease entered into before July 1, 1950, does not make the rental income taxable.

The third exclusion limits the application of the tax on certain rental income where only a part of the property is rented out under long-term leases. In these cases the tax is imposed only if either of two conditions is present:

(a) the rents derived from long-term leases represent 50 percent or more of the total rental payments received, or the space occupied by such leaseholders represents 50 percent or more of the rented area, or

(b) the rental payments derived from any single long-term lease-holder represent 10 percent or more of the total rents or the space occupied by any single long-term leaseholder represents 10 percent or more of the area rented out.

Thus, no tax would be imposed where over half of the property is rented out on a short-term basis, if the long-term leases which do exist are spread out among relatively numerous leaseholders.

The fourth exclusion relates to cases where an exempt organization has borrowed funds to build a building primarily designed for its own use, but has extra space which it desires to rent out under long-term leases.

B. "Feeder" organizations

The bill provides that no organization operated primarily for the purpose of carrying on a trade or business (other than the rental of real estate) for profit shall be exempt under section 101 merely on the grounds that all of its profits are payable to one or more organizations exempt from tax under this section. This amendment is not intended to affect the exemptions now provided for farm cooperatives, subsidiaries of these cooperatives, or investment subsidiaries exempt under section 101 (12), (13), and (14).

The effect of this amendment is to prevent the exemption of a trade or business organization under section 101 on the grounds that an organization actually described in section 101 receives the earnings from the operations of the trade or business organization.

This provision is applicable with respect to taxable years beginning after December 31, 1950.

C. Exemption for past years (sec. 302)

The bill as agreed to in conference adds three provisions dealing primarily with the exemption of organizations in prior years. The first of these provides that with respect to years beginning prior to January 1, 1951, no organization shall be denied exemption under section 101 (1), (6), or (7) merely because it is deriving income from a trade or business if this income would not be taxed in future years under this bill as unrelated business income, or merely because the income is rental income from real property.

Under the second of these provisions, the filing of an informational return (Form 990) is to be considered as the filing of a return for the purpose of starting the 3-year period of limitations on the assessment of deficiencies with respect to those organizations which would be exempt under section 101 if they were not carrying on a trade or business for profit. Organizations not required to file Form 990 are treated for this purpose as if they had done so. This second provision does not apply, however, in those cases where prior to September 20, 1950, a deficiency has been asserted or taxes have been assessed or paid. Subject to these limitations, this second provision has the effect with respect to past years of barring any action with respect to years prior to 1947 to deny exemption to any organization under section 101 merely because it was carrying on a trade or business if the organization complied with the provisions of the law relating to the filing of information returns.

Third, it is also provided that a deduction for a gift or bequest to an organization prior to January 1, 1951, may not be denied if the limitations provided in the first or second provision described above prevent the denial of an exemption under section 101 to the organization to which the contribution was made.

The statement of the managers on the part of the House also includes the following statement:

> The conferees were unable to consider the question of taxability for years prior to 1951 of income derived by a college or university from the conduct of a trade or business whether carried on directly by the institution or through a subsidiary. This matter is in litigation and was not in conference. However, it is the view of the conferees that undue hardship will arise, if such institutions are required to pay taxes on income which has already been spent to carry out their educational programs; and the conferees express the hope that this matter may be reviewed in subsequent legislation.

D. *Provisions relating to transactions prohibited in the case of trusts and exempt foundations (the part of sec. 331 which inserts sec. 3813 in the code, and the part of sec. 321 which inserts sec. 162 (g) (2) in the code)*

The bill provides that if certain types of organizations exempt under section 101 (6) (and trusts claiming charitable deductions under sec.

162 (a)) engage in specified "prohibited transactions" they lose their exemption (or their unlimited charitable deduction in the case of trusts claiming deductions under sec. 162 (a)).

The prohibited transactions are defined as including transactions in which an organization—

(1) lends any part of its income or corpus without adequate security or at an unreasonable rate of interest to donors (including testators), members of their families, or a corporation which they control,

(2) pays any compensation to such persons in excess of a reasonable allowance for personal services actually rendered,

(3) makes any part of its services available to such persons on a preferential basis,

(4) makes any substantial purchase of securities or other property from such persons for more than adequate consideration,

(5) sells any substantial part of its securities or other property to such persons without adequate consideration, or

(6) engages in any other transaction which results in a substantial diversion of its income or corpus to such persons.

Exemption or the unlimited charitable deduction under section 162 (a) is denied in the case of an organization or trust participating in a prohibited transaction only with respect to years subsequent to the year in which it receives notification of a violation except where the prohibited transaction was entered into with the purpose of diverting funds involving a substantial proportion of the assets or income of the organization. In the latter case exemption may be denied retroactively. An organization or trust which has engaged in a prohibited transaction may regain its exempt status (or the unlimited charitable, etc., deduction under sec. 162 (a)) by presenting information to the Commissioner of Internal Revenue which satisfies him that it is unlikely knowingly to participate again in one of these transactions.

For deduction of contributions to donors, the bill requires that the organization or trust be exempt at the time the contribution is made, unless the donors (or their families) personally are involved in one of these transactions for the purpose of diverting funds from the organization and such transaction involves a substantial part of the assets or income of the organization.

The provisions discussed here affect trusts claiming charitable deductions under section 162 (a) and organizations exempt under section 101 (6) other than—

(1) Religious organizations,

(2) Educational organizations with an enrolled student body in attendance,

(3) Organizations which receive a substantial portion of their support from the Government or directly or indirectly from the general public (excluding in such computation income received by the organization in carrying on its exempt function),

(4) Organizations which are operated or principally supported by religious organizations, and

(5) Organizations providing medical or hospital care or medical education or medical research.

The organizations excluded from the application of these provisions are, in general, what might be called "public" organizations.

These provisions are applicable to taxable years beginning after December 31, 1950, or with respect to gifts or bequests made after that date.

E. Provisions Relating to Types of Accumulations Prohibited in the Case of Trusts and Exempt Foundations (the part of sec. 331 which inserts sec. 3814 in the code and the part of sec. 321 which inserts sec. 162 (g) (4) in the code)

The bill as agreed to in conference denies exemption to any organization exempt under section 101 (6) where the income accumulated in the current and prior years—

(1) is unreasonably large, or is held for an unreasonable period of time, in view of the exempt purposes for which the funds are intended to be used, or

(2) is used to a substantial degree for purposes other than the organization's exempt purpose, or

(3) is invested in such a manner as to entail the risk that the funds will be lost and thus not be available for the exempt purpose of the organization.

In considering the above factors the income accumulated in prior years, as well as the current year, are taken into consideration. Exemption under this provision in the case of organizations not meeting these tests is lost only for the 1 year involved. If in the next year the accumulations of the current and prior years' income meet these tests the organization is again exempt. The initial determination as to whether or not the above tests are met will be made by the Bureau of Internal Revenue, but the ordinary judicial remedies are available to the organization where it disagrees with this determination. An organization denied exemption under this provision would still be eligible for the 5-percent deduction for charitable contributions available to ordinary corporate taxpayers (or a 15-percent charitable deduction if taxable like an individual). This provision applies to taxable years beginning after December 31, 1950.

A provision is also incorporated in the bill which in a similar manner denies the charitable, etc., deduction to trusts claiming deductions under section 162 (a) if their accumulations do not meet similar tests.

F. Publicizing accumulated investment income (sec. 341)

The bill as agreed to in conference also incorporates a provision requiring that information disclosing the extent of accumulations of income of certain tax-exempt organizations be made available to the public.

The organizations required to file this information include all organizations exempt under section 101 (6) now required to file information returns (Form 990) under section 54 (f) of the code, and also trusts claiming charitable, etc., deductions under section 162 (a) of the code. In general this means that all private foundations and trusts are subject to this provision.

The information required in the case of a section 101 (6) organization (which the Commissioner of Internal Revenue may require in such detail as he deems desirable) is the organization's:

1. Gross income for the year,
2. Expenses attributable to such income,
3. Disbursements out of current income for its educational, charitable, etc., purpose,
4. Accumulation of income within the year,
5. Prior accumulations of income,
6. Disbursements out of principal, and
7. Balance sheet.

Trusts claiming charitable, etc., deductions under section 162 (a) will be required to submit similar information.

This provision is effective with respect to taxable years beginning after December 31, 1949.

INDEX

Index

U.S.S.R., 42, 79, 87
Utah, 60, 61

VACATION services, 116
Vaccination, 22
Vassar College, 201
Venezuela, 75
Vermont, 61
Veterans: educational aid, 189, 191–192,
 203–204; government aid, 44, 46, 121,
 189, 191–192, 203–204, 267; tax ex-
 emption for organizations, 23, 232,
 271
Veterans Administration, 44
Victory Clothing Drive, 78
Vincent, G. E., 98n
Virginia, 61
Vocational guidance, 116
Vocational training, 24
Voluntary Action (Beveridge), 48n, 116n
Voluntary agencies, 111–133; budgets
 of, 124–133; defined, 111; health,
 120–123; local, 115–116; national,
 113–115; number, 21; overhead in,
 119–120; recreation, 123–124
Voluntary Foreign Aid, 77n, 83n, 84n
Voluntary Health Agencies (Gunn, Platt),
 123
Voluntary War Relief During World War II,
 82n
Volunteers: as fund-collectors, 134–136,
 140, 159; as workers, 42, 111, 135

WAGE-EARNERS, as contributors, 63
War chests, 75, 144, 149
War Prisoners' Aid, 149
War Production Board, 47n
War Relief Control Board, 82, 83, 149,
 169
War Relief Service, 85, 86
Ward, Wells and Dresham, 138
Washington, D. C., 61, 88, 247
Washington, George, 197
Washington, state of, 61
Washington and Lee University, 197,
 201
Waterbury Foundation, 285
Watertown Foundation, 286
Ways and Means Committee, House of
 Representatives, 49
WCTU. *See* National Woman's Chris-
 tian Temperance Union
Wealth of Nations (Smith), 198
Wealthy, gifts of, 37, 56–60, 68–69, 157,
 292
Welfare Council, New York, 164
Welfare Department of New York City,
 47

Welfare Federation of Los Angeles Area,
 147
"Welfare state," 48
West, The, 109
West Virginia, 61
Westinghouse Educational Foundation,
 202
Wheelock, Eleazar, 190
Whitman, William, 28
Widows: aid to, 22, 28, 29, 30, 32, 33,
 102; widow's mite, 34, 36, 52
Widowers, aid to, 29
Will, Folsom and Smith, 138
Williamsport Foundation, 287
Wills, 69, 94
Wilmington, 91
Wilson, Mrs. Woodrow, 210
Winston, Ellen, 10
Winston-Salem Foundation, 286
Wisconsin, 61
*Wohltätigkeit und Armenpflege im Vorchrist-
 lichen Altertum* (Bolkestein), 31n
Wolfe, Thomas, 211
Woll, Matthew, 62
Wordsworth, William, 254n
Work relief, 46
Workhouses, 41
World Council of Churches, 85
World Peace Foundation, 232
World Student Service Fund, 202
World War I: effects, 18, 63, 64, 164,
 190; relief abroad, 75, 138, 246;
 scholarships, 202
World War II: costs, 47; effects, 18,
 195n, 207; relief abroad, 75, 77, 169,
 170; memorials, 200, 210; and re-
 search, 229
Writing, support of, 211, 212, 250
Wyoming, 61

XENODOCHIA, 33
Xenophon, 32

YALE *Law Journal*, 168n
Yale University, 107, 201, 224, 228
Yearbook of Philanthropy, 211n
YMCA. *See* Young Men's Christian
 Associations
Young Adult Council, 124
Young, Donald, 7, 215, 227
Young Men's Christian Associations,
 124, 140, 141, 187
Young Women's Christian Associations,
 124, 141, 187
Youngstown Foundation, 286
Youth Commission, N. Y., 48
Yugoslavia, 170
YWCA. *See* Young Women's Christian
 Associations